Media and Civil Society in 21st-Century Conflict

Media and Civil Society in 21st-Century Conflict

E. L. Gaston, editor

International Debate Education Association

New York, London & Amsterdam

Published by
The International Debate Education Association
105 East 22nd Street
New York, NY 10010

This book is published with the generous support of the Open Society Foundations.

Special thanks to Samantha Schott for research support.

Library of Congress Cataloging-in-Publication Data
Media and civil society in 21st century conflict/E.L. Gaston, editor.
    pages cm
  ISBN 978-1-61770-095-8
  1. Mass media and war. 2. War in mass media 3. Civil society.
4. Humanitarian assistance. 5. Television broadcasting of news. 6. Conflict management. I. Gaston, E. L., editor of compilation.
  P96.W35M338 2014
  302.23—dc23   2014000301

Composition by Brad Walrod/Kenoza Type, Inc.
Printed in the USA

 IDEBATE Press

Contents

Introduction

As the nature of war has changed, so has the role of civilians in it. Analysis of war has tended to view the actors in war as belonging to one of two camps: the fighters, also called combatants, and noncombatants, or civilians. *Media and Civil Society in 21st-Century Conflict* focuses on actors who fall squarely into neither camp. They are civilians under any technical legal definition, but they are not bystanders or victims. They are unquestionably shaping the outcomes of war, but they are not fighters, or even the strategists or supporters of warfare. This third category is made up of the aid workers, human rights advocates, journalists, and citizen activists who are ever more present in conflict zones worldwide. They are witnesses to the suffering of war, often the vital link providing information to a now-global public of what is happening at the front lines. They are the voice for the voiceless, advocating for a cessation of conflict or at least for restraint from inhumane or unnecessary acts of violence. They may be civilians' only hope, the lifeline providing food, water, or shelter in a shattered environment. And in an ever more interconnected and globalized world, the way that media, civil society, and nongovernmental actors engage with conflict can be as important as what happens on the battlefield.

But while the authors in this anthology outline some of the impressive work accomplished by these actors, they also raise important doubts and caveats concerning such achievements. When well-meaning people are faced with the difficult and complex challenge of limiting or documenting the effects of war, there may be as many failings as there are good intentions. Efforts intended to mitigate suffering or stop violence have been used to fuel conflict, and efforts to improve knowledge and public understanding have instead provided opportunities to misinform. Given the difficulty of humanizing or mitigating the scourge of war, can they succeed? And given the potential for unintended consequences that may completely undermine their purpose, do they run the risk of harming as much as they've helped?

"DO-GOODERS" IN CONFLICT

The calculations of war have changed in the modern era. In the past, conflict was dominated by state actors fighting over territory, or access to wealth and resources. War was governed (more or less effectively) by treaties between equals, and the international system was premised on an idea of state sovereignty. But globalization and modern technological advances have challenged many of those fundamental precepts—eroding borders and notions of sovereignty, and making the physical territory less important than controlling the less tangible landscape of economic or social networks.

The power of states has declined vis-à-vis that of individuals—those seeking to help as well as those seeking to harm. Technological advances have made weapons with the potential to cause immense harm more widely available, such that individuals or non-state actors have the ability to cause a level of harm and destruction that previously could only have been perpetrated by a state. A small amount of high-impact explosives activated by a cell phone can cause mass casualties; an Internet virus launched from a single computer can wreak immense economic destruction. With more potent weapons and the greater ability for individuals to coordinate and collaborate to wage war against states, asymmetric threats from non-state actors (typically terrorists, insurgent or guerrilla groups, or criminals) and intrastate violence now dominate modern conflict.

But just as the roles of states and their aggressors have changed, so has the role of the civilian within war. War is not waged on discrete battlefields, with armies charging each other in uniform. Instead, because of the changing tactics of non-state actors, conflict is more often found in the local shopping mall, down a main city boulevard, or in an important commercial target. Given these changing modes of warfare, the civilian is much more central to modern warfare, equally as a potential hostage or victim to calculated violence—a weapon in these asymmetric conflicts—or as a potential ally helping to counter threats that could come from anywhere, and everywhere, including within the civilian population.

Because of their engagement with the civilian population, three categories of civilians who feature in this book play a much more prominent role in these new modes of warfare. The first category is humanitarian organizations that provide food, water, shelter, medical assistance, and other basic humanitarian necessities to civilians in the midst of conflict or crises. They are motivated to do so because they believe that responding to such extreme suffering is a basic duty of humanity. But because what happens to the civilian population is more central to modern war-fighting strategy, groups like these, with the ability to help the population, have become either an important ally or the next target. As one scholar of humanitarian assistance, Janice Gross Stein, has argued, providing aid can be particularly critical in the counterinsurgency and civil war situations that are the most common type of warfare today:

The aim of much contemporary military strategy in civil wars is make the civilian population hostage, and, if possible, to prevent or undo the effects of emergency relief and the protection of civilians. . . . Civilians, and those humanitarian NGOs who would protect them, become the objects of military action. They and their resources stand not apart from, but directly on the battlefield. Becoming part of the battle challenges all the fundamental precepts of humanitarian action.[1]

The second category—human rights NGOs, activists, and lawyers—has also grown in importance. Although there are overlaps and organizations that do both types of work, human rights organizations are generally distinct from humanitarian organizations. They tend not to provide direct assistance, but focus on advocating for a specific cause. For example, they might argue for ending the practice of using children as soldiers, for limiting tactics that result in civilian deaths in warfare, or for the international community to intervene in a country where atrocities are ongoing. As a result, they often become the de facto mediators between the civilian population and warring parties, representing civilian voices or concerns to warring parties or to a broader population.

Many argue that human rights actors have a bigger impact not only because of the changing modes of warfare, but also because of changing geopolitical dynamics. Since the end of the Cold War in 1991, there has been even greater space for consideration of human rights in foreign policy because foreign policy is no longer held hostage to the larger geopolitical conflict between the United States and the Soviet Union. In addition, the work of human rights groups has the potential for greater impact because civilians and their advocates have a much louder voice through modern media. With now-pervasive, around-the-clock media coverage, humanitarians and human rights advocates, along with the civilians they are trying to help, are increasingly before the public eye, in ways that foreign policy decision-makers cannot ignore. Media coverage of mass atrocities, displacement, or other humanitarian emergencies may spur international action to relieve or stop suffering. Media portrayals of torture or cruel treatment of detainees may outrage domestic publics, who then pressure politicians, policymakers, and sometimes even non-state actors to enact limitations or restrictions that they would not otherwise adopt.

But the media are not just a mouthpiece or a vehicle. The journalists—both traditional media and emerging citizen journalists—are themselves a more central actor in conflict, and form the third category in this compendium. Many are inspired by what they see as their duty to increase public understanding and accountability for what happens in war. Meanwhile, the globalization of media and new social platforms allows more diverse voices to provide information and critiques than ever before. Larger numbers of citizen journalists, freelancers, and NGOs are also reporting on what happens in war, providing fresh viewpoints and critiques that might have been ignored or gone unheard in past eras of warfare. A potential downside to this more open media environment, though, is that those who wish to perpetuate war, or who simply provide bad information or misinformed commentary, can equally access a global audience.

Given the changes in conflict dynamics, the potential for limiting war or mitigating its costs are huge. But there are also significant risks to this type of work. The same media spotlight that has the potential to force warring parties to spare lives or to change tactics can motivate other attacks or violence. Insurgent or terrorist groups have frequently staged public attacks or atrocities designed to capture global media attention as a means of winning a strategic victory against more militarily powerful state actors, or to gain a platform for their political cause. In September 2013, for example, armed men linked with the Somalia-based terrorist group al-Shabaab attacked a shopping mall outside Nairobi, opening fire on civilians and taking hostages as a way to make a global public statement about their cause.

And as they become more important to the strategy of a conflict, journalists, NGOs, and aid workers can become the direct targets. The significant success in protecting civilian lives or creating effective humanitarian campaigns is intermixed with personal tragedies among those engaged in this type of work. Civilian aid workers have been targeted at record levels in countries like Afghanistan, Iraq, Pakistan, Somalia, Sudan, and Yemen. Meanwhile, by some standards, attacks on journalists have quadrupled since the 1990s—the result not only of changed tactics by warring parties but also the blurring of lines between traditional journalism, citizen activism, and partisan groups. Despite the risks, these actors tend to believe that the personal sacrifice is worth it in order to reduce suffering from war or improve public awareness.

OVERVIEW OF THE ANTHOLOGY

Media and Civil Society in 21st-Century Conflict explores how aid workers, human rights advocates, journalists, and civilian activists are engaging with modern conflict. While some of the authors describe important ways in which these actors are shaping modern conflict dynamics for the better—easing the suffering of affected civilians, limiting harm or atrocities, or improving public understanding—others discuss ways in which these efforts have fallen short, or have created unintended consequences as serious as those they are trying to address.

In Part 1, Humanitarian Aid Dilemmas, the authors focus on challenges facing those who try to provide impartial humanitarian aid and ask: Does aid do as much harm as good? Can humanitarian aid remain truly neutral in modern conflict?

It is hard to argue against the motivation and mission of humanitarians, who try to bring relief to those in great distress, often at great personal risk. Yet some critics contend that the presence of humanitarian aid may make the situation worse. As the anecdotes Philip Gourevitch offers in the "Alms Dealers: Can You Provide Humanitarian Aid Without Facilitating Conficts?" illustrate, aid intended as a balm to limit suffering has been used to prolong war, enabling fighters to keep fighting, or providing an alibi for political inaction.

Gourevitch's article is a book review of *The Crisis Caravan: What's Wrong with Humanitarian Aid?*—a damning critique by Linda Polman, who argues that the aid industry not only enables war to continue, but it does so because humanitarian aid has become a global business and tending to war victims is profitable. In "Aid and War: A Response to Linda Polman's Critique of Humanitarianism," the Overseas Development Institute argues that while more can be done to improve accountability and enforce standards, "none of these innovations really gets to the heart of the problem, namely that humanitarian assistance alone cannot ensure that belligerents will behave well towards aid workers or their beneficiaries, or listen to calls to respect human rights and international humanitarian law."[2]

Another common dilemma for humanitarians is how to preserve their ideal of providing neutral, impartial aid, staying above and apart from the politics of a conflict. Skeptics have questioned whether such neutrality is even possible, given the way aid affects conflict environments. As Gourevitch notes, "The scenes of suffering that we tend to call humanitarian crises are almost always symptoms of political circumstances, and there's no apolitical way of responding to them—no way to act without having a political effect."[3]

But many NGOs argue that such neutrality—if respected—would help protect humanitarians and improve the impact of their work. Elizabeth Ferris, author of "9/11 and Humanitarian Assistance: A Disturbing Legacy," cautions that U.S. counterterrorism policies in the last decade, and U.S. use of humanitarian aid strategically, have eroded the perception of neutrality that has traditionally protected humanitarian workers from being attacked. However, Paul O'Brien, in "Politicized Humanitarianism: a Response to Nicolas de Torrente," counters that the effectiveness of neutrality in making humanitarians immune from attack depends on the conflict zone. In some situations, aid or the presence of Western NGOs may be inherently political, and receiving support from those parties to the conflict that enable humanitarian aid and civilian protection is not necessarily a bad response on the part of humanitarians.

Part 2, Speaking Truth to Power: NGO Advocacy Campaigns, explores whether advocacy campaigns can actually change policies, tactics, and warring-party behavior in order to save civilian lives, to stop atrocities or end abuses. Do seemingly successful advocacy campaigns really prevent suffering in war, or do they merely distract from meaningful political action? Can human rights campaigns live up to their promise?

Human rights advocates and researchers are often the first on the ground, documenting or bearing witness to what happens. One NGO leader engaged in this type of work, Sarah Holewinski, argues in "Speaking for Civilians in War" that acting as a voice for the victims—directly to warring parties and to the public at large—can lead to changes that result in sparing civilian lives.

While changing the behavior of state parties has been one of the major successes of NGOs in this field, one of the major challenges they face is how to restrain non-state actors, who are often responsible for the greater amount of civilian harm or violations in war. Claudia Hofmann and Ulrich Schneckener, in "NGOs and Nonstate Actors: Improving Compliance with International Norms," argue that two organizations, the International Committee of the Red Cross and Geneva Call, have demonstrated that the conduct of non-state actors can be improved, but only with non-state actors who are concerned about their reputation or legitimacy.

Bonnie Docherty, in "Influence and Collaboration: Civil Society's Role in Creating International Humanitarian Law," points out that NGOs not only hold armed actors to account under existing law, but also play an important role in driving and influencing *new* law to place a greater emphasis on humanitarian considerations. She evaluates NGO involvement in the development of the 2008 international Convention on Cluster Munitions. The greater humanitarian focus within its provisions illustrates the positive role that NGOs can have in extending rights protections in times of conflict, she argues.

Many human rights and humanitarian aid campaigns try to portray the suffering of victims and the ongoing costs of conflict and of humanitarian crises in hopes that this will generate public pressure on powerful states to intervene. But is public awareness the answer to seeming global indifference to such suffering? "If machetes (rise and) fall in Africa and no American voters are listening, do American politicians care?" asks Andrew Stobo Sniderman, in the opening query to "A Brief History of 'Save Darfur.'"[4] In reviewing a recent book on the topic, Sniderman argues that a U.S.-based citizen campaign that tried to motivate intervention to stop a genocide in Darfur made historic strides, but questions whether it ultimately was effective. The global public and critical policymakers were made aware that millions continued to die, suffer injuries or displacement, but intervention along the lines that the campaign proposed did not happen.

Kate Cronin-Furman and Amanda Taub, in "Solving War Crimes with Wristbands: The Arrogance of 'Kony 2012,'" critique NGOs' heavy emphasis on raising public awareness, arguing that awareness cannot substitute for meaningful engagement. In addition, they fear that constantly bombarding the public with scenes of destruction, misery, and death may desensitize people to suffering without necessarily increasing incentives to halt violence.

Pressing further on the value of public awareness, the articles in Part 3, Public Scrutiny and the Drumbeat to War, question whether increased public discourse results in greater accountability, fewer abuses, and, in the end, fewer senseless wars. As the media landscape has widened, are the new sources of information adding public value or simply adding more noise?

Public scrutiny of the legality of conduct in war has become much more important in modern conflict—a trend that many human rights actors applaud because of its potential to increase public pressure and accountability. But in "Lawfare: A Decisive Element of 21st-Century Conflicts?," Charles Dunlap, Jr. argues that perceptions of compliance with law have become so important to many state militaries that law can be used against them as a tactic of war. Instead of improving human rights, heightened consideration for law among modern militaries can perversely give an advantage to non-state actors who are more abusive and least likely to respect international law: Terrorist and insurgent groups can use a country's adherence to law as a tactical advantage, for example, by provoking media coverage that suggests that militaries have committed war crimes. Other critics have argued that litigation against state parties in courts creates bad policies or unintended consequences—for example, making it easier for a state to kill than to capture a suspected enemy combatant because detention appeals and litigation are more likely than post hoc tactical reviews.

In "Lawfare in the Courts: Litigation as a Weapon of War?" Nikolaus Grubeck examines whether the use of litigation (so far primarily by human rights lawyers and organizations) can be considered a "weapon of war." He finds that litigation on questions of war is ad hoc, and uncoordinated, and is generally not deployed by enemies of the state being charged, so it cannot be a weapon per se. And in fact, it need not necessarily be viewed as a military disadvantage. In practice, Grubeck argues, the conduct of litigation is unlikely to be used against Western countries as part of a concerted strategy, and "[i]nsofar as fair and independent oversight by the courts of conduct in war can help visibly uphold the rule of law, overall it is likely to strengthen, not weaken democratically mandated armed forces."[5]

Most NGOs, lawyers, and activists assume that the greater availability of media coverage has a positive value, because they assume that public attention will drive policymakers to more humane policies or practices. But Piers Robinson in "The CNN Effect: Can the News Media Drive Foreign Policy?" and Peter Viggo Jakobsen in "Focus on the CNN Effect Misses the Point: The Real Media Impact on Conflict Management Is Invisible and Indirect" question whether media attention really does drive foreign policy. The common assumption has been that heavy media attention encouraging intervention can lead to international action, while negative coverage can force modern democracies to beat a retreat. As Jakobsen quotes former U.S. assistant secretary of state for human rights and democracy John Shattuck: "The media got us [the United States] into Somalia and then got us out."[6] Yet, despite this assumption, both articles provide evidence that at least when it comes to military intervention, media is not as important in driving decision making as is commonly assumed. It may be decisive in only a small number of cases and in certain phases of a conflict.

Finally, public scrutiny of war is growing in no small part because of developments in social media and the increasing number of citizen journalists. In "Could Twitter Have Prevented the Iraq War?" Eric Boehlert argues that these new voices can act as a "media equalizer," counterbalancing what is too often a complicit and unquestioning press corps, in halting the resort to war. He maintains that if the Twitterati had been around in 2003, the United States would not have found it as easy to make a case for war in Iraq because it would have been checked by a global citizenry of fact checkers and those with different perspectives and information. In "When Lines Between NGO and News Organization Blur," Glenda Cooper acknowledges the contribution of new voices—not only citizen journalists but also NGOs—but points out these new voices may not be unbiased, and that the loudest voices, rather than the neediest ones, will succeed in attracting international attention and aid.

The final section, Part 4, The Cost of Making a Difference: Balancing Risk in Modern Conflict, examines the increasing risks that journalists and NGO workers face in modern conflict. Does the value of greater public information and awareness, or the effort to prevent suffering (however successful), justify the fact that some will have to make the "ultimate sacrifice"?

Each year over the past decade, the number of journalists who have become casualties to war—from IEDs in Iraq, targeted killings in Pakistan, aerial assaults in Libya, or being caught in the cross fire in Syria—has climbed. Getting to the truth often requires journalists to put their own lives at risk. But some argue that modern media demands for blood and action, and journalists' own ambition, are what leads them to go too far, endangering not only their own lives but others, as Tunku Varadarajan discusses in "The Price of a Scoop: Two Dead." He questions whether journalists are too reckless in their quest to be first for the information, while admitting that journalism cannot be a risk-free enterprise. The second article in the section, "Embedded Journalism: A Distorted View of War," by Patrick Cockburn, illustrates some of the limitations to public understanding when conflict situations are so dangerous that they force journalists to limit their reporting to traveling alongside the military. While "embedding," as the practice is known, provides a measure of access, it runs the risk of skewing the coverage in ways that undermine the fundamental purpose of reporting in these zones.

Like journalists, the aid workers or representatives of NGOs are not immune from the increased risk of operating in conflict areas. They are frequently killed, kidnapped, threatened, or arrested, and aid facilities bombed, sabotaged, or shut down, as Scott Baldauf describes in "Helpers in a Hostile World: The Risk of Aid Work Grows." "Aid groups have to make decisions based largely on whether the reward of making a difference—in saving lives at Somali refugee camps, for instance—is worth the risk of losing staff members in what appear to be targeted attacks."[7] How these groups draw the line between protecting staff and ensuring access begs some of the larger questions of the book, as this balancing act sometimes requires making compromises with those who are furthering the war.

CONCLUSION

This anthology is designed to provide the uninitiated reader with an introduction to some of the most dynamic actors in modern conflict.[8] However, given its introductory nature, this compendium can provide only a brief glimpse into what are extremely complex and diverse debates within popular and academic literature. The issues presented in each of the articles in this anthology could be expanded into a book or multiple books on their own (and have been).[9]

As you read each article, try to put yourself in the place of the aid workers, activists, and journalists who figure in it, and to identify the contradictions or dilemmas they face as they go about their work. While many of these actors are motivated by a desire to do right and to help in some of the worst hellholes on earth, likely none would argue that they do so perfectly or that the situations they face are clear-cut. This type of work is challenging—often impossibly so—and, given the instability in war, frequently doomed to setback and failure.

Does the good outweigh the bad? Can these journalists, activists, and humanitarian workers succeed in speaking truth to power, and limiting the scourge of war? And even if they do not quite live up to their highest aspirations, is there a better alternative? After all, what kind of world would it be if there were not those who sought to limit the costs of conflict.

NOTES

1. Janice Gross Stein, "In the Eye of the Storm: Humanitarian NGOs, Complex Emergencies, and Conflict Resolution," *Peace and Conflict Studies* 8, no. 1 (May 2001): 21. Aid workers are also more prominent because the sheer numbers of them in conflict zones has increased. As Stein notes, "This growth is a direct outcome of the restructuring of the state and welfare systems by northern donors during the 1980s. In some countries, official development assistance has effectively been privatized." Ibid., 17–19.

2. The Humanitarian Policy Group, Opinion: "Aid and War: A Response to Linda Polman's Critique of Humanitarianism," Overseas Development Institute, May 2010, 144.

3. Philip Gourevitch, "Alms Dealers: Can You Provide Humanitarian Aid Without Facilitating Conflicts?," *New Yorker*, October 11, 2010, 106.http://www.newyorker.com/arts/critics/atlarge/2010/10/11/101011crat_atlarge_gourevitch?printable=true&currentPage=all#ixzz2c97Ea3LG.

4. Andrew Stobo Sniderman, "A Brief History of 'Save Darfur': The Darfur Lobby was Historic; But Was It Effective?," *Columbia Journalism Review*, March 16, 2011, http://www.cjr.org/critical_eye/a_brief_history_of_save_darfur.php?page=all.

5. Nikolaus Grubeck, "Lawfare in the Courts: Litigation as a Weapon of War?" in this volume, p. 130.

6. Peter Viggo Jakobsen, "Focus on the CNN Effect Misses the Point: The Real Media Impact on Conflict Management Is Invisible and Indirect," *Journal of Peace Research* (2000): 132 (citing John, Shattuck, "Human Rights and Humanitarian Crises: Policy-Making and the Media," in R.I. Rotberg and T. Weiss, *From Massacres to Genocide: the Media, Public Policy, and Humanitarian Crises*, 169–175 [Washington, DC: Brookings Institution Press, 1996], 174).

7. Scott Baldauf, "Helpers in a Hostile World: The Risk of Aid Work Grows," *Christian Science Monitor*, February 10, 2012, p. 2, http://www.csmonitor.com/World/Global-Issues/2012/0210/Helpers-in-a-hostile-world-the-risk-of-aid-work-grows.

8. Another casualty of the condensed, introductory nature of this book relates to terminology. This book alternately refers to situations or crises arising in "wartime" or sometimes in the context of "counterterrorist" operations. In reality, there is an increasingly murky line between armed conflict or war, and counterterrorism, or law-enforcement struggles. These legal debates are the focus of another compendium by this author, E.L. Gaston, *The Laws of War and 21st-Century Conflict* (New York: IDEBATE Press, 2012). This book will generally refer to this spectrum of situations as "armed conflict," "war," or "warfare," with specific reference to counterterrorism situations or tactics where relevant. In discussing humanitarians' activities in these zones, this book will sometimes refer to "crisis" or "emergency situations." In part, this also reflects the legal ambiguities in many of these situations—the same area may go through cycles of violence or relative calm that complicate, at any given time, categorization as conflict or pre- or post-violence. Aid workers may be engaged at any and all points in this cycle of violence.

9. Although the literature on humanitarian aid, human rights advocacy, and their interrelationships with the evolving media landscape are endless, a few key resources that were useful in developing the themes of this compendium include Jo Becker, *Campaigning for Justice: Human Rights Advocacy in Practice* (Palo Alto, CA: Stanford University Press, 2012); David Kennedy, *The Dark Side of Virtue: Reassessing International Humanitarianism* (Princeton, NJ: Princeton University Press, 2005); Aryeh Neier, *The International Human Rights Movement: A History* (Princeton, NJ: Princeton University Press, 2012); David Rieff, *A Bed for the Night:*

Humanitarianism in Crisis (New York: Simon & Schuster, 2002); Margaret E. Keck and Kathryn Sikkink, *Activists beyond Borders: Advocacy Networks in International Politics* (Ithaca, NY: Cornell University Press, 1998); Fiona Terry, *Condemned to Repeat? The Paradox of Humanitarian Action* (Ithaca, NY: Cornell University Press, 2002); John Tirman, *The Deaths of Others: The Fate of Civilians in America's Wars* (New York: Oxford University Press, 2011).

Part 1:
Humanitarian Aid Dilemmas

Aid workers can be found in some of the most challenging and dangerous environments in the world—sewing up the wounded, feeding the hungry, sheltering those who have lost their homes to natural or man-made disasters. Their work is unquestionably difficult, desperately needed, and often thankless. And yet, for all their impressive work, does humanitarianism have a dark side? Is it at risk of becoming politicized, and aiding and abetting the agenda of war fighters? Even worse, in putting a Band-Aid on civilian suffering, does humanitarian aid prolong war?[1]

BIRTH OF THE HUMANITARIAN MOVEMENT

In 1859, a Swiss merchant named Henry Dunant witnessed the aftermath of the battle of Solferino, a decisive and bloody battle in the second Italian war for independence. Horrified at the neglect of wounded soldiers, he began a movement that would lead to the formation of the first and one of the most significant international humanitarian aid organizations, the International Committee of the Red Cross (ICRC), and the development of principles that still dominate international humanitarian law and humanitarian aid.[2]

Dunant argued that providing medical care and support to those who were not actively taking part in the conflict—which included not only civilians but also wounded soldiers and prisoners of war—was a moral obligation. While they were engaged in conflict, he conceded, soldiers could be targeted, but when they were taken out of the fight—by virtue of being wounded or taken prisoner—helping them was an act of basic humanity. This was a revolutionary concept at the time. Only minimal medical facilities and resources were available for wounded soldiers, and those offering medical care to a soldier might easily find themselves targeted by the other side as aiding the enemy. Dunant revolutionized care in wartime and gained recognition for the idea that those providing aid *neutrally* to all sides and parties should not be targeted because they were fulfilling society's duty to help those in need.

Dunant's ideas and activities were eventually codified into international law and led to the emergence of a new cadre of nongovernmental organizations focused on providing humanitarian aid—medical assistance, food, water, shelter, and other basic subsistence needs—during periods of conflict or humanitarian crises. Beginning with the ICRC and the affiliated Red Cross and Red Crescent societies,[3] a model of aid organizations emerged dedicated to the principle of providing relief and assistance impartially, neutrally, and independent of parties to the conflict.

UNINTENDED CONSEQUENCES AND DO NO HARM

Since Dunant's time, thousands of aid organizations—both local and international—have emerged. They are present in the majority of conflict zones and emergency situations worldwide, providing medical aid and humanitarian support in places where the most basic resources would otherwise not be available. Aid workers, laboring for little or no pay, often far from their homes and at great personal risk, have come to the rescue in crisis after crisis—providing shelter, food, and water after natural disasters, delivering lifesaving medical support for civilians caught in war, or reuniting and supporting families separated by famine, war, or disease. The work of nongovernmental organizations (NGOs) may go beyond immediate, emergency support, for example supporting longer-term camps and services for refugees or displaced persons, or providing development or medical assistance that might prevent disasters or better equip communities to respond to them when they happen.

Given that their work aids millions in the most desperate of situations every year, it is difficult to take issue with the track record of humanitarians. Yet some critics worry that even the best-intentioned humanitarianism may be doing as much harm as good. By addressing the needs of conflict-affected populations, humanitarian aid mitigates the costs of war that might otherwise force the end of a conflict. Supporting humanitarian aid can act as an "out" that allows the international community or more powerful states to do something about the humanitarian suffering without intervening militarily or politically, which many argue would result in a more sustainable solution. NGO-provided aid, shelter, or medical support may be wasted, misused, embezzled, or may be the crutch that prevents local communities from developing their own long-term support means.

In some situations, armed groups use humanitarian aid to support their own fighters. For example, following the 1994 Rwandan genocide, aid organizations provided relief to the millions of refugees who fled to refugee camps in the nearby Democratic Republic of the Congo. But in addition to those civilians who fled, many former government officials and leaders of armed groups who had organized and perpetrated the genocide also took refuge in the camps. They used the camps as a base to carry out attacks against the new Rwandan government and the armed groups that had defeated them, and to perpetrate more abuses and atrocities against the local population and other refugees.

The dilemmas created by providing humanitarian aid are the focus of the first article in this section, "Alms Dealers: Can You Provide Humanitarian Aid Without Facilitating Conflicts?," by journalist Philip Gourevitch. The point of departure for Gourevitch is *The Crisis Caravan: What's Wrong with Humanitarian Aid?*, by humanitarian aid critic Linda Polman. Polman's book offers a scathing view of the aid industry. She argues that in many cases the money and media attention that tend to follow NGOs can be an incentive for armed groups to perpetuate atrocities. By way of example she points to fighters in the Sierra Leone civil war who, she says, may have conducted mass amputations of the civilian population to attract international attention and money toward the Sierra Leone crisis.

Polman accuses the aid sector as a whole of ignoring these unintended consequences because the continuation of war serves its interests (NGOs whose mission is to bandage wounds would have no job if there were no wounds to bandage). As Gourevitch summarizes Polman's argument: "Sowing horror to reap aid, and reaping aid to sow horror . . . is 'the logic of the humanitarian era.'"[4] Because aid workers are perceived to be doing good, they are not held to account, Polman asserts.

Gourevitch notes that Polman's "polemic" approach leaves out the good that humanitarians have done in many situations. But in his years as a foreign correspondent, he often saw situations that smacked of facilitating ongoing conflict. He reflects on a visit to a town called Kitchanga in eastern Congo, where he spent a night observing a medical clinic run by Médecins Sans Frontières (one of the most prominent global medical humanitarian aid organizations). He marveled that the humanitarian doctors had been able to save a young boy whose "neck had been chopped through to the bone," only to later discover that the same doctors had also treated the armed fighters likely responsible for the boy's injuries. "And I wondered: If these humanitarians weren't here, would that boy have needed them?"[5]

Polman ultimately concludes that in such situations, rather than risk feeding the conflict, humanitarians would do better to withdraw, regardless of the humanitarian suffering that would result. But many humanitarians, including the Humanitarian Policy Group authors in the second article, "Aid and War: A Response to Linda Polman's Critique of Humanitarianism,"[6] reject this all-or-nothing approach. They agree with some of Polman's critiques—that aid is big business, that some of it is squandered or stolen, and that it can sometimes create "perverse and at times catastrophic effects."[7] Nevertheless, they argue that, contrary to Polman's assertion that NGOs are unaccountable or unreflective of the consequences of their work, incidents like the Rwandan refugee crisis sparked an "existential crisis" within the humanitarian aid world that led to "a radical and sustained rethinking of the nature, purpose and practice of aid."[8]

Further they argue that Polman oversimplifies the situation facing NGOs:

It is not sufficient to say, as Polman seems to on Rwanda, that withdrawing or withholding aid will somehow induce combatants to see sense and stop killing. In reality, complex emergencies are precisely that—complex constellations of social, political, ethnic and historical problems, within which humanitarian aid is only one element among many. For all the terrible mistakes that have been made, the larger failures arguably lie with others, not least donor governments and the political and security organs of the UN.[9]

THE POLITICIZATION OF AID

While much has changed since Dunant's time, aid organizations still consider the three principles of independence, neutrality, and impartiality that Dunant established to be the bedrock of the humanitarian ethic, enabling humanitarian organizations to provide truly need-based aid without being swayed by the politics of a crisis situation. Critics like Polman argue that an overemphasis on neutrality is part of the problem, because it blinds humanitarian actors to situations in which their aid perpetuates, or is part of, a conflict. "Whether you're being manipulated by the Sudanese regime or coalition forces in Afghanistan, you are always an instrument of war," she argued in a *Guardian* interview (not included in this book).[10] The critique is that even if humanitarians intend to provide aid neutrally or impartially, their presence and the aid they provide inevitably have an impact, which may not be neutral or impartial in its effect.

But many NGOs counter that the problem is not that the concept of neutrality is outdated or inappropriate as an operating principle, but that since Dunant's time, state parties who should be helping to uphold this principle have instead taken actions that undermine it, and put humanitarians and their work at risk. As Cornelio Sommaruga, former president of the ICRC, frames the problem: "Politicians and governments have abused humanitarianism to disengage from their own responsibilities, and, in doing so, have provoked an enormous and grave confusion."[11]

In the third article in this section, "9/11 and Humanitarian Assistance: A Disturbing Legacy," Elizabeth Ferris argues that the United States' response to the September 11, 2001, attacks has limited the space to provide neutral and impartial humanitarian aid. As part of a strategy to win hearts and minds in counterinsurgency operations in Iraq and Afghanistan, the U.S. government has become more engaged in humanitarian activity—both by funding massive amounts of humanitarian and development aid and by directly distributing some humanitarian supplies through U.S. troops. Where it has funded the aid, it has tried to take credit, or asked NGOs relying on those funds to let the population know whom the support is coming from. In this way, Ferris argues, the United States has tried to co-opt the work of NGOs "as a tool of U.S. foreign policy."[12] This has had the effect, or at least the perception, of militarizing aid in many key conflict zones, which in turn makes it difficult for NGOs to maintain their independence and neutrality.

In "Politicized Humanitarianism: A Response to Nicolas de Torrente," Paul O'Brien explores the quandary for NGOs on the other end of this aid dilemma: should aid organizations accept humanitarian aid funding from warring parties in countries in which they are part of the fight? Are NGOs who do so also to blame for imperiling NGOs' neutrality, or undermining the success of their work? O'Brien is responding to an article (not included in this volume) by Nicolas de Torrente, former director of the U.S. office of Doctors Without Borders. Torrente argued that NGOs who accepted U.S. funding in Iraq damaged the credibility of assistance and made humanitarian groups vulnerable to targeting.[13] O'Brien rejects the assumption that aid is completely apolitical. In some conflicts, the presence of aid is inevitably part of the conflict because warring parties' objectives are to support or block support to the civilian population. Thus groups that have the ability to help the population have become either an important ally or the next target.

Because of this dynamic in Afghanistan—with the United States and NATO allies seeking to support humanitarian aid, and the Taliban or other armed groups deliberately putting civilians and aid workers at risk—humanitarian aid workers cannot be neutral; and maybe they should not be, O'Brien counters. "What is going on in Afghanistan and Iraq is not the politicization of aid—which is a tautology—but a diminishing consensus on the political value of humanitarian independence. . . . In contexts such as Afghanistan and Iraq, humanitarians are unlikely to convince warring parties that they should be left alone because their aid is of no political or military importance."[14] Where their interests align with the United States (for example, in Afghanistan both the United States and NGOs generally sought to limit harm and ensure humanitarian access), O'Brien argues taking U.S. funding should not be problematic. There is no one-size-fits-all approach to humanitarian engagement in conflict zones, he argues.

What some characterize as politicization of aid is simply a response to engaging in that environment.

Given the moral imperative for this type of work and the difficulties within these crisis situations, the dilemmas humanitarian workers face may not be easy to resolve. Reflecting on recent pressures for the humanitarian aid community to be more political—to withdraw from some situations, or to abandon neutrality—David Rieff, a prominent thinker on humanitarianism and its unintended consequences, writes:

> In most cases, humanitarianism is best advised to focus on saving lives, whatever the compromises it has to make along the way. Let it tend to the victims and remind the luckier corner of the world of the incalculable suffering, misery, and grief that literally billions of people feel every day of their lives.... The tragedy of humanitarianism may be that for all its failings and limitations, it represents what is decent in an indecent world. Its core assumptions—solidarity, a fundamental sympathy for victims, and an antipathy for oppressors and exploiters—represent those rare moments of grace when we are at our best. So many people, including relief workers, now speak of "mere" charity, "mere" humanitarianism—as if coping with a dishonorable world justly, and a cruel world with kindness, were not honor enough.[15]

As you read these selections, consider the following questions:

- Where there is a risk of extending the conflict or having aid manipulated by warring parties, should aid organizations withdraw? What are the arguments for and against?

- Polman argues that NGOs are blind to the consequences of their actions and never held to account. What sort of accountability mechanisms would be appropriate for this type of work?

- What sort of checks do you think would be important to ensure that humanitarian organizations are balancing the possible side effects or consequences of their presence against the intended benefits?

- Do you agree with authors like Ferris that actions by warring parties like the United States have undermined the principle of neutrality, limiting humanitarian space? Or would some of those limitations have happened regardless because of the surrounding conflict dynamics?

- Is it problematic for humanitarian organizations to take aid money from states that are party to the conflict? What if the funds support work they independently believe is important?

- Is Dunant's principle of neutrality outdated? Or is the problem that state actors have stopped respecting and helping to preserve neutral, humanitarian operating space, as many NGOs argue? How would you support either argument?

NOTES

1. See Andrew Anthony, "Does Humanitarian Aid Prolong War?," *Guardian*, April 24, 2010, http://www.theguardian.com/society/2010/apr/25/humanitarian-aid-war-linda-polman.

2. For more on Dunant's early motivations and work in this period, and the continued engagement of the International Committee of the Red Cross in later decades, see International Committee of the Red Cross, "From the Battle of Solferino to the Eve of the First World War," December 28, 2004, http://www.icrc.org/eng/resources/documents/misc/57jnvp.htm; G. François Bugnion, "The Role of the Red Cross in the Development of International Humanitarian Law: The International Committee of the Red Cross and the Development of International Humanitarian Law," *Chicago Journal of International Law* 5, no. 191 (Summer 2004).

3. ICRC field staff regularly monitor the treatment of prisoners of war and remind warring parties of their obligations under international law. For more on their role and activities, see Alain Aeschlimann, "Protection of Detainees: The ICRC's Action Behind Bars," International Committee of the Red Cross, Publication Ref. 0861, September 20, 2005, http://www.icrc.org/eng/resources/documents/publication/p0861.htm; "Protection of Civilians in Conflict—the ICRC Perspective," address by Angelo Gnaedinger, ICRC director-general, Humanitarian and Resident Coordinators' Retreat, Geneva, May 9, 2007, http://www.icrc.org/eng/resources/documents/statement/children-statement-140507.htm.

4. Philip Gourevitch, "Alms Dealers: Can You Provide Humanitarian Aid Without Facilitating Conflicts?," *New Yorker*, October 11, 2010, p. 105, http://www.newyorker.com/arts/critics/atlarge/2010/10/11/101011crat_atlarge_gourevitch?printable=true&currentPage=all#ixzz2eSlIhNac.

5. Ibid., 109.

6. The Overseas Development Institute opinion is directly responding to Polman's critiques made in her book *War Games: The Story of Aid and War in Modern Times*, which is a different book than the one discussed in the article by Gourevitch, but with many of the same critiques.

7. The Humanitarian Policy Group, Opinion: "Aid and War: A Response to Linda Polman's Critique of Humanitarianism," Overseas Development Institute, May 2010, p. 144.

8. Ibid.

9. Ibid., 145.

10. Anthony, "Does Humanitarian Aid Prolong War?"

11. David Rieff, *A Bed for the Night: Humanitarianism in Crisis* (New York: Simon & Schuster, 2002), 26.

12. Elizabeth Ferris, "9/11 and Humanitarian Assistance: A Disturbing Legacy," *Up Front* blog, http://www.brookings.edu/blogs/up-front/posts/2011/09/01-sept11-ferris.

13. See Nicolas de Torrente, "Humanitarian Action under Attack: Reflections on the Iraq War," *Harvard Human Rights Journal* 17 (2004): 1–30.

14. Paul O'Brien, "Politicized Humanitarianism: A Response to Nicolas de Torrente," *Harvard Human Rights Journal* 17 (2004): 32.

15. David Rieff, "Humanitarianism in Crisis," *Foreign Affairs* (November/December 2002): 121.

Alms Dealers: Can You Provide Humanitarian Aid Without Facilitating Conflicts?

*by Philip Gourevitch**

In Biafra in 1968, a generation of children was starving to death. This was a year after oil-rich Biafra had seceded from Nigeria, and, in return, Nigeria had attacked and laid siege to Biafra. Foreign correspondents in the blockaded enclave spotted the first signs of famine that spring, and by early summer there were reports that thousands of the youngest Biafrans were dying each day. Hardly anybody in the rest of the world paid attention until a reporter from the *Sun*, the London tabloid, visited Biafra with a photographer and encountered the wasting children: eerie, withered little wraiths. The paper ran the pictures alongside harrowing reportage for days on end. Soon, the story got picked up by newspapers all over the world. More photographers made their way to Biafra, and television crews, too. The civil war in Nigeria was the first African war to be televised. Suddenly, Biafra's hunger was one of the defining stories of the age—the graphic suffering of innocents made an inescapable appeal to conscience—and the humanitarian-aid business as we know it today came into being.

"There were meetings, committees, protests, demonstrations, riots, lobbies, sit-ins, fasts, vigils, collections, banners, public meetings, marches, letters sent to everybody in public life capable of influencing other opinion, sermons, lectures, films and donations," wrote Frederick Forsyth, who reported from Biafra during much of the siege, and published a book about it before turning to fiction with "The Day of the Jackal." "Young people volunteered to go out and try to help, doctors and nurses did go out to offer their services in an attempt to relieve the suffering. Others offered to take Biafran babies into their homes for the duration of the war; some volunteered to fly or fight for Biafra. The donors are known to have ranged from old-age pensioners to the boys at Eton College." Forsyth was describing the British response, but the same things were happening across Europe, and in America as well.

Stick-limbed, balloon-bellied, ancient-eyed, the tiny, failing bodies of Biafra had become as heavy a presence on evening-news broadcasts as battlefield dispatches from Vietnam. The Americans who took to the streets to demand government action were often the same demonstrators who were protesting what their government was doing in Vietnam. Out of Vietnam and into Biafra—that was the message. Forsyth writes that the State Department was flooded with mail, as many as twenty-five thousand letters in one day. It got to where President Lyndon Johnson told his Undersecretary of State, "Just get those nigger babies off my TV set."

That was Johnson's way of authorizing humanitarian relief for Biafra, and his order was executed in the spirit in which it was given: stingily. According to Forsyth, by the war's end, in 1970, Washington's total expenditure on food aid for Biafra had been equivalent to "about three days of the cost of taking lives in Vietnam," or "about twenty minutes of the Apollo Eleven flight." But Forsyth, who was an unapologetic partisan of the Biafran cause, reserved his deepest contempt for the British government, which supported the Nigerian blockade. Even as Nigeria's representative to abortive peace talks declared, "Starvation is a legitimate weapon of war, and we have every intention of using it," the Labour Government in London dismissed reports of Biafran starvation as enemy propaganda. Whitehall's campaign against Biafra, Forsyth wrote, "rings a sinister bell in the minds of those who remember the small but noisy caucus of rather creepy gentlemen who in 1938 took it upon themselves to play devil's advocate for Nazi Germany."

The Holocaust was a constant reference for Biafra advocates. In this, they were assisted by Biafra's secessionist government, which had a formidable propaganda department and a Swiss public-relations firm. The cameras made the historical association obvious: few had seen such images since the liberation of the Nazi death camps. Propelled by that memory, the Westerners who gave Biafra their money and their time (and, in some cases, their lives) believed that another genocide was imminent there, and the humanitarian relief operation they mounted was unprecedented in its scope and accomplishment.

In 1967, the International Committee of the Red Cross, the world's oldest and largest humanitarian nongovernmental organization, had a total annual budget of just half a million dollars. A year later, the Red Cross was spending about a million and a half dollars a month in Biafra alone, and other N.G.O.s, secular and church-based (including Oxfam, Caritas, and Concern), were also growing exponentially in response to Biafra. The Red Cross ultimately withdrew from the Nigerian civil war in order to preserve its neutrality, but by then its absence hardly affected the scale of the operation. Biafra was inaccessible except by air, and by the fall of 1968 a humanitarian airlift had begun. The Biafran air bridge, as it was known, had no official support from any state. It was carried out entirely by N.G.O.s, and all the flying had to be done by night, as the planes were under constant fire from Nigerian forces. At its peak, in 1969, the mission delivered an average of two hundred and fifty metric tons of food a night. Only the Berlin airlift had ever moved more aid more efficiently, and that was an Air Force operation.

The air bridge was a heroic undertaking, and a stunning technical success for a rising humanitarian generation, eager to atone for the legacies of colonialism and for the inequities of the Cold War world order. In fact, the humanitarianism that emerged from Biafra—and its lawyerly twin, the human-rights lobby—is probably the most enduring legacy of the ferment of 1968 in global politics. Here was a non-ideological ideology of engagement that allowed one, a quarter of a century after Auschwitz, not to be a bystander, and, at the same time, not to be identified with power: to stand always with the victim, in solidarity, with clean hands—healing hands. The underlying ideas and principles weren't new, but they came together in Biafra, and spread forth from there with a force that reflected a growing desire in the West (a desire that only intensified when the Berlin Wall was breached) to find a way to seek honor on the battlefield without having to kill for it.

Three decades later, in Sierra Leone, a Dutch journalist named Linda Polman squeezed into a bush taxi bound for Makeni, the headquarters of the Revolutionary United Front rebels. In the previous decade, the R.U.F. had waged a guerrilla war of such extreme cruelty in the service of such incoherent politics that the mania seemed its own end. While the R.U.F. leadership, backed by President Charles Taylor, of Liberia, got rich off captured diamond mines, its Army, made up largely of abducted children, got stoned and sacked the land, raping and hacking limbs off citizens and burning homes and villages to the ground. But, in May, 2001, a truce had been signed, and by the time Polman arrived in Sierra Leone later that year the Blue Helmets of the United Nations were disarming and demobilizing the R.U.F. The business of war was giving way to the business of peace, and, in Makeni, Polman found that former rebel warlords—such self-named men as General Cut-Throat, Major Roadblock, Sergeant Rape Star, and Kill-Man No-Blood—had taken to calling their territories "humanitarian zones," and identifying themselves as "humanitarian officers." As one rebel turned peacenik, who went by the name Colonel Vandamme, explained, "The white men are soon gonna need drivers, security guards, and houses. We're gonna provide them."

Colonel Vandamme called aid workers "wives"—"because they care for people," according to Polman, and also, presumably, because they are seen as fit objects of manipulation and exploitation. Speaking in the local pidgin, Vandamme told Polman, "Them N.G.O. wifes done reach already for come count how much sick and pikin [children] de na di area." Vandamme saw opportunity in this census. "They're my pikin and my sick," he said. "Anyone who wants to count them has to pay me first."

This was what Polman had come to Makeni to hear. The conventional wisdom was that Sierra Leone's civil war had been pure insanity: tens of thousands dead, many more maimed or wounded, and half the population displaced—all for nothing. But Polman had heard it suggested that the R.U.F.'s rampages had followed from "a rational, calculated strategy." The idea was that the extreme violence had been "a deliberate attempt to drive up the price of peace." Sure enough, Polman met a rebel leader in Makeni, who told her, "We'd worked harder than anyone for peace, but we got almost nothing in return." Addressing Polman as a stand-in for the international community, he elaborated, "You people looked the other way all those years. . . . There was nothing to stop for. Everything was broken, and you people weren't here to fix it."

In the end, he claimed, the R.U.F. had escalated the horror of the war (and provoked the government, too, to escalate it) by deploying special "cut-hands gangs" to lop off civilian limbs. "It was only when you saw ever more amputees that you started paying attention to our fate," he said. "Without the amputee factor, you people wouldn't have come." The U.N.'s mission in Sierra Leone was per capita the most expensive humanitarian relief operation in the world at the time. The old rebel believed that, instead of being vilified for the mutilations, he and his comrades should be thanked for rescuing their country.

Is this true? Do doped-up maniacs really go a-maiming in order to increase their country's appeal in the eyes of international aid donors? Does the modern humanitarian-aid industry help create the kind of misery it is supposed to redress? That is the central contention of Polman's new book, "The Crisis Caravan: What's Wrong with Humanitarian Aid?" (Metropolitan; $24), translated by the excellent Liz Waters. Three years after Polman's visit to Makeni, the international Truth and Reconciliation Commission for Sierra Leone published testimony that described a meeting in the late nineteen-nineties at which rebels and government soldiers discussed their shared need for international attention. Amputations, they agreed, drew more press coverage than any other feature of the war. "When we started cutting hands, hardly a day BBC would not talk about us," a T.R.C. witness said. The authors of the T.R.C. report remarked that "this seems to be a deranged way of addressing problems," but at the same time they allowed that under the circumstances "it might be a plausible way of thinking."

Polman puts it more provocatively. Sowing horror to reap aid, and reaping aid to sow horror, she argues, is "the logic of the humanitarian era." Consider how Christian aid groups that set up "redemption" programs to buy the freedom of slaves in Sudan drove up the market incentives for slavers to take more captives. Consider how, in Ethiopia and Somalia during the nineteen-eighties and nineties, politically instigated, localized famines attracted the food aid that allowed governments to feed their own armies while they further destroyed and displaced targeted population groups. Consider how, in the early eighties, aid fortified fugitive

Khmer Rouge killers in camps on the Thai-Cambodian border, enabling them to visit another ten years of war, terror, and misery upon Cambodians; and how, in the mid-nineties, fugitive Rwandan *génocidaires* were succored in the same way by international humanitarians in border camps in eastern Congo, so that they have been able to continue their campaigns of extermination and rape to this day.

And then there's what happened in Sierra Leone after the amputations brought the peace, which brought the U.N., which brought the money, which brought the N.G.O.s. All of them, as Polman tells it, wanted a piece of the amputee action. It got to the point where the armless and legless had piles of extra prosthetics in their huts and still went around with their stubs exposed to satisfy the demands of press and N.G.O. photographers, who brought yet more money and more aid. In the obscene circus of self-regarding charity that Polman sketches, vacationing American doctors turned up, sponsored by their churches, and performed life-threatening (sometimes life-taking) operations without proper aftercare, while other Americans persuaded amputee parents to give up amputee children for adoption in a manner that seemed to combine aspects of bribery and kidnapping. Officers of the new Sierra Leone government had only to put out a hand to catch some of the cascading aid money.

Polman might also have found more heartening anecdotes and balanced her account of humanitarianism run amok with tales of humanitarian success: lives salvaged, epidemics averted, families reunited. But in her view the good intentions of aid—and the good that aid does—are too often invoked as excuses for ignoring its ills. The corruptions of unchecked humanitarianism, after all, are hardly unique to Sierra Leone. Polman finds such moral hazard on display wherever aid workers are deployed. In case after case, a persuasive argument can be made that, over-all, humanitarian aid did as much or even more harm than good.

"Yes, but, good grief, should we just do nothing at all then?" Max Chevalier, a sympathetic Dutchman who tended amputees in Freetown for the N.G.O. Handicap International, asked Polman. Chevalier made his argument by shearing away from the big political-historical picture to focus instead, as humanitarian fundraising appeals do, on a single suffering individual—in this instance, a teen-age girl who had not only had a hand cut off by rebels but had then been forced to eat it. Chevalier wanted to know, "Are we supposed to simply walk away and abandon that girl?" Polman insists that conscience compels us to consider that option.

The godfather of modern humanitarianism was a Swiss businessman named Henri Dunant, who happened, on June 24, 1859, to witness the Battle of Solferino, which pitted a Franco-Sardinian alliance against the Austrian Army in a struggle for control of Italy. Some three hundred thousand soldiers went at it that day, and Dunant was thunderstruck by the carnage of the combat. But what affected him more was the aftermath of the fight: the battlefield crawling with wounded soldiers, abandoned by their armies to languish, untended, in their gore and agony. Dunant helped organize local civilians to rescue, feed, bathe, and bandage the survivors. But the great good will of those who volunteered their aid could not make up for their incapacity and incompetence. Dunant returned to Switzerland brooding on the need to establish a standing, professionalized service for the provision of humanitarian relief. Before long, he founded the Red Cross, on three bedrock principles: impartiality, neutrality, and independence. In fund-raising letters, he described his scheme as both Christian and a good deal for countries going to war. "By reducing the number of cripples," he wrote, "a saving would be effected in the expenses of a Government which has to provide pensions for disabled soldiers."

Humanitarianism also had a godmother, as Linda Polman reminds us. She was Florence Nightingale, and she rejected the idea of the Red Cross from the outset. "I think its views most absurd just such as would originate in a little state like Geneva, which can never see war," she said. Nightingale had served as a nurse in British military hospitals during the Crimean War, where nightmarish conditions—septic, sordid, and brutal—more often than not amounted to a death sentence for wounded soldiers of the Crown. So she was outraged by Dunant's pitch. How could anyone who sought to reduce human suffering want to make war less costly? By easing the burden on war ministries, Nightingale argued, volunteer efforts could simply make waging war more attractive, and more probable.

It might appear that Dunant won the argument. His principles of unconditional humanitarianism got enshrined in the Geneva Conventions, earned him the first Nobel Peace Prize, and have stood as the industry standard ever since. But Dunant's legacy has hardly made war less cruel. As humanitarian action has proliferated in the century since his death, so has the agony it is supposed to alleviate. When Dunant contemplated the horrors of Solferino, nearly all of the casualties were soldiers; today, the U.N. estimates that ninety per cent of war's casualties are civilians. And Polman has come back from fifteen years of reporting in the places where aid workers ply their trade to tell us that Nightingale was right.

The scenes of suffering that we tend to call humanitarian crises are almost always symptoms of political circumstances, and there's no apolitical way of responding to them—no way to act without having a political effect. At the very least, the role of the officially neutral, apolitical aid worker in most contemporary conflicts is, as Nightingale forewarned, that of a caterer: humanitarianism relieves the warring parties of many of the burdens (administrative and financial) of waging war, diminishing the demands of governing while fighting, cutting the cost of sustaining casualties, and supplying the food, medicine, and logistical support that keep armies going. At its worst—as the Red Cross demonstrated during the Second World War, when the organization offered its services at Nazi death camps, while maintaining absolute confidentiality about the atrocities it was privy to—impartiality in the face of atrocity can be indistinguishable from complicity.

"The Crisis Caravan" is the latest addition to a groaning shelf of books from the past fifteen years that examine the humanitarian-aid industry and its discontent. Polman leans heavily on the seminal critiques advanced in Alex de Waal's "Famine Crimes" and Michael Maren's "The Road to Hell"; on Fiona Terry's mixture of lament and apologia for the misuse of aid, "Condemned to Repeat?"; and on David Rieff's pessimistic meditation on humanitarian idealism, "A Bed for the Night." All these authors are veteran aid workers, or, in Rieff's case, a longtime humanitarian fellow-traveller. Polman carries no such baggage. She cannot be called disillusioned. In an earlier book, "We Did Nothing," she offered a prosecutorial sketch of the pathetic record of U.N. peacekeeping missions. Then, as now, her method was less that of investigative reporting than the cumulative anecdotalism of travelogue pointed by polemic. Her style is brusque, hardboiled, with a satirist's taste for gallows humor. Her basic stance is: *J'accuse.*

Polman takes aim at everything from the mixture of world-weary cynicism and entitled self-righteousness by which aid workers insulate themselves from their surroundings to the deeper decadence of a humanitarianism that paid war taxes of anywhere from fifteen per cent of the value of the aid it delivered (in Charles Taylor's Liberia) to eighty per cent (on the turf of some Somali warlords), or that effectively provided the logistical infrastructure for ethnic cleansing (in Bosnia). She does not spare her colleagues in the press, either, describing how reporters are exploited by aid agencies to amplify crises in ways that boost fund-raising, and to present stories of suffering without political or historical context.

Journalists too often depend on aid workers—for transportation, lodging, food, and companionship as well as information—and Polman worries that they come away with a distorted view of natives as people who merely suffer or inflict suffering, and of white humanitarians as their only hope. Most damningly, she writes: "Confronted with humanitarian disasters, journalists who usually like to present themselves as objective outsiders suddenly become the disciples of aid workers. They accept uncritically the humanitarian aid agencies' claims to neutrality, elevating the trustworthiness and expertise of aid workers above journalistic skepticism."

Maren and de Waal expose more thoroughly the ignoble economies that aid feeds off and creates: the competition for contracts, even for projects that everyone knows are ill-considered, the ways in which aid upends local markets for goods and services, fortifying war-makers and creating entirely new crises for their victims. Worst of all, de Waal argues, emergency aid weakens recipient governments, eroding their accountability and undermining their legitimacy. Polman works in a more populist vein. She is less patient in building her case—at times slapdash, at times flippant. But she is no less biting, and what she finds most galling about the humanitarian order is that it is accountable to no one. Moving from mess to mess, the aid workers in their white Land Cruisers manage to take credit without accepting blame, as though humanitarianism were its own alibi.

Since Biafra, humanitarianism has become the idea, and the practice, that dominates Western response to other people's wars and natural disasters; of late, it has even become a dominant justification for Western war-making. Biafra was where many of the leaders of what de Waal calls the "humanitarian international" got their start, and the Biafra airlift provided the industry with its founding legend, "an unsurpassed effort in terms of logistical achievement and sheer physical courage," de Waal writes. It is remembered as it was lived, as a cause célèbre— John Lennon and Jean-Paul Sartre both raised their fists for the Biafrans—and the food the West sent certainly did save lives. Yet a moral assessment of the Biafra operation is far from clear-cut.

After the secessionist government was finally forced to surrender and rejoin Nigeria, in 1970, the predicted genocidal massacres never materialized. Had it not been for the West's charity, the Nigerian civil war surely would have ended much sooner. Against the lives that the airlifted aid saved must be weighed all those lives—tens of thousands, perhaps hundreds of thousands—that were lost to the extra year and a half of destruction. But the newborn humanitarian international hardly stopped to reflect on this fact. New crises beckoned—most immediately, in Bangladesh—and who can know in advance whether saving lives will cost even more lives? The crisis caravan rolled on. Its mood was triumphalist, and to a large degree it remains so.

Michael Maren stumbled into the aid industry in the nineteen-seventies by way of the Peace Corps. "In the post-Vietnam world, the Peace Corps offered us an opportunity to forge a different kind of relationship with the Third World, one based on respect," he writes. But he soon began to wonder how respectful it is to send Western kids to tell the elders of ancient agrarian cultures how to feed themselves better. As he watched professional humanitarians chasing contracts to implement policies whose harm they plainly saw, he came to regard his colleagues as a new breed of mercenaries: soldiers of misfortune. Yet, David Rieff notes, "for better or worse, by the late 1980s humanitarianism had become the last coherent saving ideal."

How is it that humanitarians so readily deflect accountability for the negative consequences of their actions? "Humanitarianism flourishes as an ethical response to emergencies not just because bad things happen in the world, but also because many people have lost faith in both economic development and political struggle as ways of trying to improve the human lot," the social scientist Craig Calhoun observes in his contribution to a new volume of essays, "Contemporary States of Emergency," edited by Didier Fassin and Mariella Pandolfi (Zone; $36.95). "Humanitarianism appeals to many who seek morally pure and immediately good ways of responding to suffering in the world." Or, as the Harvard law professor David Kennedy writes in "The Dark Sides of Virtue" (2004), "Humanitarianism tempts us to hubris, to an idolatry about our intentions and routines, to the conviction that we know more than we do about what justice can be."

Maren, who came to regard humanitarianism as every bit as damaging to its subjects as colonialism, and vastly more dishonest, takes a dimmer view: that we do not really care about those to whom we send aid, that our focus is our own virtue. He quotes these lines of the Somali poet Ali Dhux:

A man tries hard to help you find your lost camels.
He works more tirelessly than even you,
But in truth he does not want you to find them, ever.

In May of 1996, in the hill town of Kitchanga in the North Kivu province of eastern Congo (then still called Zaire), I spent a night in a dank schoolroom that had been temporarily set up as an operating room by surgeons from the Dutch section of Médecins Sans Frontières. A few days earlier, a gang from the U.N.-sponsored refugee camps for Rwandan Hutus—camps that were controlled by the killers, physically, politically, economically—had massacred a group of Congolese Tutsis at a nearby monastery. Members of the M.S.F. team had been patching up some of the survivors. A man with a gaping gunshot wound writhed beneath the forceps of a Belarusian doctor, chanting quietly—"Ay, yay, yay, yay, yay, yay"—before crying out in Swahili, "Too much sorrow."

Everyone knew that the Hutu génocidaires bullied and extorted aid workers, and filled their war chests with taxes collected on aid rations. Everybody knew, too, that these killers were now working their way into the surrounding Congolese territory to slaughter and drive out the local Tutsi population. (During my visit, they had even begun attacking N.G.O. vehicles.) In the literature of aid work, the U.N. border camps set up after the Rwandan genocide, and particularly the Goma camps, figure as the ultimate example of corrupted humanitarianism— of humanitarianism in the service of extreme inhumanity. It could only end badly, bloodily. That there would be another war because of the camps was obvious long before the war came.

Aid workers were afraid, and demoralized, and without faith in their work. In the early months of the crisis, in 1994, several leading aid agencies had withdrawn from the camps to protest being made the accomplices of *génocidaires*. But other organizations rushed to take over their contracts, and those who remained spoke of their mission as if it had been inscribed in stone at Mt. Sinai. They could not, they said, abandon the people in the camps. Of course, that's exactly what the humanitarians did when the war came: they fled as the Rwandan Army swept in and drove the great mass of people in the camps home to Rwanda. Then the Army pursued those who remained, fighters and noncombatants, as they fled west across Congo. Tens of thousands were killed, massacres were reported—and this slaughter was the ultimate price of the camps, a price that is still being paid today by the Congolese people, who chafed under serial Rwandan occupations of their country, and continue now to be preyed upon by remnant Hutu Power forces.

Sadako Ogata, who ran the U.N. refugee agency in those years, and was responsible for all the camps in Congo, wrote her own self-exculpating book, "The Turbulent Decade," in which she repeatedly falls back on the truism "There are no humanitarian solutions to humanitarian problems." She means that the solution must be political, but, coming from Ogata, this mantra also clearly means: no holding humanitarianism accountable for its consequences. One of Ogata's top officers at the time said so more directly, when he summed up the humanitarian experience of the Hutu Power-controlled border camps and their aftermath with the extraordinary Nixonian formulation "Yes, mistakes were made, but we are not responsible."

It is a wonder that the U.N. refugee chiefs' spin escaped Linda Polman's notice: it's the sort of nonsense that gets her writerly pulse up. But Polman does effectively answer them. "As far as I'm aware," she remarks, "no aid worker or aid organization has ever been dragged before the courts for failures or mistakes, let alone for complicity in crimes committed by rebels and regimes."

Aid organizations and their workers are entirely self-policing, which means that when it comes to the political consequences of their actions they are simply not policed. When a mission ends in catastrophe, they write their own evaluations. And if there are investigations of the crimes that follow on their aid, the humanitarians get airbrushed out of the story. Polman's suggestion that it should not be so is particularly timely just now, as a new U.N. report on atrocities in the Congo between 1993 and 2003 has revived the question of responsibility for the bloody aftermath of the camps. There can be no proper accounting of such a history as long as humanitarians continue to enjoy total impunity.

During my night at the schoolroom surgery in Kitchanga, the doctors told me about a teen-age boy who had been found naked except for a banana leaf, which he had plastered over the back of his head and shoulders. When the leaf fell away, the doctors saw that the boy's neck had been chopped through to the bone. His head hung off to the side. I saw the boy in the morning. He was walking gingerly around the schoolyard. The doctors had reassembled him and stitched him back together. And he was not the only one they had saved. This was the humanitarian ideal in practice—pure and unambiguous. Such immense "small mercies" are to be found everywhere that humanitarians go, even at the scenes of their most disastrous interventions. What could be better than restoring a life like that? The sight of that sewed-up boy was as moving as the abuses of the humanitarian international were offensive. Then, later that day, the doctors I was travelling with told me that, to insure their own safety while they worked, they had to prove their neutrality by tending to *génocidaires* as well as to their victims. And I wondered: If these humanitarians weren't here, would that boy have needed them?

*Philip Gourevitch is an award-winning, regular contributor to the *New Yorker* and former editor of the *Paris Review*.

Gourevitch, Philip. "Alms Dealers: Can You Provide Humanitarian Aid Without Facilitating Conflicts?" *New Yorker*, October 11, 2010. http://www.newyorker.com/arts/critics/atlarge/2010/10/11/101011crat_atlarge_gourevitch?printable=true&currentPage=all#ixzz2c97Ea3LG.

Aid and War: A Response to Linda Polman's Critique of Humanitarianism

by the Humanitarian Policy Group at the Overseas Development Institute*

Dutch journalist Linda Polman has some sharp things to say about humanitarian aid in an interview in the *Observer* newspaper promoting her book *War Games: The Story of Aid and War in Modern Times*. Many of Polman's criticisms of the practice of humanitarian action are valid, and echo those levelled at aid workers in the 1990s. Yet progress has been made over the last decade and the picture is not quite as bleak as painted. More importantly, on the fundamental question of the relationship between humanitarian aid and conflict, Polman's critique is based on an incomplete understanding of the scope and purpose of humanitarianism, and what sets it apart from other forms of intervention in conflicts and complex emergencies.

First, the areas where we agree. Relief aid is, as Polman says, big business. Although accurate figures are difficult to obtain, analysts at Development Initiatives estimate that the humanitarian aid sector globally was worth at least $18 billion in 2008 (Development Initiatives, 2009). In the same year, the sector employed almost 300,000 people (Stoddard et al., 2009). One of the biggest players, World Vision International, spent over $6.5 million on relief assistance in 60 countries that year, distributing over half a million tonnes of food to 8.5 million people. In short, a lot of money and jobs are involved.

Polman is also right that aid has had perverse and at times catastrophic effects, most notably in Goma's refugee camps in 1994. She is right too that competition between agencies distorts the aid enterprise by forcing agencies to go where the money is, not necessarily where the greatest needs are. It is also true that, in complicated crises like Afghanistan, aid work is now identified with the overall Western political and strategic effort. The notion of rich aid workers living in luxury compounds while those around them struggle to survive is grotesque and the destabilising effects of their high wages on local economies are well known. So too are allegations of sexual abuse.

Then there are the problems Polman doesn't mention. No one really knows, for instance, how much relief aid is diverted by agency staff, leaving aside what is taken by thugs, militias and politicians. Nor do agencies really know how to target help to the very poorest in a society. Very often, everyone receives something in the belief that a little is better than nothing. And then we complain when those who don't want the food, seeds or tools we have given them sell them to others who do.

We tell donors that they're not giving enough, while simultaneously telling ourselves that giving too much creates aid dependency, as if humanitarian assistance were the only resource for people in times of crisis (Harvey and Lind, 2005). A lack of contextual knowledge, plus cultural insensitivity, often lead to inappropriate, unwanted or unsustainable projects. Displaced people are still herded into massive camps because delivering aid is easier and cheaper when they are in one place, despite evidence that camps are often incubators of disease and crime, and often develop into more-or-less permanent communities. At higher policy levels, we worry that humanitarian aid may become a substitute for the state, freeing governments of their responsibility to their own people.

Where we part company with Polman is in her diagnosis of the cause of these ills, her verdict on the sector's efforts to improve and her assessment of the power of humanitarian aid to shape the social and political environment in the world's poorest and most distressed states. According to Polman, the root of humanitarianism's apparent crisis lies in its preoccupation with neutrality, one of the basic principles of the sector. In her view, aid workers use neutrality to sidestep any moral or legal responsibility for the detrimental effects of aid.

This misrepresents what neutrality means in this context. It does not mean dodging responsibility for humanitarian agency actions, or standing aloof from suffering. As an operating principle, neutrality means staying apart from warring parties, thereby protecting agencies' access to war-affected people and ensuring the safety of their staff. By not taking sides, so the theory goes, agencies do not present a threat and should be treated with respect. Granted there are many examples where neutrality has failed, and some aid workers, reflecting on the role of aid in Iraq and Afghanistan in particular, wonder whether it still has value. But a commitment to neutrality does not allow humanitarian agencies to behave as they like, nor does it give them permission to duck responsibility and accountability for what they do.

Second is Polman's claim that, while aid workers know the problems, competition between agencies makes them unwilling to address them. Not so. The crisis in Rwanda in 1994, like the Biafran war some 30 years earlier, was an existential crisis in humanitarianism. The painful truth that relief aid was supporting people guilty of genocide led to a radical and sustained rethinking of the nature, purpose and practice of aid. A vast evaluation looked in rigorous detail at the Rwanda response (DANIDA, 1996), and a widely accepted code of conduct was developed governing aid agencies' work (Borton, 1994), along with a humanitarian charter and a plethora of standards and guidelines covering everything from shelter reconstruction to psychosocial care. Frameworks of action have sought to ensure that, post-Rwanda, aid at a minimum does no harm (Anderson, 1999), and the idea of protecting people in the immediate crisis (going beyond the provision of food and shelter) is more prominent in humanitarian discourse, even if there is precious little agreement on what protection is (O'Callaghan and Pantuliano, 2007). At a systemic level, new mechanisms are trying to improve coordi[nation] and cut out wasteful duplication, and agencies are more aware of the need to work with local governments and groups.

On the ground, much effort has been put into making humanitarian action accountable to its recipients, as well as to its donors, and aid agencies try to consult people on who should get aid and how. Efforts to work with representative local institutions, make people aware of their aid entitlements, set up complaints mechanisms and monitor delivery aim to ensure that aid reaches its intended destination. Innovations, such as the provision of cash instead of food, are meant to enhance choice and preserve people's dignity (Harvey, 2007), and new products and techniques, such as community-based therapeutic care, have improved targeting and treatment (Collins, 2004). Aid projects are now routinely evaluated and impacts assessed, and the sector is more professional and managerial in its approach. Humanitarianism has, in short, become much more complex, sophisticated and reflective than Polman's arguments suggest.

No standards or codes, however, can guarantee effective action on the ground, and humanitarianism remains messy and imperfect. Nonetheless, these are not negligible changes, and show that, in principle at least, thoughtful practitioners are aware of the shortcomings of the past and are conscious of the need to fix them. The trouble is that none of these innovations really gets to the heart of the problem, namely that humanitarian assistance alone cannot ensure that belligerents will behave well towards aid workers or their beneficiaries, or listen to calls to respect human rights and international humanitarian law.

It is not sufficient to say, as Polman seems to on Rwanda, that withdrawing or withholding aid will somehow induce combatants to see sense and stop killing. In reality, complex emergencies are precisely that—complex constellations of social, political, ethnic and historical problems, within which humanitarian aid is only one element among many. For all the terrible mistakes that have been made, the larger failures arguably lie with others, not least donor governments and the political and security organs of the UN.

Influencing the course and conduct of conflict is ultimately the business of politicians, diplomats and soldiers, not aid workers, whose main concern is with the victims of conflict and abuse. Aid workers know all too well the failures, limitations and risks of aid in complex environments, not least because they are often at the sharp end when things go wrong, and they have taken important steps to overcome the problems they face. More needs to be done, but this should not mean making the perfect the enemy of the good, abandoning our common humanity and leaving the victims of conflicts and crises to fend for themselves.

References

Anderson, Mary B. (1999) *Do No Harm: How Aid Can Support Peace—Or War.* Boulder, CO: Lynne Rienner.

Borton, J (ed.) (1994) *Code of Conduct for the International Red Cross and Red Crescent Movement and NGOs.* HPN Network Paper 7. London: ODI.

Collins, S. (2004) *Community-Based Therapeutic Care.* HPN Network Paper 48. London: ODI.

DANIDA (1996) *The International Response to Conflict and Genocide: Lessons from the Rwanda Experience.* Various authors. Copenhagen: DANIDA.

Development Initiatives (2009) *Summary GHA Report* (http://bit.ly/summGHA).

Harvey, P. (2007) *Cash-Based Responses in Emergencies.* HPG Report 24. London: ODI.

Harvey, P. and Lind, J. (2005) *Dependency and Humanitarian Relief: A Critical Analysis.* HPG Report 19. London: ODI.

Harvey, P., Stoddard, A., Harmer, A., Taylor, G. (2010) *The State of the Humanitarian System Report.* London: ODI/ALNAP. (http://bit.ly/SOHSrep)

Humanitarian Exchange (2010) 'Humanitarian Protection,' *Humanitarian Exchange* special issue, no. 46, March. London: ODI.

O'Callaghan, S. and Pantuliano, S. (2007) *Protective Action: Incorporating Civilian Protection into Humanitarian Response.* HPG Report 26. London: ODI.

Polman, L. (2010) *War Games: The Story of Aid and War in Modern Times.* New York: Viking.

Stoddard, A., Harmer, A. and DiDomenico, V. (2009) 'Providing Aid in Insecure Environments: 2009 Update,' HPG Policy Brief 34. London: ODI.

*The **Overseas Development Institute** is the United Kingdom's leading independent think tank on international development and humanitarian issues.

The Humanitarian Policy Group, Overseas Development Institute. "Aid and War: A Response to Linda Polman's Critique of Humanitarianism." *Opinion* 144. May 2010. Overseas Development Institute, London.

Used by permission.

9/11 and Humanitarian Assistance: A Disturbing Legacy

by Elizabeth Ferris*

Counterterrorism policies implemented since the attacks on September 11, 2001 have fundamentally, perhaps irreversibly, changed the international humanitarian system. For almost 150 years, humanitarian action has been grounded in a few basic principles: that humanitarian agencies are independent of governments, neutral in political conflicts and impartial in the way they distribute assistance. Adherence to these principles has enabled humanitarians to work in the world's most dangerous areas and to help victims on all sides of a conflict. However, for the past decade, these principles have come under increasing threat as policymakers try to use humanitarian assistance in support of the struggle against terrorists and insurgents.

The post-9/11 determination to apprehend the terrorists responsible for the attacks on the United States and to prevent other terrorist actions has impacted humanitarian work in many ways, but three developments stand out: the increasingly active role of the U.S. military as a provider of humanitarian relief; efforts to use U.S. non-governmental organizations (NGOs) as a tool of U.S. foreign policy; and the criminalization of humanitarian diplomacy in cases where negotiations with non-state actors are necessary for humanitarian access. While the intentions of these actions to stop terrorists are certainly laudable, the consequences of these actions have been devastating for humanitarian actors.

1) THE INCREASINGLY ACTIVE ROLE OF THE U.S. MILITARY AS A PROVIDER OF HUMANITARIAN RELIEF

The U.S. military's involvement in humanitarian assistance certainly predates the 9/11 attacks, but the scale and intentionality of its involvement have since increased to the point that such assistance is now a standard "tool" in counterinsurgency operations. From Provincial Reconstruction Teams and Commanders' Emergency Response Funds to the formation of U.S. Africa Command (AFRICOM), military provision of humanitarian relief is used to support military objectives. While international military involvement in natural disasters—such as the earthquake in Haiti or the floods in Pakistan last year—is not as controversial, when the military provides assistance in settings in which it is actively engaged in conflict, the message is clear that such assistance is neither neutral nor independent of foreign policy objectives. The U.S. military has now become a major stakeholder in the humanitarian system which raises many questions: Are the traditional principles of neutrality, independence and impartiality still valid—or possible? How do humanitarian agencies relate to the military on the ground? What does it mean when the face of US humanitarian aid is now a soldier's?

2) THE EFFORTS TO USE U.S. NON-GOVERNMENTAL ORGANIZATIONS (NGOs) AS A TOOL OF U.S. FOREIGN POLICY

In the days following 9/11, the U.S. government made it clear that American NGOs receiving U.S. government funds were instruments of U.S. foreign policy. References by then-US Secretary of State Colin Powell that NGOs were 'force multipliers' and by the USAID Administrator Andrew Natsios that NGOs were expected to act as arms of the U.S. government made it difficult, indeed impossible, for U.S. humanitarian NGOs to claim that they were independent of their government's policy, particularly when they were supported with U.S. funding. Things became even stickier with the implementation of a partner vetting system by the U.S. government which requires nonprofit organizations applying for USAID funding to provide personal information on NGO staff and partner organizations, with even more onerous requirements in place for countries such as Iraq and Afghanistan. While the intention is to prevent U.S. government funds from being diverted to terrorists, in practice this means that NGOs are seen as reporting to the U.S. government on their contacts in the field. This has put the NGOs in an extraordinarily difficult position vis-à-vis their own local staff, their local implementing partners and the international NGO community.

3) THE CRIMINALIZATION OF HUMANITARIAN DIPLOMACY— PARTICULARLY IN CASES WHERE NEGOTIATIONS WITH NONSTATE ACTORS ARE NECESSARY FOR HUMANITARIAN ACCESS

Finally, since 9/11, legislation has expanded both the statutory definition of a terrorist organization and the interpretation of what it means to provide 'material support' to such organizations. The damages caused by this expanded understanding are manifold. On an individual level, it has severely restricted the U.S. refugee resettlement program, whereby a woman who provided water to an insurgent holding a gun to her head or a father who paid ransom to free his kidnapped child from a nonstate actor is deemed ineligible for resettlement on the grounds of having provided material support to terrorists. Although there have been some waivers to these restrictions, laws on material support have been upheld by the U.S. Supreme Court, most notably in the 2010 decision of *Holder vs. the Humanitarian Law Project*. In this case, the Humanitarian Law Project, a U.S.-based nonprofit, had wanted to provide training in international humanitarian law and peaceful conflict-resolution mechanisms to the Kurdistan Workers Party (PKK). But the PKK has been designated as a terrorist organization by the State Department and even efforts to provide them with training in human rights were judged by the Supreme Court to constitute material support and hence to be a crime punishable by a 15-year prison sentence.

The fact is that negotiating with nonstate actors to gain access to civilians affected by conflict has long been a necessity for humanitarians working in conflict zones—a necessity which has now become criminalized when these nonstate actors are designated as terrorist organizations. This raises questions of whether humanitarian agencies need to retain criminal defense counsel to help them in preparing and planning operations in conflict areas where insurgent forces are active. The reality, of course, is that these areas are precisely those where humanitarian need is often the greatest.

Although it has certainly taken the lead, the United States is not alone in adopting counterterrorism legislation which negatively impacts humanitarian actions. But it is a shame that these counterterrorist efforts are making it even more difficult for humanitarian agencies seeking to uphold basic principles of neutrality, independence and impartiality while assisting people in desperate need. What a terrible legacy of 9/11.

*Elizabeth Ferris is the codirector of the Brookings-LSE Project on Internal Displacement and a senior fellow in Foreign Policy, where her work encompasses a wide range of issues related to internal displacement, humanitarian action, natural disasters, and climate change. Her book *The Politics of Protection* examines the challenges—and limitations—of protecting vulnerable populations from the ravages of war and natural disasters.

Ferris, Elizabeth. "9/11 and Humanitarian Assistance: A Disturbing Legacy." *Up Front.* http://www.brookings.edu/blogs/up-front/posts/2011/09/01-sept11-ferris.

Politicized Humanitarianism: A Response to Nicolas de Torrente

by Paul O'Brien*

Nicolas de Torrente raises a dilemma for humanitarians: how do they continue to reach people in need when western policy makers want to assimilate them into their political and military agendas on the one hand and anti-western extremists want to kill them on the other? He believes that humanitarians can and should resolve this dilemma by rediscovering their apolitical roots. If humanitarian nongovernmental organizations (NGOs) can prove themselves politically neutral, impartial and independent, then perhaps belligerents will once again allow them to save lives and relieve humanitarian suffering.

De Torrente is right to urge humanitarians to respond to what he calls the "politicization of aid," but he is wrong to suggest that a return to classic humanitarianism offers our only hope.[1] Learning lessons from post-Taliban Afghanistan as well as Iraq, this Response concludes that humanitarians need something more than political agnosticism. Challenging three of de Torrente's theoretical conclusions, this Response argues that (1) humanitarianism is and should be political, (2) humanitarians can and should speak out about the justice and injustice of war, and (3) accepting funding from belligerents in war can make both principled and pragmatic good sense.

I. HUMANITARIANISM IS AND SHOULD BE POLITICAL

De Torrente, and classic humanitarians more generally, confuse politics and partisanship. Humanitarianism is a political ideology and always has been. "Humanity," "impartiality," "independence," and "neutrality" are all political values. Politics, at its essence, concerns the decision-making process through which policy makers allocate resources and power. Humanitarian action channels resources and power in a certain direction and in a certain way—to save the lives of the neediest in conflicts. The decision in 1949 to mandate legally the protection of civilians in war was a profoundly political step,[2] just as it is political to mandate the redistribution of resources from the powerful to the marginalized, or from one country's taxpayers to save lives in another.

De Torrente fails to recognize that what is going on in Afghanistan and Iraq is not the politicization of aid—which is a tautology—but a diminishing consensus on the political value of humanitarian independence. That independence has always relied upon belligerents accepting the notion that humanitarianism should not substantially alter the military outcome or political consequence of a conflict. In contexts such as Afghanistan and Iraq, humanitarians are unlikely to convince warring parties that they should be left alone because their aid is of no political or military importance. With belligerents increasingly willing to either co-opt or attack humanitarian work, his response that "humanitarian action is not a political project"[3] rings like an honorable lament for the past, but no longer provides adequate guidance to humanitarian actors in highly politicized settings. To remain relevant in such contexts, classic humanitarianism must answer difficult questions:

1. Is claiming to be "beyond" politics the most effective path for most humanitarians? At the heart of classic humanitarianism is a call for humility—what de Torrente calls "the limited, modest yet vitally important ambition to ensure that the most vulnerable are not sacrificed in times of conflict and crisis."[4] Classic humanitarians argue they can at least give those in need a "bed for the night",[5] they do not rebuild lives or restore livelihoods, but they can save them for another day, for another set of future actors.

This argument makes sense for Médecins Sans Frontières (MSF), given its primary focus on emergency medicine, but is less relevant or meaningful for other humanitarians. Many other international aid agencies have multiple mandates focused not just on saving lives through health interventions, but also on helping the living to rebuild after they are saved, by fighting extreme poverty, educating children, providing food and adequate nutrition, and helping people to feed themselves. These larger mandates are born not out of a lack of humility, but out of a strong sense that ensuring human survival is simply not enough.[6]

2. What if all humanitarian NGOs in Afghanistan had adopted a limited and classical humanitarian mandate? The vast majority would have left Afghanistan following the last humanitarian crisis of 2002 because saving lives was no longer the main concern.[7] As a result, many children would have gone without education.[8] The reconstruction effort, already compromised by insecurity, would have all but ground to a halt.[9] NGOs would have refused to engage in projects such as the National Solidarity Program (NSP), designed to alleviate poverty, because NSP also aimed to legitimize the central government as a service provider.[10] Although humanitarian work in Afghanistan has moved beyond the 'life and death' political choices of emergency response work and towards the far more explicitly political work of post-conflict reconstruction, it remains crucial to the people of Afghanistan.[11] NGOs that participate in such work cannot claim to be apolitical. Rather, they need to understand and articulate how their political solidarity with the people they serve trumps any political obligations they may have to their donors or to the sovereign governments where they work.

3. *Is classic humanitarianism humble when it claims to be "beyond" politics?* De Torrente's argument assumes that the humanitarian space necessary to help those in need is dictated in large part not by warring parties, but by the decisions of NGOs to accept or refuse funding. In the Iraq context, he holds humanitarians partly culpable for the politicization of aid because they conceded its inevitability.[12] Perhaps it would be more humble to acknowledge that humanitarians do not control or even significantly influence humanitarian space and to adapt to the new environment that politically partisan aid use presents, recognizing that we are but one small voice in a complex political matrix. We cannot dictate the humanitarian future of threatened populations, but we may be able to influence them by engaging in political debate.

II. HUMANITARIANS SHOULD SPEAK OUT ON THE JUSTICE OF WAR AND OBLIGATIONS OF BELLIGERENTS IN WAR

Classic humanitarianism was born of a pragmatic accommodation: war is inevitable, and while operating in conflict zones and promoting justice *in* war, humanitarians must pass no political judgment on the justice *of* war. De Torrente argues that MSF was right not to engage publicly on the justness of the wars in Iraq or Afghanistan. He believes that French and British NGOs should not have challenged the justness of the Iraq invasion because they jeopardized their ability to reach people in need when the war started.[13]

In making this argument, de Torrente assumes that the benefits of apolitical humanitarian action in war will always outweigh the good that can be done through political engagement on the justness of war. That is a matter of judgment, not of principle. If one believes that belligerents listen to humanitarians and constrict humanitarian space as a result, it is at least possible that they are influenced by humanitarian perspectives on the justice and injustice of war.

Additionally, de Torrente offers no evidence to indicate that belligerents make the connection between NGOs taking a political stand on war and the restriction of humanitarian space.[14] When attacks on the NGO community in Afghanistan went from one a month in late 2002 to almost one a day one year later,[15] no one suggested that extremists were targeting NGOs because of their political views.[16] In fact, if their aim was to terrorize humanitarians, then the more innocent and apolitical their targets, the more effective they would be. In reality, it is far more likely that NGOs were being targeted simply because they were Western soft targets.

De Torrente's response to the deteriorating security situation in Iraq is to call for more effective measures by the United States as part of its responsibilities as an Occupying Power.[17] Although the U.S. military is not necessarily in the same position as an occupying force in Afghanistan, de Torrente's plea for greater security is equally relevant in Afghanistan because it acknowledges the fundamental need for basic security as a precursor to reconstruction. Recognizing this need for security, CARE has been one of the NGOs calling for expansion of international military forces outside of Kabul. The aim of CARE's advocacy in repeated policy briefs and more than three hundred interviews with the international press in 2002 and 2003 is to promote the security rights and reconstruction needs of ordinary Afghans.[18] In fact, CARE's advocacy repeatedly urged international military forces to avoid blurring the lines between military and civilian activities and, to date, has refused to work alongside them or to accept any form of armed protection for their activities.[19]

CARE believes, and NATO has confirmed,[20] that NGOs have been instrumental in keeping discussions alive on the need for greater international investment in security in Afghanistan. As long as most of Afghanistan faces a security vacuum and is increasingly ruled by local militia leaders and drug lords, CARE plans to urge the international community to fulfill their promises to Afghans to provide security.[21] While de Torrente himself does acknowledge the importance of increased security in Iraq, MSF's silence on this issue in Afghanistan has been surprising considering its policy of speaking out on rights issues and its purpose to promote international humanitarian law.[22] In light of ground developments in places like Afghanistan and Iraq, classic humanitarians should at least ask themselves whether their struggle to remain beyond politics shuts the door after the horse has bolted, leaving the barn inside burning.

III. HUMANITARIANS SHOULD CONSIDER
TAKING FUNDING FROM BELLIGERENTS

Finally, de Torrente argues that NGOs should refuse politically motivated funding and challenges U.S. NGOs for compromising their humanitarian independence by accepting money from the United States when it is one of the belligerents. But his argument fails to answer four important questions:

    1. *If classic humanitarians refuse funding from the U.S. government and as a result needs are not met, are they not violating their commitment to impartiality?* The only

legitimate basis for refusing to take funding from a warring party is that ultimately it will do more harm than good for intended beneficiaries. But one cannot reach that conclusion without a complex, political cost-benefit analysis that contemplates refusing to respond to needs because of the source of the support. Such a calculation, to use de Torrente's words, "challenges the essence of humanitarian action as a neutral and impartial endeavor."[23]

2. *When is public funding not politically motivated?* In 2002 and 2001, MSF received 19% of its funding from governments and international organizations (like the European Union).[24] While MSF avoids the direct tarnish of belligerent funding, can it argue that the other public funding it receives in contexts other than Iraq, where it is privately funded, is purely altruistic and humanitarian in purpose? The fact that Iraq today (and Afghanistan before it) receives such a disproportionately high percentage of humanitarian funding is a testament to the political nature of that support.

3. *What if there is a coincidence of interests between humanitarian NGOs and the U.S. government in Afghanistan and Iraq?* What if the U.S. government as part of its military and civilian strategy in Afghanistan and Iraq aims to relieve suffering? In signing the International Federation of the Red Cross Code of Conduct, many NGOs commit to "formulate [their] own policies and implementation strategies and . . . not seek to implement the policy of any government, *except in so far as it coincides with* [their] *own independent policy.*"[25] The appropriate question is not whether NGOs take funding. Rather, the question is whether taking funding from a belligerent compromises the "single-minded purpose of alleviating suffering, unconditionally and without any ulterior motive."[26] Admittedly, that standard challenges U.S.-funded NGOs that seek political solidarity with the poor in Iraq and Afghanistan to ensure they are not used to further political or military objectives contrary to their missions. But de Torrente goes too far to claim that taking U.S. money for humanitarian purposes in those contexts will necessarily do more harm than good.

Moreover, de Torrente appears to want to have it both ways when it comes to the United States. On the one hand, he chastises the U.S.-led Coalition in Iraq for "the manner in which [it sought] to make the minimization of harm and the provision of relief for Iraqis an integral part of its political and military agenda. . . ."[27] Yet he consistently refers to U.S. obligations under humanitarian law,[28] which in fact include the minimization of harm and the provision of relief.[29] Following de Torrente's argument, it is not clear what would constitute a proper and politically realistic motive for a state to meet its obligations under humanitarian law.

4. If NGOs do not accept funding from belligerents, who will ensure the quantity and quality of humanitarian response? MSF, for example, has a limited capacity to respond to the humanitarian crises in Afghanistan and Iraq because it does not take funding from belligerents, and the donor willing to provide the most significant funding for those countries' reconstruction has been the United States. De Torrente's proposal, if adopted by other NGOs, would leave private contractors (whose single-minded purpose is profit) and the military (whose purpose is the security of their own nationals) to fight poverty and rebuild Afghanistan and Iraq with U.S. money.

Already in Afghanistan, there are serious concerns that the privatization and militarization of aid is robbing the Afghan people of an important opportunity to lift themselves out of poverty. The real debate there is not whether humanitarianism is political, but whether the political agendas of Presidents Karzai and Bush to win reelection is wasting precious reconstruction resources in Afghanistan on high-profile, hardware projects implemented by businesses and soldiers to achieve short-term, political gains without adequate consideration of the software required to make those hardware projects function effectively for Afghans over the long-term. This is a profoundly political debate. Unless humanitarian NGOs who care about the long-term impact on poverty remain engaged, that trend may well worsen in the coming months.

IV. Conclusion

If humanitarian organizations continue to uphold a classic humanitarian model, they will undoubtedly continue to save lives and protect the innocent in conflict. But one size does not fit all in the humanitarian world. CARE and other organizations are committed to addressing not only the tragic symptoms of conflict, but also its root causes. Not all wars are inevitable. Nor is global poverty inevitable. Politicized humanitarians should seek to influence the political root causes of conflict and poverty by working alongside the powerful states, but they should do so with the humble recognition that their efforts will have limited influence.

The "with us or against us" political culture in today's foreign policy, to which de Torrente refers, makes politics a singularly unattractive field with which to engage. But engage we must, for politics are too important to be left to politicians.[30] The fiction of humanitarian neutrality may still have currency for some organizations in some settings, but it can no longer be relied upon for all humanitarians in highly politicized contexts such as Afghanistan and Iraq. In such environments, politicized humanitarianism is both right and realistic.[31]

NOTES

The author would like to thank Kathleen Campbell, Antonio Donini, Volker Heins, Kevin Henry, David Rieff, and Abby Stoddard for their valuable insights.

1. Nicolas de Torrente, cite to 17 Harv. Hum. Rts. J., at 1 [hereinafter de Torrente]. De Torrente's article appears earlier in this issue of the *Harvard Human Rights Journal.*

2. Modern humanitarian law, embodied in the Geneva Conventions, was essentially a novel political ideology that extended the protection of humanitarian law not just to wounded soldiers but to civilians. Following both the specific targeting of the marginalized, disabled, and "racially inferior" by Nazi Germany and the dropping of atomic bombs on civilians by the United States to achieve its military goals, the ideology that civilians should be protected in warfare was a radical departure for the international community and was designed to achieve political consensus that such massive civilian casualties should never happen again.

3. De Torrente at 5.

4. De Torrente at 28.

5. For the most influential recent argument for classic humanitarianism, see David Rieff, A Bed for the Night, Humanitarianism in Crisis (Simon & Schuster 2002). For an interesting critique of David Rieff's arguments, see Hugo Slim, Is Humanitarianism Being Politicized, A Reply To David Rieff, Speech at The Dutch Red Cross Symposium on Ethics in Aid, The Hague, (Oct. 8, 2003) (on file with the author).

6. In Hugo Slim's words, "[t]here are good and bad ways to save people that are determined by wider moral goods around their personal, social and economic dignity. You can't just save and leave. You can't just save by cruelly concentrating people in camps . . . . You can't just save people without an eye to their continued protection or their future livelihood." *Quoted in* Rieff, *supra* note 2, at 3.

7. MSF, to its credit, continued to characterize the situation in Afghanistan as a crisis warranting a humanitarian response. Throughout Afghanistan, medical and nutritional needs remain serious, as reconstruction of the public services is slow to start and conflict continues to affect the south and southeastern parts of the country. MSF maintains assistance programs in 16 of Afghanistan's 32 provinces with a staff of 107 international and 1380 national personnel. Médecins Sans Frontières, MSF *programs around the world, in* MSF International Activity Report 2002–2003, *available at* http://www.msf.org/content/pagecfm?articleid=E0478D42-6DDB-4CCE-8EF89204603CFCB8.

8. CARE, for example, facilitates education programs for 45,000 children, but aims to integrate those programs into the Afghan government school system as the government's capacity increases. Another NGO, the Swedish Committee for Afghanistan, is educating more than 250,000 students. The Afghan government recognizes that in the short term, it must rely heavily upon NGOs and the U.N. as educational service providers while it focuses on "policy making, regulating and monitoring service delivery, facilitating the roles of others, and contracting for services." Afghan Government, *Securing Afghanistan's Future*, Consultation Draft (not for citation) at 24, *available at* http://www.af/recosting/ (Jan. 29, 2004).

9. There are more than 2000 NGOs registered with the Ministry of Planning in Afghanistan (although active NGOs with reasonable capacities and genuinely non-profit missions probably number in the low hundreds). Yet those NGOs continue to provide many of the non-emergency but essential services that Afghans desperately need. Many work closely with the Afghan state to build their long-term capacity as a social safety net for the poor.

10. The NSP is a major government program which aims to allocate $140 million to almost 8000 communities this Afghan fiscal year (Mar. 2003–Mar. 2004). Participating communities are required to select committees to determine the most pressing needs towards which funding will be allocated. These election processes are viewed by many as a means to engage communities in political decision-making.

11. As de Torrente acknowledges, even the most rigidly classical humanitarians do not treat their principles as "sacrosanct straitjackets." De Torrente at 5. When I worked in Western Uganda,

for example, I noted how MSF staff trained government medical staff as a matter of course, even during the conflict between the Ugandan government and anti-government rebels in 2001.

12. De Torrente at 7–8.

13. There is a certain irony in de Torrente's position because MSF has had a well-respected reputation in Afghanistan for being willing to take sides on behalf of the marginalized. They even embraced the political consequences of these stances. As Rony Brauman, one of MSF's founders, wrote in 1998:

> For ten years, together with the teams of other French organizations, the 550 MSF doctors and nurses who relayed each other on Afghan territory were the only foreign humanitarians assisting the population on the side of the Afghan resistance fighters. Because of its rarity, *the medical assistance offered by MSF gave the Afghans valuable psychological and political support. The foreign doctors were their link with the West to make the international community aware of their struggle*, especially from the fall of 1981 onward, when the Red Army began to bomb the hospitals in which MSF was working. *At the time, MSF denounced the Soviet acts and encouraged journalists to visit Afghanistan.*

Rony Brauman & Joelle Tanguy, *The Médecins Sans Frontières Experience* § 12 (1998) (emphasis added), *available at* http://www.doctorswithoutborders.org/publications/other/themsfexperience.shtml.

14. While he concedes the possibility that aid workers are targeted because of what they are, not what they do, he believes this risk can be mitigated by "establishing transparent relationships with local authorities and communities based on an unambiguous humanitarian identity." De Torrente at 6. Again, the implication is that humanitarians control the way they are perceived.

15. *See* CARE, *Good Intentions Will Not Pave the Path to Peace, available at* http://www.careusa.org/newsroom/specialreports/afghanistan/09152003_afghanistanbrief.pdf (Sept. 15, 2003) [hereinafter *Good Intentions*].

16. In Afghanistan, two international aid workers have been killed since the fall of the Taliban. One worked for the ICRC, the most apolitical of all humanitarian agencies; the other worked for the U.N., the humanitarian actor most closely politically allied to the Karzai regime. *See* Carlotta Gall, *In Afghanistan, Helping Can Be Deadly*, N.Y. TIMES, Apr. 5, 2003, at B13, and David Rhode, *Slain Frenchwoman Buried in Afghanistan*, N.Y. TIMES, Nov. 21, 2003, at A8. In Iraq as well, the two most significant attacks on humanitarians have been on the ICRC and the United Nations. *See* Dexter Filkins & Alex Berenson, *Suicide Bombers in Baghdad Kill at Least 34*, N.Y. TIMES, Oct. 28, 2003, at A1, and Dexter Filkins & Richard A. Oppel Jr., *Huge Suicide Blast Demolishes U.N. Headquarters in Baghdad; Top Aid Officials Among 17 Dead*, N.Y. TIMES, Aug. 20, 2003, at A1.

17. De Torrente at 16.

18. *See, e.g.*, CARE, *Rebuilding Afghanistan, A Little Less Talk, A Lot More Action, available at* http://www.careusa.org/newsroom/specialreports/afghanistan/09302002_policybrief.pdf (Oct. 1, 2002); CARE, *A New Year's Resolution to Keep: Secure a Lasting Peace in Afghanistan, available at* http://www.careusa.org/newsroom/specialreports/afghanistan/01132003_policybrief.pdf (Jan. 13, 2003); *Good Intentions, supra* note 11.

19. An area of shared concern between MSF and CARE is the U.S. military's public references to NGOs as an integral part of the U.S.'s larger political and military effect in Afghanistan. *See* de Torrente at 3. CARE's concern, however, is motivated *not* by a belief that we are beyond politics (or can convince belligerents in Afghanistan that we are beyond politics), but because these messages inaccurately portray our political reasons for being in Afghanistan. CARE works in Afghanistan to promote the human rights (including political, economic, and security rights) and aspirations of the poor and marginalized. Claims by the United States that we are here as part of the "war on terror" not only undermine CARE's security, but also CARE's pro-poor political philosophy.

20. I attended a presentation by NATO on February 17, 2004 at which the reason given for NATO plans to expand ISAF was advocacy by NGOs.

21. For example, this author was interviewed for the U.S. television magazine show *60 Minutes* and said the following:

> LESLIE STAHL: . . . [A]nti-Americanism is starting to simmer among the Afghan people?

> MR. O'BRIEN: They're frustrated, and they do at some level look at the international community and the United States in particular and say, "You made promises to us. You told us we'd have peace in Afghanistan. Now I don't feel safe in my town," and that frustration does lead to fingers being pointed.

> *60 Minutes* (CBS television broadcast, May 4, 2003).

22. A December 2003 MSF press release criticized NGO advocacy for increased security in Afghanistan in terms similar to those of de Torrente. "Several NGOs have called for the extended deployment of military forces under NATO command to provide 'security' for their operations and this message may also have contributed to the erosion of the image of NGOs as independent and neutral actors." Press Release, MSF, MSF Suspends Activities in Zhare Dasht Camp, Afghanistan, Violence Against Aid Workers in Afghanistan Esclates [sic], *available at* http://www.msf.org/countries/page.cfm?articleid=0B153B94-535B-4A4D-8F25979E498C2B0A (Dec. 4, 2003). This statement was all the more surprising considering MSF's well-known policy of *temoignage*. As the MSF Web site notes, "*Temoignage* is a French term that encompasses the MSF commitment to testimony, open advocacy and outright denunciation when working with endangered populations throughout the world." *Médecins Sans Frontières*, Temoignage and the MSF movement, *available at* http://www.msf.org/about/index.cfm?indexid=B439CEF3-BFBB-11 D4-B1FD0060084A6370 (last updated June 19, 2001).

23. To slightly adapt de Torrente's own argument, it implies that aid may be selectively allocated to certain groups of victims, or withheld from others, depending on *the source of the aid*, instead of being allocated according to, and proportionate to, needs alone.

24. *Médecins Sans Frontières, Finances, projects and volunteers, in* MSF International Activity Report 2002–2003, *available at* http://www.msf.org/content/page.cfm?articleid=94AF43A9-3265-4758-99F69015EF6C3554. In addition to the E.U., MSF's report names the governments of Belgium, Denmark, Luxembourg, the Netherlands, Norway, Spain, Sweden, and the United Kingdom "among others" as funding sources. *Id.* Historically, MSF has also received funding from the United Nations High Commissioner for Refugees and the United States Office of Foreign Disaster Assistance. *See* Brauman & Tanguy, *supra* note 9, § 8.

25. International Federation of Red Cross and Red Crescent Societies for the ICRC, *Annex IV: The Code of Conduct for the International Red Cross and Red Crescent Movements and NGOs in Disaster Relief*, at principle 4 (Sept. 15, 1995).

26. De Torrente at 5.

27. *Id.* at 3.

28. De Torrente's comment that the U.S. should "fulfill its obligations under IHL in a straightforward and systematic manner instead of viewing the conduct of warfare and provision of assistance primarily through the prism of a 'hearts and minds' agenda" is difficult to understand. De Torrente at 25. Is he suggesting that the United States should not consider or take into account how Iraqis will perceive U.S. military and humanitarian interventions? It is hard to imagine such a suggestion resonating with U.S. policy makers.

29. Article 59 of Geneva Convention IV places this burden firmly upon the Occupying Power, stating:

> If the whole or part of the population of an occupied territory is inadequately supplied, the Occupying Power shall agree to relief schemes on behalf of the said population, and shall facilitate them by all the means at its disposal. Such schemes, which may be undertaken either by States or by impartial humanitarian organizations such as the International Committee of the Red Cross, shall consist, in particular, of the provision of consignments of foodstuffs, medical supplies and clothing.

> Geneva Convention Relative to the Protection of Civilian Persons in Time of War of Aug. 12, 1949, 6 U.S.T. 3516, 3556, 75 U.N.T.S. 287, 326.

30. Charles de Gaulle, former President of France, famously remarked: "I have come to the conclusion that politics are too serious a matter to be left to the politicians." *See* James B. Simpson, Simpson's Contemporary Quotations, *available at* http://www.bartleby.com/63/17/617.html (last visited Feb. 28, 2004).

31. For an account of how politicized humanitarianism is already having an impact in Afghanistan, see generally Paul O'Brien, *Old Woods, New Paths and Diverging Choices for NGOs, in* NATION BUILDING UNRAVELED?: AID, PEACE AND JUSTICE IN AFGHANISTAN (Antonio Donini et al. eds., Kumarian Press 2004).

*Paul O'Brien has been the advocacy coordinator for CARE in Afghanistan since November 2001, based in Kabul. Before that he was CARE's Africa policy adviser, based in Kampala.

O'Brien, Paul. "Politicized Humanitarianism: A Response to Nicolas de Torrente." *Harvard Human Rights Journal* 17 (2004): 31–39.

Part 2:
Speaking Truth to Power: NGO Advocacy Campaigns

One of the more dynamic subsets of nongovernmental organization (NGO) activity in the last few decades has been advocacy in armed conflict or counter-terrorism situations. In many conflicts, NGOs have successfully shifted public discourse and thinking toward greater consideration of the human costs, potentially preventing thousands, if not millions, of civilian casualties, and deterring the commission of other atrocities in war. Yet while human rights NGOs have certainly increased their voice and influence over the conduct of war, critics and self-doubters among them worry that sometimes human rights campaigns that appear to be successful ultimately deliver no greater protection to those suffering on the ground. Can NGOs really have an impact when faced with the realities of global politics and the bad intentions of warmongers and fighters worldwide?

New Modes of NGO Advocacy in Conflict

Although nongovernmental actors have been trying to change the behavior of warring parties at least since Dunant's time, in the last few decades NGOs have become much more prominent in shaping conflict dynamics. NGOs working on laws of war and human rights violations in conflict are engaged both on the ground and at an international level in conflict situations around the world. They can be found at the tip of the spear, investigating the direct impact of munitions on civilians, or in the halls of the United Nations, taking part in treaty negotiations or urging humanitarian intervention.

This area of human rights advocacy has arguably been one of the most successful within the post–Cold War period. NGO advocacy in conflicts such as the U.S. and NATO intervention in Kosovo (1998–99) and Afghanistan (2001–present) and the Israeli conflict with Hezbollah in 2006 have significantly changed the focus of state warring parties to include greater attention to international humanitarian law standards and the reduction of civilian casualties. Aryeh Neier, a leader within the human rights movement, maintained that NGO advocacy in the last two decades "has significantly reduced the numbers killed in some conflicts, as the combatants must modify their conduct in order to gain support in the arena of public opinion."[1] While he notes that this has not been effective in all conflicts, "the magnitude of civilian casualties... [during the first decade of the 21st century] is dwarfed by the vast number killed in the years after World War II, before there was an international human rights movement that took up a focus on armed conflict."[2]

One way that NGOs have expanded their role and influence in conflict is simply by acting as information providers. One of the biggest challenges to greater accountability for misconduct in war is the lack of information or evidence about what is going on. An air strike or a roadside explosion may take place far from major population centers. Civilians affected by conflict may be isolated and unable or afraid to communicate what happened to them. Some patterns of abuse or misconduct may not be visible to the public at all. For example, in cases of detention abuse, the misconduct is happening behind closed doors, heavily fortified and protected by the perpetrator in question (the warring party). Without information about what has happened or is happening in conflict, it can be difficult to assess whether warring parties are following international law and even more difficult to make a case for changing bad behavior.

To fill this gap, NGOs working in this area spend significant time and resources investigating allegations of misconduct and gathering information from the field, often at great risk to themselves. In the first article, "Speaking for Civilians in War," Sarah Holewinski, the executive director of the Center for Civilians in Conflict, describes how gathering such information and using it to limit harm in war have increased the influence of NGOs in modern conflict:

> The NGO community has become go-to experts for the media when covering a conflict, a resource for policymakers as they grapple with how to address a particular aspect of a conflict... and a trusted leader for the public at large, which may offer donations or volunteer on a cause they care about.[3]

A frequent goal of this information gathering is to raise the awareness of the public, which can increase pressure on warring parties to improve their behavior, or may simply encourage members of the public to provide financial or other support that would help victims.

NGOs also use the information they gather to directly confront warring parties and suggest changes in behavior. By directly engaging with militaries involved in conflict, Holewinski asserts, NGOs have been able to bring about tangible changes that save civilian lives. "NGOs are changing how warring parties behave in conflict, how states engage in war, and how civilians—the ordinary people trying to go about their lives in the midst of bullets and bombs—can make it through, unharmed," she argues.[4]

The examples Holewinski provides focus primarily on how NGOs try to change the behavior of state actors. However, other organizations focus on getting non-state actors to conform to international norms and standards, as explored in "NGOs and Nonstate Armed Actors: Improving Compliance with International Norms," by Claudia Hofmann and Ulrich Schneckener. On its face, the idea of getting insurgent groups or rebel fighters to follow standards set out in international treaties may seem even more quixotic than trying to regulate war in the first place. But two organizations—the International Committee of the Red Cross (ICRC) and Geneva Call—have demonstrated that it is possible in some situations. These organizations work to build a relationship of trust with the non-state actors, teach them about standards under international law, make moral or practical arguments for why these standards should be followed, offer concrete suggestions for how to apply them, and reinforce lessons through monitoring and repeated exposure. In this way, they persuade non-state actors to adopt international standards and principles as their own, a process Hofmann and Schneckener call "norm diffusion."

Hofmann and Schneckener argue that ICRC and Geneva Call are most successful when the non-state groups with whom they are dealing value their public reputation, possibly because they seek to ultimately take part in government, or need support from the local population to survive and continue fighting. However, not all groups fit this model, so there are limits to what non-state norm diffusion can achieve. Even where groups do value their public reputation and seek legitimacy, they may not value it enough to comply with all dictates of international law or to cease fighting altogether. "The primary intent of such initiatives is not necessarily more peace, but rather less violence, particularly regarding civilians and, more generally, the prevention of an increasing erosion of international humanitarian law during conflicts," as Hofmann and Schneckener explain.[5]

In addition to these inherent limitations vis-à-vis non-state actors, Hofmann and Schneckener note that the positive role played by actors like ICRC and Geneva Call may be limited in the future by other developments in modern conflict. Revisiting some of the arguments made by Elizabeth Ferris in Part 1, the authors caution that U.S. laws in the wake of September 11 that criminalized contact with non-state actors may shut down an important avenue for enforcing international norms and standards in warfare. This model of norm diffusion depends on NGOs being able to work directly with non-state actors, including offering them some benefits such as humanitarian assistance or other technical advice, which they cannot do if such actions are criminalized.

Rewriting the Laws of War

The types of activities discussed so far—spreading information about what is happening on the ground, and directly advocating that warring parties conform to international norms and standards—are primarily (although not solely) focused on changing warring parties' behavior in the midst of conflict.[6] They are part of enforcing the *existing* norms and rules of international law. But many NGOs also try to shape the norms and rules themselves, with the goal of reforming the laws of war and state policies to prevent civilian deaths or unnecessary suffering in future conflicts.

The third article illustrates how NGOs help create and shape the rules that govern armed conflict. In "Influence and Collaboration: Civil Society's Role in Creating International Humanitarian Law," Bonnie Docherty describes the role that international NGOs played in building momentum for a new treaty prohibiting the use, stockpiling, and transfer of cluster munitions. Cluster munitions are a class of weapons that disperse dozens to hundreds of mini-bomblets over a large area. They cover such a wide territory that they may strike both military and civilian targets indiscriminately. Many cluster munitions also have a high "dud" rate, and when they fail to explode on contact, they leave thousands of unexploded munitions that are hazardous to civilians for decades after the conflict has ended.

After years of failed efforts to ban cluster munitions, a number of NGOs together with state partners initiated a new international treaty to restrict the use of cluster munitions. On May 30, 2008, 94 states signed the new Convention on Cluster Munitions (CCM). Docherty argues that NGOs' success in building momentum toward the CCM, and the emphasis on humanitarian needs within the CCM provisions, demonstrate "the power NGOs can exercise to influence the creation of international law with a humanitarian focus . . . while preserving states' role in diplomacy."[7] She points out that this is only one example of how NGO engagement in the field of disarmament and arms regulation has shifted the emphasis toward greater humanitarian protection than in the past centuries of legal regulation.

Critics have argued that in prioritizing the humanitarian view NGOs may ignore the bigger picture or overrepresent one perspective at the expense of others in treaty development. For example, as Docherty cites, two authors from the conservative Heritage Foundation, Steven Groves and Ted R. Bromund,[8] critiqued NGO engagement in the process that led to the CCM for usurping the legitimate roles of representative governments by "unelected and self-nominated NGOs."[9] Docherty counters that "civil society brought to the table voices often forgotten in traditional diplomacy, but it did not claim to represent the whole world."[10]

THE LIMITS TO REINING-IN WAR

In addition to NGO efforts to change the way war is conducted, a significant amount of advocacy relates to whether force should be used at all. NGOs or other citizens or activists try to stop military engagement altogether or, where they think the cause is justified, try to encourage military intervention.

Military intervention unleashes incredibly destructive forces and often results in mass deprivation of rights, however well conducted or however just the cause that motivated it. So why would humanitarians and rights proponents ever argue *for* the use of military force? In the face of mass human rights abuses or extreme humanitarian crises, many argue that the international community should do something.[11] Following World War II, as the horrors of the Holocaust, the genocide of an estimated 6 million Jewish men, women, and children, became clear, the international community promised to "never again" stand by in the face of mass atrocities. Yet in many cases those perpetrating genocide, allowing or creating a humanitarian crisis, or committing other severe rights abuses can only be stopped by force. In these cases, many argue that the international community not only has a right to intervene in other states' affairs, but it has a responsibility to do so, a "responsibility to protect."[12] For example, in 2013, the U.S. representative to the United Nations, Samantha Power—a long-standing proponent of giving teeth to the phrase "never again"—argued that diplomacy had so far failed to stop the Syrian regime from attacking its own civilians on a mass scale, including with banned chemical weapons. She asserted that use of military force was the only course left:

> We should agree that there are lines in this world that cannot be
> crossed, and limits on murderous behavior, especially with weapons of
> mass destruction, that must be enforced.... The alternative is to give
> a green light to outrages that will threaten our security and haunt our
> conscience, outrages that will eventually compel us to use force anyway
> down the line, at far greater risk and cost to our own citizens. If the last
> century teaches us anything, it is this.[13]

Prior to her government service, Power was a journalist and activist whose widely acclaimed book *A Problem from Hell: America and the Age of Genocide*, denounced global inaction in crisis after crisis following World War II—from the Khmer Rouge in Cambodia in the 1970s to Saddam Hussein's attacks on Iraqi Kurds in the 1990s to the failure to act during the 1994 Rwandan genocide. With a particular focus on U.S. inaction, she argued that lack of significant pressure from the American public allowed U.S. government officials to justify doing nothing in each of these cases.

The fourth article, "A Brief History of 'Save Darfur,'" by Andrew Stobo Sniderman, discusses the success of a movement that tried to test Power's theory: could NGOs or civil society change the calculations for going to war by building concerted pressure on policymakers? Sniderman reviews a book by Rebecca Hamilton that documents the "Save Darfur" campaign, a U.S.-based campaign for humanitarian intervention in the Darfur region in western Sudan. By 2003, repressive government tactics and fighting between the Sudanese government and rebels had already resulted in nearly half a million killed and over 2 million displaced in Darfur. Outraged that the "never again" standard was once again being flouted, a strange-bedfellows mixture of university students, right-wing religious advocates, and anti-genocide activists banded together to try to stop the killing.

By many standards, the Save Darfur campaign was wildly successful: from 2003 to 2010 it built a mass movement, captured frequent and high media attention, and succeeded in pressuring significant U.S. and global policymakers. However, despite these achievements, it was ultimately not enough to change the facts on the ground in a far-off land. "Even an engaged superpower could not dictate terms to a ruthless regime flush with petro-dollars," notes Sniderman.[14]

The reflections in Hamilton's book and Sniderman's critiques raise a sobering question: for all the good intentions, do humanitarian or human rights campaigns live up to their promise? Many rights advocates argue that mobilizing the public and putting a greater spotlight on atrocities can change the course of action, reduce violence, and improve the lives of those they are championing. But Sniderman is not so sure:

> Some claim that unprecedented social media makes faraway atrocities ever harder to ignore (dude, people are dying on my iPhone), and that the human rights community has cracked the code for political impact (ape the National Rifle Association, but for genocide). There is something to this, but certainly less than its proponents claim, as the muted response to the far-greater human toll in Congo demonstrates.[15]

In the final article, "Solving War Crimes with Wristbands: The Arrogance of 'Kony 2012,'" Kate Cronin-Furman and Amanda Taub discuss another campaign to stop atrocities that seemed successful on the surface but may have ultimately fallen short. In doing so, they raise deeper questions about the value of awareness-raising and public advocacy. Cronin-Furman and Taub evaluate the effect of an online advocacy video Kony 2012, produced by the organization Invisible Children, which documented the abuses of the Ugandan guerrilla group the Lord's Resistance Army (LRA) led by Joseph Kony. Although Kony 2012 focused on a relatively obscure conflict, the video immediately vaulted to worldwide notice, with millions of viewers on the Internet. It sparked a mass social media response and an outpouring of public support for doing something to stop Joseph Kony—exactly the type of widespread public attention that many NGOs try to achieve. The mass attention to *Kony 2012* was followed by the United States dispatching 100 Special Forces to hunt for him.

Notwithstanding *Kony 2012*'s enormous virtual popularity, Cronin-Furman and Taub question whether it ultimately made any difference for those subject to the LRA's abuses. They contend that these campaigns mobilize "a demand to do *something*" without taking into account the messy consequences that may result. "The t-shirts, posters, and wristbands of awareness campaigns like Invisible Children's do not mention that death and failure often lie along the road to permanent solutions, nor that the simplest 'solutions' are often the worst."[16]

They argue that a culture of easy awareness—showing support simply by changing a status on Facebook, or "retweeting" a link—can have a negative effect, serving as a substitute for meaningful engagement that might actually address the issues being highlighted. In addition, they worry that NGOs do so much awareness-raising that it dilutes the impact of such activities, and may create the unintended consequence of forestalling political action. "Treating awareness as a goal in and of itself risks compassion fatigue—most people only have so much time and energy to devote to far-away causes—and ultimately squanders political momentum that could be used to push for effective solutions."[17]

Such reservations provide an important check on the more optimistic view of NGO activities in the first three articles. While NGOs undoubtedly have made enormous contributions to limiting the scourge of war, there are limits to what can be accomplished. After all, NGOs in this field are engaging in some of the most challenging global problems, by definition those that were so complex and entrenched that they escalated into war.

As you read these selections, consider the following questions:

- Did you find the authors' descriptions of activities they are engaged in compelling? Are there certain types of activities (advocacy to fighters, treaty development, public awareness) that you think non-state actors should not be engaged in? Why or why not?

- Could you see some of the strategies described in the Holewinski or the Hofmann and Schneckener article working? Do you think NGOs can persuade fighters to take greater care around civilians or to treat prisoners with respect? Do you think these kind of NGO activities could produce unintended consequences or counterreactions? Why or why not?

- Is it important for NGOs to be engaged in the rule-making of war, such as treaty development and modification, so as to bring a more humanitarian perspective? Or could state parties adequately represent these views and balance them against other concerns?

- Viewing all the articles together, clearly some NGO activities or campaigns are more successful than others. What type of situations might be more conducive to successful advocacy or public awareness campaigns?

- In pushing for humanitarian intervention, some argue that in certain situations war is the only way to stop mass atrocities or to reinforce international norms of protection. Do you agree with this position? Can war be an effective way to enforce peace? Why or why not?

- Cronin-Furman and Taub criticize many public-awareness campaigns as a poor substitute for actual political action. However, even if they do not always motivate direct action, might awareness campaigns have other positive effects, for example shaping long-term foreign policy decision-making patterns or simply increasing public knowledge?

- Would you sign on to a Facebook or Twitter campaign to support intervention in a situation like the genocide in Darfur or to stop Joseph Kony's Lord's Resistance Army? Why or why not?

NOTES

1. Aryeh Neier, *The International Human Rights Movement: A History* (Princeton, NJ: Princeton University Press, 2012), 16–17.

2. Ibid., 17.

3. Sarah Holewinski, "Speaking for Civilians in War," in this volume, p. 64.

4. Ibid.

5. Claudia Hofmann and Ulrich Schneckener, "NGOs and Nonstate Actors: Improving Compliance with International Norms," United States Institute of Peace, Special Report 284 (July 2011), 2.

6. Undoubtedly the more that standards are enforced during conflict, the more it increases the strength of norms and their ability to exert authority over other warring parties in future conflicts. Thus strategies that focus on warring-party conduct during conflict also have a preventive role.

7. Bonnie Docherty, "Influence and Collaboration: Civil Society's Role in Creating International Humanitarian Law," in this volume, p. 92.

8. Steven Groves and Ted R. Bromund, "The United States Should Not Join the Convention on Cluster Munitions," Heritage Foundation backgrounder, no. 2550, April 28, 2011, http://www.heritage.org/research/reports/2011/04/the-united-states-should-not-join-the-convention-on-cluster-munitions, p. 20, as quoted in Docherty, "Influence and Collaboration," 90.

9. Groves and Bromund, "United States Should Not Join," 21.

10. Docherty, "Influence and Collaboration," 90.

11. In some cases, the end goal may not be full-scale military engagement, or may be measures short of the use of force. Depending on the circumstances, activists may press for diplomatic engagement, economic sanctions, or only a limited use of military force—for example the use

of airpower to block the aggressor state from firing on civilians. In the case of the 1995 geno-cide of the Tutsi minority group in Rwanda (an estimated 800,000 killed), some argued that U.S. or UN intervention could have been as simple as jamming radio signals, since local radio broadcasts exhorted crowds to attack Tutsis with machetes, a significant cause of death.

12. The concept of a legitimate humanitarian intervention gained such wide currency that in 2000, the Canadian government established a commission to review what was seen as an emerging norm of "responsibility to protect." The commission's findings argued that where a state fails to protect its citizens from mass human rights abuses, it loses some of its sovereignty rights. In cases of extreme violations of such rights, the international community not only may intervene legitimately but has the responsibility to do so, first diplomatically, or economically, and then using armed force as a last resort.

13. Remarks on the Syrian conflict by Ambassador Samantha Power, U.S. permanent representa-tive to the United Nations, at the Center for American Progress, Washington, DC, September 6, 2013, http://usun.state.gov/briefing/statements/213901.htm.

14. Andrew Stobo Sniderman, "A Brief History of 'Save Darfur,'" *Columbia Journalism Review*, March 16, 2011, http://www.cjr.org/critical_eye/a_brief_history_of_save_darfur.php?page=all.

15. Ibid.

16. Kate Cronin-Furman and Amanda Taub, "Solving War Crimes with Wristbands: The Arro-gance of 'Kony 2012,'" March 8, 2012, *Atlantic*, http://www.theatlantic.com/international/archive/2012/03/solving-war-crimes-with-wristbands-the-arrogance-of-kony-2012/254193/.

17. Ibid.

Speaking for Civilians in War

*by Sarah Holewinski**

In today's wars, there are no clear battlefields, no trenches or fields demarcated for the fighting. Instead, combat zones are ordinary neighborhoods, with the homes and shops and schools of ordinary people caught in the line of fire. These people are considered under international law to be "civilians." The world's governments came together after the horrors of the Second World War to deem civilians off limits, not to be targeted or involved in the conflict, to the extent that such a thing is possible. Still, in just the past decade, civilians in Afghanistan, Iraq, Mali, Pakistan, Somalia, and Syria, to name a few places, have seen their streets transformed by war. They've lost property, jobs, and loved ones. Often the only people who will speak for them or try to get them help are nongovernmental organizations (NGOs).

NGOs working inside conflict zones and on war as a pressing human rights issue are a diverse group, both in the reasons why they do their work and in the way they do their work. Motivations for working in such a tragic, difficult field range from a desire to speak for the powerless to righting injustices, from religious conviction to a more academic interest in the strategies of making peace. The daily work of NGOs is just as wide-ranging. Some groups, like Human Rights Watch, publicize violations of human rights to shame the perpetrators into changing their behavior. A group like Amnesty International has millions of members worldwide and speaks on their behalf against injustices. Other groups like CARE, Save the Children, and MercyCorps are focused on bringing aid supplies like water, food, shelter, and medical care to families suffering through a war.

The parties in warfare have changed drastically between the end of the last century and today, as have their roles. In World Wars I and II, militaries usually wore uniforms to signal their fighting status; doctors and nurses wore their white coats with the red cross emblem to signal their jobs to heal. Aid for people harmed in the conflict was often given by either the Red Cross (one of the first formal humanitarian organizations) or by the local population. Interested citizens formed committees to provide limited relief to civilians or to speak out in public on behalf of war victims, but formal NGOs with a specific mandate to do so were few and far between.

Today, the battlefield is muddled. Armed actors may be uniformed military, but they are just as likely to be rebel groups, militias, and criminal gangs who have an interest in not identifying themselves, often by wearing civilian clothes and blending into the population. The Red Cross is still going strong in most conflict zones, providing much-needed aid and services to the displaced or wounded, and reminding warring parties of their obligations under international law. But a new crop of aid and advocacy efforts has emerged in warfare in the form of the NGO, marking a significant shift in parties involved on the battlefield and in the halls of power.

The relatively recent flood of NGOs as actors onto the battlefield gives civilians in war something they have had only intermittently throughout history: a formal group of committed professionals working, around the clock, on their behalf. The way that wars are fought has been significantly altered for the better because NGOs apply the right kind of pressure at the right time to the right people in power.

HUMANITARIAN RELIEF: HELPING WHERE NO ONE ELSE WILL

Although the mandates and activities of NGOs vary widely, NGOs engaged in helping civilians in conflict are involved in two broad types of activity: the provision of humanitarian aid, and advocacy (with the aim to influence policy on behalf of civilians). When states are weak or fail, such as in times of armed conflict, the government often cannot or will not provide basic services to its citizens. NGOs are increasingly stepping in to fill the void in providing basic health care, food, and shelter. Somalia is a good case in point. In the absence of a functioning government, since the year 2000 more than 90 NGOs stepped in to provide for the local population. Some NGOs also provide more-advanced services such as irrigation assistance for crops, small business creation for income generation, or training of local civilians in how to detect and disarm an unexploded land mine, just to name a few. In South Sudan, the International Rescue Committee provided aid to survivors of horrific sexual violence and is now helping the population rebuild in the Yiba refugee camp by providing training and assistance in education, human rights, and reintegration of the displaced.

This can be extremely dangerous work for NGO staff, many of whom face land mines, suicide bombers, reprisals from militant groups who don't want them there, and cross fire on a daily basis. The Catch-22 is that the more a neighborhood needs help, the more dangerous it is likely to be for the NGO that provides it. Self-protection is one reason humanitarian NGOs abide by the values of neutrality and independence, solely focused on providing help to vulnerable people, regardless of that population's political affiliation, religion, or philosophy about the conflict. Aligning themselves with a particular side or view might make them a target, and undermine their ability to help those most in need.

Despite the many millions of people helped by these efforts in the midst of horrific conflicts, NGO efforts to provide aid in warfare are not without criticism. Remaining neutral in times of great moral crisis makes NGOs a target for ideologues on either side of the conflict. Commentators ask, "How can you not take a side?" And since funding for massive humanitarian aid to the tune of millions of dollars must often be mobilized from wealthy governments, humanitarian organizations are sometimes caught up in politics despite their best efforts to avoid them. For example, an NGO may find itself conflicted about taking a particular donor government's money to provide aid to a population even as that same government is providing the weapons that are harming the very population in need. Another criticism is that humanitarian organizations may create dependency among the local population in a war zone and hamper the ability of a fledgling government or local humanitarian groups to help their own citizens or neighbors. This criticism is particularly focused, obviously, on international NGOs that work across a broad range of conflicts and may at some point leave. No matter how skilled or expert such NGOs may be in providing aid in times of crisis, if they aren't part of a larger effort to make sure the population can be cared for in the long term—whether by the government or by local groups—their good and valuable work may be criticized as a temporary Band-Aid.

Finally, humanitarian organizations have been criticized for working in an ad hoc manner, meaning that any given NGO may be doing its work in the same place as other NGOs doing similar work. This was a major critique of the 2010 efforts to rebuild Haiti following the devastating earthquake there. NGOs flew in by the hundreds with supplies, medicine, makeshift shelters, and staff, but they were uncoordinated, causing confusion and possibly less-effective assistance for those in need. Mechanisms are being developed to combat this problem. For example, the United Nations Office for Coordination of Humanitarian Affairs is coordinating aid groups working in places like South Sudan. Nevertheless, coordination remains rudimentary in other places where it could save lives or at least avoid duplication of aid efforts.

While all these critiques are important and must be taken seriously by the humanitarian community, it should be noted that aid professionals are overwhelmingly both well-intentioned and skilled. They are trying to go about their lifesaving work in tremendously challenging political environments, many aspects of which they cannot and should not be expected to control. As essential as it is for humanitarian organizations to ensure they abide by the old maxim "do no harm," their presence in conflict zones is just as essential for civilians with few others to turn to.

ADVOCACY: SPEAKING OUT FOR THE VOICELESS IN WAR

A relatively new area of work for NGOs is advocacy. NGOs use advocacy to try to change the policies of nations in a particular conflict for the benefit of the civilian population caught up in it. Efforts like these have existed throughout the past century, but were never formalized. Passionate individuals or ad hoc groups would try to make their way into the halls of the United Nations or protest outside the White House to advocate for a particular cause. Consider the work of Mr. Raphael Lemkin, who during World War II coined and defined the word "genocide" at the United Nations, or the black-and-white images of women chaining themselves to the White House gates for suffrage. Now, myriad organizations have been created to professionally advocate for causes both large and small. The International Center for Transitional Justice based in New York advocates for particular processes—for example, truth commissions, reparations programs, or sometimes criminal prosecutions—to be followed when the fighting has stopped, to bring about reconciliation and prevent future cycles of violence. Geneva Call, based quite obviously in Geneva, advocates with non-state actors to uphold the laws of war when engaged in an armed conflict. My own organization, the Center for Civilians in Conflict, works directly with militaries to better recognize civilians on the battlefield, so they can be avoided and helped if harmed. As advocates, we hope that our efforts to change policies and behaviors will mean more people will emerge from war unharmed or with the help they need.

In our short history of just ten years, the Center for Civilians in Conflict has seen remarkable change happen because NGOs like ours who work for civilians in war took up their cause and advocated in smart ways. For example, advocacy groups including Human Rights Watch advocated for the United Nations to push Somalia to end the use of child soldiers. These NGOs publicized the practice both at the UN in New York and also in the media—a tactic called "name and shame," meaning to name the perpetrators of a warfare violation and to shame them into changing their behavior. That public advocacy combined with a threat from the United States that it would end funding for Somalia's military if child soldiers continued to be used pressured the Somali government into signing a 2012 action plan to end the practice.

The processes for creating change differ from one NGO to another, and from one conflict to another. As already mentioned, some NGOs use the "name and shame" technique, which can bring about terrific results when a state or an armed group doesn't want to be seen as harming a civilian population. Naming and shaming may also bolster other levers for change, such as providing public pressure for peace negotiations or justice tribunals. Other NGOs, like my own and Geneva Call, engage directly with militaries, governments, or armed groups outside of the spotlight in order to persuade them to pay attention to the civilian populations caught in warfare and create compassionate, smart policies to match.

Regardless of the approach taken—whether a public campaign or a behind-the-scenes push—NGO advocacy is more powerful when it begins with and is based on bearing witness to the reality on the ground. Any advocacy with the public or with policymakers should come from real, tangible knowledge of what civilians have suffered and what has caused that suffering. Let's take my organization's work as an example of this process, from the start of advocacy to the final outcome (hopefully a policy or behavior change in favor of civilians caught in armed conflict). Over the last 10 years, Center for Civilians in Conflict staff have traveled to war zones like Afghanistan, Mali, Myanmar, Somalia, or, most recently, Syria to speak to war victims directly about their lives, their safety concerns, and their losses. Their stories are often tragic; the physical, psychological, and economic effects of combat operations on them and their families are both immediately devastating and long-lasting. We often find that their suffering is made worse when they do not receive any acknowledgment for their losses or help for recovery. They want to know why they have been harmed, particularly when so many militaries and non-state armed groups today use high-flying rhetoric about avoiding civilian harm. In addition to talking with civilians in a conflict, we visit with military and government officials, and with local and international humanitarian organizations (like those described above), so we can understand the challenges they may be having in minimizing civilian harm and suffering.

With this kind of information in hand, many NGOs will develop a public awareness campaign around the plight of civilians they've spoken with, or call out perpetrators of violence with examples of their behavior. At Civilians in Conflict, we sit down with the testimonials, data, and other information we've gathered from a conflict zone to figure out why civilians are at risk and what solutions might be available to protect them before they are harmed, or help if they've already suffered losses. Why have civilians been harmed? Could that harm have been avoided? How? What could change? It's then time to put words on paper, in the form of recommendations to the military or to a local governor or council. Advocacy NGOs like ours might even draft a suggested policy, and provide it to the public or to policymakers, making it easier for them to see what is possible and to adopt the solution being offered.

What would such a solution look like? In Somalia, African Union forces fighting al-Shabaab—a militant group associated with al-Qaeda—were causing civilian casualties by firing into crowded areas in response to incoming fire. After talking with hundreds of Somali civilians, humanitarian workers, government and United Nations officials, and military officers, we were able to identify the problem and create a detailed set of procedures for the military that would lessen the risk to civilians. Also in Somalia, we realized after talking with many Somali civilians living through the conflict that their losses were made worse when they didn't receive anything—an apology or assistance—for the harm they had suffered. In this case, we had to convince the African coalition forces that it was in their best interest to offer some form of compensation for losses they unintentionally caused to the local population. We suggested they do so by incorporating local conflict resolution traditions into our recommendations for a war victims program of assistance.

In fact, in all our advocacy efforts to protect and get help to civilians in war, we have to convince militaries around the world that harming civilians or walking away from civilian suffering is not only ethically wrong, but also strategically damaging. We might say: consider, as a military commander, that ignoring deaths or injuries or demolished homes can sow the seeds of anger among the very population whose support may be necessary to win the war. This argument is one that a military official can understand and, as such, makes it more likely that we can persuade them to change their policies to minimize civilian harm.

As a result of these kinds of engagements with policymakers and military actors, we've begun to alter the ways armed groups think about and treat civilians. When we began working in Afghanistan in 2003, American and other international forces had little notion of how damaging civilian casualties would be to their mission to stabilize the country. NGOs like Amnesty International and Physicians for Human Rights, in coalition with local groups, documented civilian casualties and began reporting them to the wider world through the media. Human Rights Watch documented violations of the laws of war, and Oxfam International created assessments of where civilians needed aid.

For our part, we concluded that commanders had no way of assessing the impact of their combat operations on the local population; they weren't keeping count of civilian casualties, and they weren't talking with village elders about what losses were occurring in their communities; they weren't apologizing for casualties; they weren't fully investigating harm to civilians; and they weren't offering any compensation or amends for civilian losses they had caused. All this had to be changed. We sat down with military commanders themselves and offered policy solutions to many of these problems, and worked with other NGO colleagues to press them to adopt what we were recommending. The advocacy effort worked—not perfectly, but it did work. American and international forces developed a system for documenting civilian casualties and investigating any possible instances of harm. They created rules for the military forces about avoiding civilian casualties, and the rates of civilian harm went down as a result. Many of the military partners also saw worth in apologizing for civilian harm when it occurred and offering something to the families for their losses. This advocacy was successful in part because international military leaders themselves realized that civilian harm was causing intense anger among ordinary Afghans and causing support for the international presence to recede. Nevertheless, NGOs can take much of the credit for bringing about such positive changes for Afghan civilians, both by publicizing the harm that was coming to local communities and by recommending smart policy solutions to the right people in power to save lives.

What we accomplished in Somalia and in Afghanistan, and what our colleague NGOs accomplish in war zones around the world, shows that change is possible. The combined strategy of seeking the truth on the ground and directly communicating civilian needs to warring parties is an effective way to protect civilians and address their needs. Elsewhere in the world, we advocated for similar changes to military operations. In Mali, a new United Nations Peacekeeping Force will have a staff member specifically focused on preventing and addressing civilian casualties, thanks to our work. In Pakistan, together with other international and local partners, we successfully pushed for a new government program of assistance for victims of conflict and terrorism.

Such examples, of which there are many more, show that, slowly, NGOs are changing how warring parties behave in conflict, how states engage in war, and how civilians—the ordinary people trying to go about their lives in the midst of bullets and bombs—can make it through, unharmed. Not all militaries or policymakers will be open to talking with NGOs. Advocates will consistently have to find smart, creative ways of making their point and eliciting change.

NGO efforts have the additional benefit of bringing the plight of civilians caught in war to the world's attention. The NGO community has become go-to experts for the media when covering a conflict, a resource for policymakers as they grapple with how to address a particular aspect of a conflict (for example, sexual violence, the use of child soldiers, the use of banned weapons, an influx of refugees), and a trusted leader for the public at large, which may offer donations or volunteer on a cause they care about. Dedicated NGO staff, many of whom put their own lives on the line to get evidence of these horrors, are directly responsible for the increased awareness of global atrocities and the assistance and relief that spring from it. Commentary from NGOs published in the media, in particular, can help to persuade the right people to do the right thing, and to inform the public about civilians' needs in conflict.

Still, criticism is leveled at advocacy NGOs in equal measure to that of the humanitarian groups, though for different reasons. Raising awareness about a conflict can be crucial to getting warring parties or governments to change their behavior, but not all the energy expended on public relations campaigns has been welcomed. For example, critics—including those from within the NGO community itself—often complain that selling colored bracelets for victims in Congo or maintaining a massive petition on a website to call attention to Darfur does little to actually help the people suffering in those conflicts; perhaps all those efforts do is make the targeted audience of buyers or petition signers feel less helpless. When it comes to documenting harm in conflict zones, critics question whether NGOs are biased in their reporting, whether they are capturing the entirety of the picture of conflict, and whether NGOs that don't come from the conflict population itself can really understand the complexities of what they are seeing on the ground. Further, advocates have been criticized for running from one conflict to another, going after the "shiny new object" to which they will devote their time and resources. Yesterday the work might have been focused on Afghanistan, when the world was paying attention, and today the work might be focused on Syria. These are all valid concerns, and NGOs deserve—both individually and as a community—to be held accountable for their actions. There are efforts under way around the clock and around the globe to analyze NGOs' impact and improve their work. Given the relatively recent proliferation of NGOs on the world's battlefields—both for aid and advocacy—their efficiency and credibility will need to evolve over time and with each challenge surmounted.

NGOs will always have an uphill battle to change the way people in power think about the powerless. Yet this is a community that is dedicated, passionate, and unwilling to give up. As individual organizations and as a coalition, NGOs are a powerful force striving for humanity in war.

*Sarah Holewinski served as executive director of the Center for Civilians in Conflict from 2006 to 2014. In 2014, she became a policy advisor to the US Ambassador to the United Nations, Samantha Power. She is a senior fellow with the Truman National Security Project and a member of the Council on Foreign Relations.

Original contribution.

NGOs and Nonstate Armed Actors: Improving Compliance with International Norms

by Claudia Hofmann and Ulrich Schneckener*

SUMMARY

- Transnational nongovernmental organizations (NGOs) have developed strategies to improve the diffusion of and general adherence to international norms among nonstate armed actors, with the goal of persuading armed actors to adapt their behavior accordingly.

- The ICRC offers trainings in international humanitarian law to armed actors that explain their responsibilities for protecting civilians in military operations. Geneva Call provides education on the effects of antipersonnel landmines and supports armed actors in their efforts to clear mined areas, destroy stockpiles, and provide victim assistance.

- The NGOs' efforts in dealing with nonstate armed actors reveal limitations and problems but also offer new avenues for states and international organizations to engage with armed groups. With greater support from the international community, NGOs' contributions could become more substantive and complement other ongoing efforts to change armed actors' behavior.

Armed actors dominate the environment during and after armed conflict in many ways apart from the conflict itself.[1] They are responsible for violence against unarmed civilians in breach of international humanitarian law and can facilitate the establishment of criminal and informal economies typically seen in postwar societies. However, they also may see themselves as representing distinct interests within the populace and may build broad support from them. Nonstate armed actors—such as rebel groups, militias, warlords, clan chiefs, terrorists, criminals, and mercenaries—can disturb, undermine, or completely truncate state- and peacebuilding processes, leading to further violence that affects the efforts of humanitarian aid workers, representatives of governments, and peacekeepers. Nonstate armed actors are defined as actors who are willing and able to use violence to pursue their objectives; are not integrated into formal state institutions, such as regular armies, presidential guards, police, or special forces; possess a certain degree of autonomy with regard to politics, military operations, resources, and infrastructure; and have an organizational structure (i.e., unlike spontaneous riots). The definition encompasses politically and ideologically motivated actors as well as profit-oriented actors.

The international community has employed a number of strategies when dealing with nonstate armed actors, ranging from counterinsurgency and containment to negotiation and mediation to integration and co-optation.[2] However, these approaches reveal that state actors, such as the affected government and third countries involved in the conflict, still have difficulties in dealing with nonstate armed actors.[3] These difficulties are often based on states' commitment to international treaties, the decisions of the UN Security Council, diplomatic customs between sovereign states, and other political considerations, such as the fear of legitimizing armed actors. Nongovernmental organizations (NGOs) and private individuals—such as elder statesmen, including influential persons and retired high officials—command more freedom and flexibility to contact armed actors or react to their requests. Accordingly, they are often involved in the facilitation of talks, informal prenegotiations, the preparation of nonpapers, and direct mediation with armed actors on different policy levels during and after conflict.

Specialized NGOs engage nonstate armed actors to reduce the violence and instability they cause during and after conflict. Two of the most prominent civil society organizations in the field are the International Committee of the Red Cross (ICRC) and Geneva Call.[4] They use different approaches in dealing with armed actors, but they have the same goal: to persuade rebel groups, militias, tribal chiefs, and other armed actors to accept international norms and change their behavior as well as their internal rules and doctrines accordingly. The international norms involve, for example, the protection of civilians, the ban of certain means of warfare (such as landmines and child soldiers), and the appropriate treatment of prisoners. The primary intent of such initiatives is not necessarily more peace, but rather less violence, particularly regarding civilians and, more generally, the prevention of an increasing erosion of international humanitarian law during conflicts.[5] These processes of persuasion and norm diffusion can also be a starting point for further engagement with armed actors that focus on the possibility of changing their self-image or identity—an approach to which actors with postconflict political aspirations may be particularly susceptible. This engagement can, in turn, positively affect a beginning or ongoing peace process and, thus, contribute to constructive conflict management. Criminalizing such NGO efforts, as through the U.S. Patriot Act with its extended definition of terrorism and terrorist organizations, passes up such constructive opportunities to work with nonstate armed groups.

This report analyzes the approaches of civil society organizations such as the ICRC and Geneva Call in communicating international norms to nonstate armed actors. It elaborates on the different methods as well as the basic conditions and factors that affect the success of their approaches in order to evaluate the strengths and limits of NGOs in constructively dealing with nonstate armed actors. Under specific circumstances armed actors can be open-minded regarding international norms, especially if they are striving to become political actors governed by normative behavior and are willing to be judged by this behavior. Such aspirations create new avenues for internal and external actors when interacting with armed actors.

NGOs' Interactions with Armed Actors

NGOs deal with armed actors in several ways as they work in the world's conflict regions.[6] Both NGOs and aid agencies have become an attractive resource for armed actors and thus continuously run the risk of instrumentalization.[7] Employees of international and local NGOs are victims of looting, blackmail, intimidation, kidnappings, and targeted attacks.[8] Often aid deliveries, vehicles, and technical equipment are stolen or extorted. That said, more constructive forms of interaction exist between NGOs and armed actors as well, ranging from ad hoc contacts and agreements to long-term cooperation that offers NGOs personnel security, access to the local population, and promotion of a peace process. For nonstate armed actors, interaction with NGOs can bring more aid to their local constituency, improving the actors' chances of gaining legitimacy, acknowledgment, and access to other internal and external actors in order to end their political isolation and marginalization.

NGOs' different activities create different reasons for interaction with armed actors (figure 1).[9] Operational services as conducted by humanitarian and development NGOs, such as Médecins Sans Frontières, CARE, InterAction, and parochial development organizations, primarily consist of tasks that aid a suffering population during and after conflict. While NGOs often work with nonstate armed actors to carry out relief projects in specific regions, contact is selective and only with regard to a dispute or an emergency; the armed actors are means to an end, as the services' main focus is the population. Public policy work concentrates mainly on lobbying, monitoring, awareness raising, and education. Organizations including Human Rights Watch, Transparency International, and the International Crisis Group denounce drawbacks and misconduct (i.e., naming and shaming), sensitize the international public to specific problems, and appeal publicly to the conflict parties to do—or not do—something. As such work focuses mainly on states and international organizations, which are in turn supposed to act against the misconduct of other actors, the engagement of

Figure 1. Modes of NGO Interaction with Nonstate Armed Actors

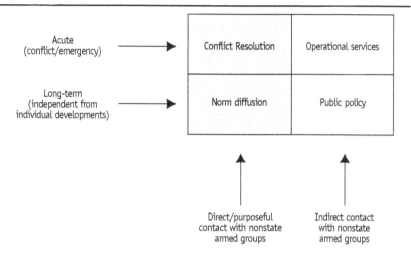

nonstate armed actors is indirect.[10] Conflict resolution, such as that conducted by the Carter Center, International Alert, or the Finnish Crisis Management Initiative (CMI), involves conflict management, the provision of good offices, and facilitation, be it in official or unofficial mission, of negotiations from the local to the international level.[11] These activities lead to direct contact with nonstate armed actors to support negotiation processes. The duration of contact depends on a favorable occasion for negotiations and does not last beyond them. Finally, norm diffusion involves persuading nonstate armed actors to adhere to specific international norms. Contact with armed actors is direct and often long-term, for example if concluded agreements regarding international norms require a monitoring process. The two organizations described in this report, the ICRC and Geneva Call, are paradigmatic for this field of action.

The typology in figure 1 only roughly characterizes NGOs themselves, as numerous NGOs engage in multiple activities simultaneously and with different intensities. The Carter Center is involved in conflict resolution but also—and more extensively—in operational services, in the fields of health and democracy. It also engages in public policy by reporting on grievances and problems and by attracting the attention of the American public. Similarly, the ICRC and Geneva Call are active in public policy and political lobbying to consolidate international humanitarian law and strengthen the ban on antipersonnel landmines. But distinguishing among categories of activity is instructive: There is a qualitative difference between delivering aid in conflict regions and lobbying political decision makers, on one hand, and supporting mediation between conflicting parties and promoting the adherence of international norms, on the other. The latter two are formative attributes of the ICRC and Geneva Call, regardless of their other activities.

The ICRC

When the ICRC was founded as a civil organization in 1863 by Henry Dunant, its main concern was to bring relief to wounded soldiers on the battlefield and to develop international treaties that would protect the wounded as well as the medical personnel assisting them. These principles still represent the foundation for the ICRC's work, though its scope has expanded considerably. The number of employees indicates the magnitude of the ICRC's efforts: Around 800 staff work at the organization's headquarters in Geneva, around 1,400 are active as specialized staff and delegates, and around 11,000 local employees work for the organization in the field. The ICRC's specific mandate is anchored in the 1949 Geneva Conventions and the 1977 Additional Protocols, in which the organization is given specific rights and tasks during and after armed conflict, such as visiting prisoners of war, supplying food and other necessities for the civil population, reuniting families, and searching for missing persons. Furthermore, according to the Statutes of the International Red Cross and Red Crescent Movement, the ICRC also must "work for the understanding and dissemination of knowledge of international humanitarian law applicable in armed conflicts and to prepare any development thereof."[12] Legally, the ICRC is a private association formed under the Swiss civil code that is made up of fifteen to twenty-five Swiss citizens. Internationally, however, the ICRC enjoys the status of a legal entity under international humanitarian law and is, therefore, different from conventional NGOs. Accordingly, the organization possesses certain privileges—such as exemptions from taxes and customs—similar to those of other international organizations. Most important, however, is immunity regarding courts of law, including international war crimes tribunals and the International Criminal Court.

The ICRC strongly values impartiality, neutrality, and independence, and thus does not distinguish between state and nonstate conflict actors systematically or normatively. In practice, this means that the ICRC seeks out direct contact with state and nonstate armed actors, independent of whether they fight on the side of or against the government, and offers each the same services. At the time of writing, the ICRC is engaging more than one hundred nonstate armed actors in about thirty countries, concentrating particularly on the provisions encoded in Common Article 3 of the Geneva Conventions. This article concerns humane treatment for all persons in enemy hands; the prohibition of murder, mutilation, and torture as well as cruel, humiliating, and degrading treatment; and the taking of hostages and unfair trials.[13] The ICRC employs two mechanisms to increase respect for international humanitarian law in armed conflicts: formally expressing commitment to humanitarian norms and gradually implementing them. Ideally, these mechanisms are mutually supportive, and practically, they are often pursued in parallel.

First, a range of legal tools give all actors in a conflict an opportunity to make an express commitment to international humanitarian norms. This not only instills the armed-actor leadership with a sense of self-determination and responsibility, but also circumvents their feeling not to be bound by international law when they are neither involved in its creation nor allowed to sign the relevant international treaty. An express commitment may contain new legal obligations that go beyond the existing provisions (i.e., a constitutive agreement) or restate law that is already binding in noninternational conflict (i.e., a declaratory agreement). In 1992, the parties to the conflict in Bosnia and Herzegovina concluded a declaratory agreement vowing respect for the provisions of Common Article 3 of the Geneva Conventions and adding provisions regulating the protection of the wounded, sick, and shipwrecked; of hospitals and medical units; and of the civilian population. Similar agreements were made in Yemen in 1962 and Nigeria in 1967. Constitutive agreements were concluded with the government of El Salvador and the Frente Farabundo Martí para la Liberación Nacional (FMNL) in 1990, and between the government of the Philippines and the National Democratic Front of the Philippines (NDFP) in 1998, accepting human rights norms that went beyond the commitments of Common Article 3 and Additional Protocol II.

Unilateral declarations give armed actors another opportunity to express commitment to international humanitarian norms and human rights independent from any other party. In September 1987 the Coordinadora Guerrillera Simón Bolívar (CGSB), a short-lived umbrella organization of rebel groups in Colombia, declared its intention to respect international humanitarian norms. In 1991 and 1996, the ICRC received declarations from the National Democratic Front of the Philippines. Such agreements have also been part of cease-fire or peace agreements. The 2002 cease-fire agreement between the government of Angola and the União Nacional para a Independência Total de Angola (UNITA) contained an additional section that guaranteed the halting of all force movements in the reinforcement or occupation of new military positions. The cease-fire agreement between the government of the Democratic Socialist Republic of Sri Lanka and the Liberation Tigers of Tamil Eelam (LTTE), also in 2002, included an additional article on protecting the population against hostile acts, such as torture, intimidation, abduction, extortion, and harassment.

The second mechanism represents the main part of the ICRC's concept. It follows the premise that, if violations are to be avoided, rules and regulations need to become an integral part of the behavior of armed actors in military operations. Generally, the process begins by disseminating information about existing humanitarian regulations, as it cannot be assumed that armed actors have comprehensive knowledge of international law or its implications for their operations. Subsequent work addresses four dimensions in particular: doctrine, education and training, equipment, and effective sanctions. Ideally, changes in these four dimensions are mutually reinforcing, so that the entire process is a comprehensive approach requiring continual and long-term interaction with an armed actor, accounting for the time the actor needs to execute and implement all necessary organizational changes. To influence behavior, international humanitarian norms have to become a common and integral part of an actor's doctrine. For this to happen, the humanitarian norms have to be incorporated into all directives, procedures, rules of behavior, and handbooks concerning the training, terminology, and decision-making processes of fighters, strategically and tactically. Special handbooks need to be compiled that speak to the relevant levels and specializations of the armed organization, such as different levels of command or fighters in populated areas. Even if no systematic curriculum exists, nonstate armed actors have some form of educational system that at least covers weapons training, which can be used for humanitarian purposes. Additionally, the ICRC offers training courses for teachers, trainers, and legal advisers of non-state armed actors. The highest level of command must equip fighters to minimize or avoid violations of international humanitarian norms, and the ICRC is authorized to inspect would-be combatants during training to determine whether they are equipped to carry out the provisions of international humanitarian law. During these training situations, the ICRC also aims to demonstrate to fighters the effects their weapons have on civilian victims. Finally, the ICRC stresses that sanctions within the group itself must not violate international law and human rights: While commanders must be able to discipline fighters, especially punish violations of rules and regulations, sanctions must be applied consistently and reasonably to demonstrate the earnestness of the leadership and their commitment to international humanitarian norms.

To subject the entire integration process to a continuous evaluation, the ICRC developed a scorecard for state military and police that records the state of an actor's integration—and violations—of international humanitarian law. The first practical applications of the scorecard have met serious challenges, such as the confidentiality of documentation necessary for an evaluation, the organizational complexity of developed military and police forces, and the need to repeat an evaluation periodically. The ICRC has not yet been able to design a corresponding scorecard for nonstate armed actors at all, as the groups in question are too different from one another to summarize according to common criteria.

Independent from which particular engagement strategy is used for a particular armed actor, the ICRC focuses on strategic argumentation.[14] To be effective, discussions and dissemination sessions with armed actors need to be adapted to the motivations and interests of the actors. They need to explain why it is in the actors' best interests to adhere to international humanitarian law. The ICRC has used several arguments in the past. First, adhering to international humanitarian law might improve actors' reputations, on the international and local levels and among their allies and constituency. Additionally, the actor may gain the moral high ground that could lead to political gains. Second, if an actor develops a reputation for treating prisoners of war well, people might surrender to it more easily. Third, while reciprocity is not necessary for international humanitarian law to apply, it is more likely that the other side will treat an actor's members well after taking them prisoner if it sees the actor treat its prisoners in a similar manner. Fourth, violations of international humanitarian law may be disadvantageous in the long run, in damage to an actor's reputation, a loss of support, or ostracism by the population. By the same logic, compliance might benefit the actor. Adherence to international humanitarian norms also may help facilitate postconflict reconciliation. Fifth, international humanitarian norms may preserve military interests; they were originally developed by military commanders, accounting for the balance between military needs and humanity. It is not only more humane, but also in the commander's interest to have well-disciplined troops and a functioning command structure. Sixth, adherence to international humanitarian law may save resources, especially in keeping infrastructure intact. Finally, recent developments in the prosecution of violations of international law during conflict, such as through the International Criminal Tribunal for Yugoslavia (ICTY), the International Criminal Tribunal for Rwanda (ICTR), and the International Criminal Court (ICC), have strengthened the international legal framework, making prosecution of violations more likely.

Whether the above mechanisms and arguments succeed in changing armed actors' behavior depends mostly on whether the ICRC is granted access to actors' leadership, and whether this contact can be maintained over a longer period. The ICRC's approach to armed actors is top down, relying on the cooperation of both political and military leadership. In its efforts, however, the ICRC is supported by its distinct status and reputation as a neutral humanitarian organization that engages nonstate armed actors in the same way it engages state actors regarding their obligations under international humanitarian law. All weapons bearers are subject to the same normative demands. This transparency awards the ICRC an exceptional credibility; at the same time, this credibility has to be reaffirmed in each individual case through the personal interactions of ICRC delegates.

Geneva Call

Geneva Call, founded in 2002, directly engages nonstate armed actors to increase their adherence to international humanitarian norms, particularly international humanitarian law and international human rights law. The NGO currently addresses three issue areas: adherence to the universal antipersonnel mine ban, respect for children in armed conflict, and respect for the rights of women in conflict. The bulk of Geneva Call's work, however, focuses on landmines, specifically in territory that nonstate armed actors control. Many nonstate armed actors maintain antipersonnel landmines as a part of their standard arsenal due to their low cost, availability, uncomplicated production, and simple use. Actors manufacture, trade, sell, and use landmines to advance their goals. Today, more than seventy states are believed to be affected by mines; in the past ten years, landmines, explosive remnants of war (ERW), and victim-activated improvised explosive devices (IED) have caused approximately 74,000 casualties. An inquiry conducted in 2006 found that forty nonstate armed actors in at least seven countries reportedly used landmines between 2003 and 2005.[15] Experts estimate that 10 to 40 percent of landmines fail to explode as intended, then remain active and make access to certain areas highly dangerous. Landmines used by nonstate armed actors in particular tend to be first-generation mines without activity limits, possibly remaining active for decades. Landmines can impede a country's development for multiple generations; simultaneously, they impair the nonstate armed actor by killing and maiming its own fighters, restricting troop movements, and diminishing support that they might otherwise have enjoyed in the affected population.

The 1997 Convention on the Prohibition of the Use, Stockpiling, Production, and Transfer of Anti-Personnel Mines and on their Destruction—otherwise known as the Ottawa Treaty—internationally regulates the use of landmines. Nonstate actors did not participate in the negotiation process and are not eligible to sign the treaty because they lack appropriate status. They are subject to the provisions of the Ottawa Treaty if their home state is a signatory party, but in practice, they often do not know about their responsibilities regarding the landmines ban and do not feel bound by them because they did not expressly agree to the provisions. Without the active inclusion and assistance of nonstate armed actors, however, the landmines problem is not being addressed in its entirety. For this reason, Geneva Call aims to persuade armed actors to change their behavior and respect the international landmines ban. For this purpose, it has designed an innovative mechanism that allows armed actors to commit to the norms of the Ottawa Treaty by signing the Deed of Commitment for Adherence to a Total Ban on Anti-Personnel Mines and for Cooperation in Mine Action between the NGO and the armed actor. The mechanism attempts to balance the shortcomings of international law by offering a parallel process for nonstate armed actors that enables them to actively enter a formal commitment to the ban of antipersonnel landmines. Under the deed, the armed actor agrees to several conditions: first, to acknowledge the norm of a total ban on antipersonnel landmines established by the 1997 Ottawa Treaty; second, to adhere to a total ban of antipersonnel landmines, which includes the complete prohibition on all use, development, production, acquisition, stockpiling, retention, and transfer of mines; third, to cooperate in and undertake stockpile destruction, mine clearance, victim assistance, mine awareness, and various other forms of mine action; fourth, to allow and cooperate in the monitoring and verification of the commitment, which entails visits and inspections by Geneva Call and other independent international and national organizations, as well as the provision of necessary information to those organizations; and fifth, to issue the necessary orders and directives to commanders and fighters, including measures for information dissemination, training, and disciplinary sanctions.

Additionally, Article 6 of the deed explains that signing the deed does not alter the legal status of the nonstate armed actor, pursuant to Common Article 3 of the Geneva Conventions. The deed itself is most commonly seen as a unilateral declaration by the armed actor, with Geneva Call and the government of the Republic and Canton of Geneva serving as witnesses. It is signed by an individual representing and acting in the name of the armed actor, often in the historic Alabama Room at the Hôtel-de-Ville in Geneva, where the Geneva Convention was signed in 1864.

Geneva Call currently engages approximately sixty armed actors. Forty-one armed actors have signed the deed, seventeen from Somalia alone and six from Myanmar. The others are from Burundi, India, Iran, Iraq, the Philippines, Sudan, Turkey, and Western Sahara.[16] Several other actors have not signed the deed but have pledged to prohibit or limit the use of antipersonnel landmines, either through individual unilateral declarations or as a part of a cease-fire agreement with the government. Still others have undertaken mine clearance and victim assistance in areas under their control. The government of Somaliland refuses to sign the deed because it considers itself to be a state and aspires to sign the Ottawa Treaty instead.

In most cases the armed actors have already begun mine clearings and other action. Geneva Call supports the implementation of the deed and monitors the progress made. In 2008, the NGO facilitated technical assistance through specialized organizations to destroy stockpiles held by two signatory groups in Western Sahara and Somalia. Two other signatories in Burundi and Sudan reported to Geneva Call the complete destruction of their stockpiles after having joined the respective government; a signatory in the Republic of Myanmar/Burma reported clearing all its landmines and mine components; one signatory reported a stockpile located in Northern Iraq as destroyed. In Somalia, Geneva Call arranged for the assistance of a specialized organization to undertake explosive ordnance disposal (EOD) and to provide emergency support to mine victims. Additionally, Geneva Call organized workshops, mine risk education (MRE) seminars, and surveys in areas under signatories' control in cooperation with partner organizations.

Geneva Call establishes contact with nonstate armed actors in three ways. First is directly, for the purpose of a dialogue on landmines, as with the Mouvement des Nigeriens pour la Justice (MNJ), the Partiya Karkerên Kurdistan (PKK), the Partîya Demokrata Kurdistan (PDK), the Patriotic Union of Kurdistan (PUK), and Al Houtis in Yemen. Second, contact has been facilitated indirectly through third parties, most commonly through local NGOs or civil society groups, but also through other nonstate armed actors, as occurred with the Mouvement des forces démocratiques de Casamance (MFDC), Palipehutu-FNL in Burundi, the Ejército de Liberación Nacional (ELN) in Colombia, the Liberation Tigers of Tamil Eelam (LTTE) in Sri Lanka, and the Partiya Jiyana Azad a Kurdistanê (PJAK). Third, some actors have contacted Geneva Call directly to begin a dialogue on antipersonnel landmines after having heard of Geneva Call's initiative, as did Chin National Front in Myanmar/Burma. Geneva Call does not begin a dialogue with an armed actor until it has thoroughly analyzed the group's character, aims, leadership, internal structure, past practices, and the like; assessed the dynamics of conflict and other factors, such as the capabilities of armed actors and their assumed commitment, to assure maximum security; considered the probability of success; and developed the right arguments that persuade the particular nonstate armed actor to give up landmines and adhere to a total ban. According to Geneva Call, armed actors are willing to sign and commit to the deed for several reasons. These include improving the quality of life in the territory controlled by them, enabling mine action programs, and protecting their constituency; improving political stability; confirming for itself that it is respected as an organization and taken seriously by an international (non-governmental) actor, coming from an internationally highly respected country (i.e., the Swiss factor); demonstrating the ability to uphold the principles of international humanitarian law and, consequently, aspiring to gain international reputation and respect; and accepting the relatively limited military utility of antipersonnel mines, which may indiscriminately wound, maim, and kill enemies, their constituencies, and their own fighters, and harm their military capacity.

To follow up allegations of deed violations, Geneva Call has developed a monitoring mechanism that can, in practice, be difficult to employ, as the parties to the conflict may not actually have an interest in verifying claims. This is true for armed actors as well as governments if allegations are only made to discredit the opposition internationally. Monitoring, therefore, may involve self-reporting and progress reports (e.g., the Polisario Front), evaluation through local NGOs and civil society (e.g., PKK in Turkey), and following up on accusations (e.g., Moro Islamic Liberation Front in the Philippines). In practice, this method may not be entirely satisfying and convincing (see, e.g., Puntland, Somalia, and the Philippines). The NGO maintains, however, that most nonstate armed actors abide by the core of the prohibitions on the use, production, acquisition, and transfer of landmines. Armed actors are also undertaking demining, stockpile destruction, mine risk education, and victim assistance, and often collaborate with specialized humanitarian organizations for this purpose. Moreover, armed actors' decisions to abstain from using landmines have in the past facilitated the ascension of states to the 1997 Ottawa Treaty, as social pressure on the state government built up once a local nonstate armed actor had signed the deed of commitment. This happened in Sudan after the signature of the Sudan People's Liberation Movement/Army (SPLM/A) and in Iraq after the ascension of the Kurdistan Democratic Party (KDP) and regional governments led by the Patriotic Union of Kurdistan (PUK). Although not party to the Ottawa Treaty, Morocco submitted a voluntary report to Geneva Call and invited the organization in 2008 to form recommendations for the government after Geneva Call had engaged the rebel Polisario Front successfully in 2005.[17]

Efforts to ban landmines have a strong technical dimension, as armed actors often need more information to avoid mistakes when handling and disposing of these weapons. Unlike the ICRC, Geneva Call does not have special status; it depends on host governments to at least tolerate its activities. But even if governments attempt to obstruct Geneva Call's efforts and refuse to give access to territory controlled by the armed actors, even state actors have an interest in controlling and containing antipersonnel landmines. They are equally affected, and responsible for protecting civilians. Whether Geneva Call's approach can be transferred to other issue areas, such as women and child soldiers, remains to be seen.

POSSIBILITIES FOR AND LIMITS TO CHANGING
ARMED ACTORS' BEHAVIOR

Despite their different sizes, histories, and goals, the ICRC and Geneva Call employ similar mechanisms regarding norm diffusion. They focus heavily on transmitting information and knowledge, including technical knowledge. They aim to persuade armed actors with arguments that speak to their particular positions in a conflict (i.e., an empathic approach). They are interested in a long-term relationship based on trust and offer targeted measures to build the armed actors' capacities in a particular field. In short, ICRC and Geneva Call explain to armed actors what they are supposed to do and why—and, furthermore, lay out concrete ways for them to implement the norms in question. Using the language developed in the literature on norm diffusion, both organizations practice first and foremost informational diffusion through strategic communication, procedural diffusion through institutionalized forms of cooperation, and transference through aid and support for implementing norms.[18] ICRC and Geneva Call work with different intensities, depending on the consistency, duration, and level of trust in the interaction with nonstate armed actors.

Both organizations benefit from their reputations as neutral and independent actors, even if not all share this perception. The ICRC's reputation is supported by the activities of the national Red Cross societies and by their special status in international humanitarian law. For Geneva Call, the Swiss factor is significant, as the organization consciously uses Switzerland's reputation as a neutral country when inviting armed actors to talks and holding conferences with all deed signatories. This alone would not be possible in many other countries, if only for the difficulties of obtaining visas for members of armed actors. Moreover, the success of the ICRC and Geneva Call depends on how the interaction with armed actors has been established. The personal commitment of the NGO representatives, the cautious handling of the interlocutors, a willingness to demonstrate empathy, and the issue of which matters should be discussed first are extremely important. Experience has shown that it is more productive to begin dialogue with more practical matters rather than delving into abstract issues of international norms. This approach gives both sides an opportunity to assess and get to know each other. To start off talks, the ICRC has used inquiries into the condition of prisoners, requesting access to specific areas or a particular checkpoint along with the offer of humanitarian assistance.

Besides the organizations' credibility and independence, their flexible but principled approaches are one of their strengths because they can be adjusted to the situation of the individual nonstate armed actor. The organizations do not offer take-it-or-leave-it programs but gradual processes through which the armed actors become acquainted with international norms step by step. Thus, the decision about whether and which norms armed actors incorporate is not a precondition for further dialogue but the result of a long-term effort that begins with awareness training and convincing. After their first steps, the ICRC and Geneva Call have developed more or less formalized forms of cooperation, depending on the actors' willingness to be part of such a process. However, practice has also shown that the degree of formalization does not indicate an actor's degree of norm adherence. A declaratory public acknowledgement of international humanitarian norms and the deed signing remain important signals but do not allow for conclusions regarding how much actors have internalized norms.

The promise of success in an interaction with a nonstate armed actor depends on external factors that may be outside the NGOs' influence. First, the timing of first contact with the phase of the conflict is significant—success is more likely if there is an ongoing peace process with existing regulations that the ICRC and Geneva Call can build on. At the same time, both organizations endeavor to intensify contact with armed actors before violence escalates (again) and before the government restricts or completely prohibits access to the armed actor. ICRC experience, in particular, shows that the earlier a channel of communication can be opened with an armed actor, the sooner a trusted relationship can be established, and the sooner the actor feels that its grievances are being considered— potentially before the lines of conflict become hardened. Such a situation can be exploited to broach the issue of protecting civilians at an early stage, in the hope that such behavior persists even if the conflict intensifies. If a conflict has already escalated and the armed actor is already conducting military operations, a dialogue on humanitarian issues is less of a priority.

Second, much depends on armed actors' abilities to cooperate with organizations such as the ICRC and Geneva Call. Their willingness to do so tends to be greater the more anchored the armed actor is in society and the more support it requires from the population. In these cases, the armed actor probably has an interest in increasing its legitimacy among civilians. This is particularly true for politically and ideologically oriented actors led by politically ambitious individuals. Additionally, a somewhat coherent and hierarchical organizational and command structure is relevant, as well as, in the case of landmines, a somewhat stable control over territory. This structure includes effective leadership as well as a regulated system for recruitment, education, and training that norm diffusion can build on. The more splintered and fragmented an armed actor, and the less assertive the leadership, the more unlikely it is that international humanitarian norms are understood, accepted, and complied with.

Both aspects touch on the issue of the sustainability of norm-diffusion processes. Although the ICRC—and Geneva Call even more so—aim to establish functioning monitoring mechanisms to supervise compliance with norms, both organizations are reaching their limits. This is due partly to the limited resources at their disposal compared with state actors. Both organizations also lack functioning sanctioning mechanisms because of their very nature. The only sanctions available to the ICRC and Geneva Call are to end any form of cooperation and publicly denounce violations of international norms. Both options have severe consequences as channels of communication are cut, contacts lost—potentially for a long time—and the possibilities diminished to at least partially improve security for the population. Additionally, such measures may negatively affect engagement with other nonstate armed actors. Thus, both the ICRC and Geneva Call sanction actors only in extreme cases.

The discrepancies between the declarations of nonstate armed actors and their actual behaviors spur the accusations—often made by governments—that armed actors are using NGOs solely to gain legitimacy and international recognition. Both the ICRC and Geneva Call know about this danger but have experiences with armed actors that put it in perspective. Often this sweeping argument is made to discredit the work of NGOs in general, mostly when the NGOs' engagement with armed actors is too successful from the government's perspective; it is not made when the engagement has no effect. Also, state actors often use this accusation to distract the international community from their own noncompliance with humanitarian norms. Furthermore, so ICRC and Geneva Call representatives argue, the gain in prestige for armed actors through cooperating with international NGOs is very small compared with the gains when armed actors change their behavior toward other (state) conflict actors, and particularly toward civilians. The problem for many states is not that NGOs fail in diffusing international norms with but that they help armed actors in a battle for the population's favor—and, thus, power in the country.

CONCLUSIONS AND RECOMMENDATIONS

The ICRC and Geneva Call approaches toward norm diffusion assume that nonstate armed actors are led by norms and values, which the organizations refer to in their statements and declarations. A fundamental reason for this assumption is that a number of nonstate armed actors value their public reputation, moral authority, and source of legitimacy, as well as the expectations that are put on them. For this reason, so the line of thought goes, their normative statements should be taken seriously and their behavior evaluated accordingly. Armed actors' self-awareness can be the start of a debate about norms and regulations, which is part of both the ICRC and Geneva Call approaches. The mechanisms these organizations have developed aim at pressuring armed actors to justify their actions. On an argumentative level, this justification becomes more difficult for the actors the more they have committed to humanitarian norms. For this reason, the declaratory acceptance of norms should be seen as a first step, opening the opportunity to entangle armed actors in an argument about the diffusion and internalization of norms—the same mechanism that is used to diffuse norms, such as human rights, among state actors.

However, the limits of the approach have also become apparent: It is more hazardous to employ the mechanism with regard to nonstate armed actors, who often need to take serious precautions for their security. Additionally, the mechanism appears particularly to affect a certain type of nonstate armed actor, namely those actors and leaders that follow a political program, see themselves as representatives of a distinct population, and are interested in providing governance in the territory controlled by them. These actors already anticipate a role in the state, either through revolution and regime change or separation. This profile suggests that NGOs can be far more effective working with classic rebel groups, clan chiefs, and militias than with terrorists, warlords, criminals, or mercenaries, who do not typically have such national-level political ambitions.

External actors dealing with nonstate armed actors need to be aware of the existing range of approaches used by different actors in the field, as well as their possibilities and limits. In any particular case, they need to know about the capabilities of all possible external actors, such as NGOs, to develop a joint effort or at least a complementing approach toward armed groups. The independent activities of NGOs in engaging nonstate armed groups in a humanitarian dialogue may facilitate a change of behavior, make such groups more approachable, and convey norms that other actors can build on, such as in future peace processes. In this respect, NGO activities may well work toward stabilization and peacebuilding even if they remain entirely independent of state efforts. However, the regulations set down in the U.S. Patriot Act specifically make it illegal for any U.S.-based civil society organization to interact with armed groups on the U.S. government's list of foreign terrorist organizations, let alone transfer knowledge to them, even if this knowledge addresses human rights norms and international humanitarian law. The so-called material support law, as part of the Patriot Act, bans any expert advice, defined as "advice or assistance derived from scientific, technical or other specialized knowledge," that would counsel groups to abandon terrorism or to use legal and peaceful means to achieve political change.[19] This argument was upheld in a U.S. Supreme Court ruling on June 21, 2010, which confirmed the ban on training, personnel, service, and expert advice and assistance to any group on the State Department list of terrorist organizations.[20] The court ruled that even advice intended to be used for peaceful purposes amounted to material support for terrorism. This expanded definition of terrorism and terrorists actively prevents U.S. NGOs from helping to reduce indiscriminate violence by armed groups. Similar problems may occur regarding the lists of terrorist organizations set up by the United Nations, the European Union, and individual countries, although no other court has issued judgments or rulings on these matters yet.

The successes that organizations such as the ICRC and Geneva Call have achieved through their norm-diffusion approach reveal the deficiencies and short-comings of the one-dimensional view of nonstate armed actors conveyed in the global war on terror. This view makes little sense conceptually and is shortsighted politically. It is necessary to differentiate among types of armed groups independent of U.S. antiterrorism efforts and to develop more flexible operational procedures that include NGO activities early on. Revising U.S. policy and legislation is advisable to allow, in particular, U.S.-based and international NGOs to use norm diffusion to reduce violence.

NOTES

1. A German edition of this paper was published as Claudia Hofmann and Ulrich Schneckener, "Verhaltensänderung durch Normdiffusion? Die Ansätze von IKRK und Geneva Call im Umgang mit bewaffneten Gruppen," *Die Friedens-Warte—Journal of International Peace and Organization* 85, no. 4 (2010), 73–98.

2. Véronique Dudouet, "Mediating Peace with Proscribed Armed Groups," Special Report no. 239, United States Institute of Peace, Washington, DC, 2010; Ulrich Schneckener, "Spoilers or Governance Actors? Engaging Armed Non-State Groups in Areas of Limited Statehood," SFB Working Papers no. 21, Berlin, October 2009.

3. Claudia Hofmann, "Engaging Non-State Armed Groups in Humanitarian Action," *International Peacekeeping* 13, no. 3 (2006), 396–409.

4. Legally, the ICRC is a private association formed under the Swiss civil code. Internationally, however, the ICRC enjoys the status of a legal entity under international humanitarian law and is, therefore, different from conventional NGOs.

5. See Leonard S. Rubenstein and Melanie D. Bittle, "Responsibility for Protection of Medical Workers and Facilities in Armed Conflict," The Lancet, no. 375 (January 2010), 329–340; Kathleen Newland, "Refugee Protection and Assistance," in P.J. Simmons and Chantal de Jonge Oudraat, eds., *Managing Global Issues: Lessons Learned* (Washington, DC: Carnegie Endowment for International Peace, 2001), 508–33.

6. See Jörn Grävingholt, Claudia Hofmann, and Stephan Klingebiel, *Development Cooperation and Non-State Armed Groups* (Bonn: Deutsches Institut für Entwicklungspolitik, 2007).

7. Mary Anderson, *Do No Harm: How Aid Can Support Peace—Or War* (Boulder: Lynne Rienner, 1999).

8. Particularly during the height of the war in Afghanistan, NGOs suffered increased attacks by nonstate armed actors. See the Afghanistan NGO Safety Office, ANSO Quarterly Data Reports, http://www.afgnso.org/index_files/Page595.htm. While this trend has often been

attributed to a loss of humanitarian space after increased civil-military cooperation on the ground, incidences of looting, blackmail, intimidation, and kidnappings of members of civil society organizations in conflict countries are common.

9. See also Tobias Debiel and Monika Sticht, *Towards a New Profile? Development, Humanitarian and Conflict-Resolution NGOs in the Age of Globalization* (Duisburg: Institut für Entwicklung und Frieden, 2005).

10. Margaret E. Keck and Kathryn Sikkink, *Activists beyond Borders: Advocacy Networks in International Politics* (Ithaca, NY: Cornell University Press, 1998).

11. See Larry A. Dunne and Louis Kriesberg, "Mediating Intermediaries: Expanding Roles of Transnational Organisations," in Jacon Bercovitch, ed., *Studies in International Mediation: Essays in Honor of Jeffrey Z. Rubin* (London: Palgrave, 2002), 194–212.

12. See Article 5.2 (g) of the Statutes of the International Red Cross and Red Crescent Movement, http://www.icrc.org/eng/resources/documents/misc/icrc-statutes-080503.htm.

13. ICRC, *Integrating the Law* (Geneva: ICRC, 2007). See also Lisbeth Zegveld, *The Accountability of Armed Opposition Groups in International Law* (Cambridge: Cambridge University Press, 2002).

14. ICRC, *Increasing Respect for International Humanitarian Law in Non-International Armed Conflicts* (Geneva: ICRC, 2008), 30–31.

15. International Campaign to Ban Landmines (ICBL), *Landmine Monitor Report 2009: Toward a Mine-Free World* (Ottawa: Mines Action Canada, 2009), http://www.the-monitor.org/lm/2009/res/Landmines_Report_2009.pdf; Anki Sjöberg, *Armed Non-State Actors and Landmines 1: A Global Report Profiling NSAs and Their Use, Acquisition, Production, Transfer, and Stockpiling of Landmines* (Geneva: Geneva Call, 2006).

16. See Geneva Call, "Anti-Personnel Mines and Armed Non-State Actors," http://www.genevacall.org/Themes/Landmines/landmines.htm.

17. Geneva Call, Annual Report 2008 (Geneva: Geneva Call, 2008), 17, http://www.genevacall.org/resources/annual-reports/f-annual-reports/2001-2010/gc-annual-report-2008.pdf.

18. Ian Manners, "Normative Power Europe: A Contradiction in Terms?" *Journal of Common Market Studies* 40, no. 2 (2002), 235–58.

19. Editorial, "Redefining 'Support' of Terrorism," *Los Angeles Times*, February 20, 2010, http://articles.latimes.com/2010/feb/20/opinion/la-ed-material20-2010feb20.

20. Holder, Attorney General, et al. v. Humanitarian Law Project et al., June 21, 2010, http://www.supremecourt.gov/opinions/09pdf/08-1498.pdf.

*Claudia Hofmann is a visiting scholar at the Center for Transatlantic Relations at the Paul H. Nitze School of Advanced International Studies at Johns Hopkins University.

Ulrich Schneckener is professor of international relations and peace and conflict studies at the University of Osnabrück, Germany.

Hofmann, Claudia, and Ulrich Schneckener. "NGOs and Nonstate Armed Actors: Improving Compliance with International Norms." Special Report, 2011. United States Institute of Peace, Washington, DC.

Used by permission.

Influence and Collaboration: Civil Society's Role in Creating International Humanitarian Law

by Bonnie Docherty*

The Ottawa Process, which produced the 1997 Mine Ban Treaty, marked a watershed in civil society's involvement in the creation of international humanitarian law.[1] While nongovernmental organizations (NGOs) had previously lobbied for legal change, their work to initiate and guide the Ottawa Process "changed a ban on anti-personnel mines from a vision to a feasible reality."[2] In 1997 the International Campaign to Ban Landmines (ICBL), the NGO coalition that led the charge, and its founding coordinator, Jody Williams, shared the Nobel Peace Prize for their role in banning these inhumane weapons.[3] Questions remained, however, about whether this process was an aberration. A leading member of the ICBL wrote, "Can lightning strike twice?"[4]

Since the adoption of the Mine Ban Treaty, civil society has proved that it will continue to be a driving force in the development of international, and particularly disarmament, law. NGOs, under the umbrella of the Cluster Munition Coalition, campaigned successfully to ban cluster munitions, another type of weapon that causes unacceptable harm. Their efforts culminated in the 2008 Convention on Cluster Munitions, which absolutely prohibits the weapons' use, production, stockpiling, and transfer.

Using the Convention on Cluster Munitions and the Oslo Process that created it as a case study, this article analyzes the contributions of civil society to international law-making and addresses associated critiques. NGOs influenced the substance of and process behind this convention in three ways. They used field reports and survivor stories to make humanitarian concerns the centerpiece of the treaty, provided technical and legal analysis that informed the drafting of provisions, and did diplomatic and grassroots advocacy to move the negotiations along. Some commentators have criticized NGOs for interfering in traditional diplomacy, which they say should be left to states. Many Oslo countries, however, willingly worked closely with NGOs and considered them valuable players in a collaborative process. These states have praised civil society as essential to the creation and long-term effectiveness of the Convention on Cluster Munitions.

Given this support and past successes, civil society seems likely to play a comparable role in the future.

BACKGROUND

The first major use of cluster munitions occurred when the United States blanketed Southeast Asia with the weapons during the Vietnam War in the 1960s and 1970s.[5] Cluster munitions are large weapons that contain dozens or hundreds of smaller weapons, called submunitions. The military values cluster munitions because of their wide area effect, which can be useful for attacking broad or moving targets. The humanitarian harm they produce, however, outweighs military benefits. Because they disperse submunitions over an area the size of a football field, cluster munitions frequently kill and injure civilians during attacks, especially in populated areas where civilians and combatants commingle. In addition, many of the submunitions do not explode on impact, becoming de facto land mines that can cause civilian casualties months or even years after a conflict. According to the *Cluster Munition Monitor 2013*, 34 countries have developed or produced more than 200 types of cluster munitions, while 91 countries have stockpiled them.[6] At least 20 government forces have used cluster munitions in 36 countries and four disputed territories.[7]

As documentation of cluster munition casualties emerged at the turn of the 21st century, the international community increasingly took notice of the threat these weapons pose. States initially tried to address the problem through the 1980 Convention on Conventional Weapons (CCW). The CCW consists of an overarching framework treaty with attached protocols that regulate specific munitions such as land mines, incendiary weapons, and blinding lasers. When CCW parties failed to advance from discussing the issue to negotiating a new protocol, a group of states went outside this traditional UN forum to establish the Oslo Process in February 2007. States hosted diplomatic conferences in Oslo, Lima, Vienna, and Wellington and final negotiations in Dublin. On May 30, 2008, 107 states, every state that had participated in the negotiations, adopted the Convention on Cluster Munitions.

This convention exemplifies a new type of law called "humanitarian disarmament." While earlier disarmament treaties focused on national security concerns, humanitarian disarmament instruments, notably the Mine Ban Treaty and the Convention on Cluster Munitions, strive to end the civilian suffering caused by problematic weapons. To achieve this goal, the Convention on Cluster Munitions includes preventive provisions, notably an absolute prohibition on cluster munitions and a deadline for stockpile destruction. It also establishes remedial measures designed to mitigate aftereffects, such as requirements to clear unexploded submunitions and assist victims of the weapons.[8] Finally, it adopts a cooperative approach to implementation through which states work together to ensure the treaty's obligations are met.

THE INFLUENCE OF CIVIL SOCIETY

Civil society was active before and during the Oslo Process.[9] In 2003 a group of NGOs founded the Cluster Munition Coalition to lead efforts to ban cluster munitions. The coalition quickly expanded and spurred states to action with its documentation and advocacy. When the Oslo Process was under way, it sent hundreds of representatives from NGOs all around the globe to the diplomatic conferences. These organizations brought to the negotiations a range of expertise in areas such as de-mining, field research, law, and victim assistance. The rules of procedure granted the Cluster Munition Coalition broad rights of participation. As a non-state actor, the coalition was not allowed to make formal proposals, vote, or adopt the final document, but it could participate in all other ways as an equal to states.

Field Reports and Survivor Stories

The Convention on Cluster Munitions became a humanitarian disarmament treaty in large part because of civil society's contributions. The release of NGO reports about the civilian harm attributable to cluster munitions generated widespread concern about the weapons' humanitarian impacts and helped lead to the Oslo Process. Human Rights Watch, in particular, published full-length reports that documented deaths, injuries, and socioeconomic effects caused by the weapons in Afghanistan (2001–2), Iraq (2003), and Lebanon (2006).[10] These reports were based on extensive field research, which included scores of interviews with survivors and witnesses as well as with de-miners, government officials, medical professionals, and members of the military. Human Rights Watch researchers also examined physical evidence to determine what types of weapons had been used, who had used them, and what kind of damage they had caused. The reports provided evidence of large numbers of civilian casualties in places such as Nadir, a neighborhood of al-Hilla, Iraq, where 38 died and 156 were wounded as the result of a 2003 U.S. attack with ground-launched cluster munitions.[11] They also related accounts of victims of unexploded submunitions, especially farmers, displaced persons, and children. In Halta, Lebanon, in 2006, for example, 14-year-old

Khodr was tossing pinecones at his 12-year-old brother Rami 'Ali Hassan Shebli. When Rami grabbed a strange piece of metal to throw back at him, the object, an Israeli submunition, exploded next to his head, killing him instantly.[12] Human Rights Watch's reports concluded that "regardless of the profile of the user, the nature of the conflict, or the type of the munition, harm from these weapons is foreseeable and unavoidable."[13] The Cluster Munition Coalition used such reports to bolster its message that cluster munitions should be banned because of the human suffering they cause.[14]

Cluster munition survivors in conjunction with the Cluster Munition Coalition furthered the humanitarian campaign by bringing their firsthand experiences to meetings of the Oslo Process.[15] They described in public speeches and private lobby sessions how they experienced life-altering injuries. Branislav Kapetanovic, a former Serbian military de-miner, lost both legs and both arms while clearing a U.S. submunition in southwest Serbia.[16] Soraj Ghulam Habib of Afghanistan lost his legs when a submunition dud exploded in a park outside Herat when he was 10 years old. Although Soraj was so seriously injured that the doctor recommended letting him die, the boy's father called for treatment that saved his life.[17] These and other stories humanized the dangers of cluster munitions for diplomats and served as a reminder of why they needed to ban the weapons.

Civil society's humanitarian message had a decisive impact on the Oslo Process and the treaty that resulted. The Oslo Declaration of February 2007 initiated the process in order to "effectively address the humanitarian problems caused by cluster munitions" through the creation of an international instrument. In this document, states committed to ban cluster munitions "that cause unacceptable harm to civilians."[18] The second paragraph of the preamble to the Convention on Cluster Munitions itself declared that states were "determined to put an end for all time to the suffering and casualties caused by cluster munitions at the time of their use, when they fail to function as intended or when they are abandoned."[19] This statement articulates the object and purpose of the treaty and has helped guide interpretation of its provisions. It also shows that humanitarian aims are at the forefront of the treaty.

The body of the Convention on Cluster Munitions includes many ground-breaking provisions to enhance civilian protection. The victim assistance provisions in particular seek to reduce the harm caused by cluster munitions. Cluster munition victims are defined broadly as including "those persons directly impacted by cluster munitions as well as their affected families and communities."[20] Article 5, the first provision of its kind in a disarmament treaty, lays out detailed obligations for affected "states parties" (states who are party to the treaty, and thus bound by its terms) to provide assistance for cluster munition victims in areas "under [their] jurisdiction or control." It states that assistance must "adequately provide age- and gender-sensitive assistance, including medical care, rehabilitation and psychological support, as well as provide for [victims'] social and economic inclusion."[21] Article 6 requires states parties to support affected states parties in meeting their victim assistance obligations.[22] With such provisions, states responded to civil society's efforts to make ending civilian suffering from cluster munitions the centerpiece of new international law.

Technical and Legal Analysis

Civil society further influenced the Convention on Cluster Munitions with its technical and legal expertise. In addition to documenting civilian harm, NGOs provided information on the characteristics of different cluster munitions, states' stockpiles of the weapons, the extent of contamination, and efforts to clear unexploded submunitions. They also analyzed existing laws and proposals for new treaty provisions.

The reaction to the report M85: An Analysis of Reliability exemplifies the influence of civil society's technical research.[23] Norwegian People's Aid, the Norwegian Defence Research Establishment, and C King Associates released the detailed study of the M85 submunition in December 2007 at the Oslo Process conference in Vienna. Many states had argued that submunitions with a self-destruct device should not be prohibited under the treaty because they were designed to have a lower failure rate and would thus minimize the post-conflict dangers of cluster munitions. This report examined Israel's use in Lebanon of the M85 with a self-destruct device. Although the M85 was supposed to have only a 1 percent failure rate, field investigations revealed that the submunition's technology was insufficient and the weapon still had about a 10 percent failure rate.[24] According to a history of the Oslo Process, "The M-85 report and its palpable impact showed how active and well-organized civil society was."[25] After the Vienna Conference, few states argued for an exception for this kind of weapon, and the Convention on Cluster Munitions ultimately encompassed it under its prohibition.

The Cluster Munition Coalition also provided legal input on the drafting of the treaty. For example, a proposal to require user states to provide assistance for clearance of areas they had contaminated before the treaty took effect generated significant controversy during the Oslo Process. While the law rarely favors retroactivity, a briefing paper published by Human Rights Watch and the Harvard Law School International Human Rights Clinic laid out legal arguments for the proposed provision. It drew from a range of bodies of law to show states that there was legal precedent for such an obligation.[26] Backed by this research, members of the Cluster Munition Coalition argued for the provision in public statements at the negotiations and during private meetings with various states. Proponents, including several states and civil society, ultimately prevailed, and the principle of user-state responsibility for clearance appeared in Article 4(4).[27] Such successes exemplify how the coalition's technical and legal analysis strengthened the convention's provisions.

Diplomatic and Grassroots Advocacy

Civil society's persistent and broad-based advocacy also advanced the creation of the Convention on Cluster Munitions. As mentioned above, NGO documentation raised awareness of civilian harm, which in turn provided an impetus for the initiation of the Oslo Process. Once the process started, the Cluster Munition Coalition worked diligently to persuade states from around the world to attend the meetings. It encouraged the participation of states with a breadth of perspectives, not just users and producers but also affected states and states with no specific ties to cluster munitions. These efforts facilitated global support for the ban that resulted. At the diplomatic conferences themselves, NGO representatives urged states forward with statements in the plenary session and ongoing lobbying behind the scenes.

Through grassroots advocacy, NGOs generated public support for a cluster munition ban, which gave governments additional motivation to take action. In Wellington, the Cluster Munition Coalition distributed flyers shaped like submunitions and made chalk outlines of willing passersby to represent victims of cluster munitions. Outside the conference hall in Dublin, survivor Soraj Ghulam Habib delivered a petition with more than 700,000 signatures to Irish foreign affairs minister Micheál Martin. During final negotiations, the Cluster Munition Coalition organized a march through the streets of the city. Civil society pressure, in whatever form it took, combined with international political will, ensured that states produced a widely accepted treaty within fifteen months, a very short period of time by international law standards.[28]

A CRITIQUE OF CIVIL SOCIETY INVOLVEMENT

Some commentators have criticized the active involvement of civil society in international law-making. In a Heritage Foundation paper encouraging the United States not to join the Convention on Cluster Munitions, for example,

Steven Groves and Ted R. Bromund condemn the Oslo Process as "NGO-led negotiations."[29] They conclude that it "threatens both the practice of serious arms control diplomacy and the sovereignty of the United States and other nation-states."[30]

Groves and Bromund contend that NGOs "sought to usurp the role of nation-states in the diplomatic process."[31] The collaborative nature of the Oslo Process disproves this claim. While NGOs played a crucial role in the creation of the Convention on Cluster Munitions, they did not, and indeed could not, act alone. States remained at the center of negotiations, and large numbers participated. Attendance peaked with 138 states at the Vienna Conference, and 107 states registered as full participants, plus 20 more as observers, for the Dublin negotiations.[32] The rules of procedure dictated that states, not NGOs, made the formal proposals for treaty language, and only states could adopt the final treaty. Moreover, international law reserves for states the power to ratify and accede to treaties.

The Heritage Foundation authors dismiss civil society's state partners as "Lilliputians," which, according to them, are small and diplomatically insignificant countries.[33] While some major users and producers chose not to join the Oslo Process meetings, the list of participants encompassed a wide range of states from six continents. Among them were more than half the world's stockpilers, and more than two-thirds of the users and producers, including the United Kingdom, one of the biggest users. More than two dozen affected states also participated.[34]

Groves and Bromund further criticize civil society for being undemocratic. They describe NGOs as "claiming to speak for the people of the world and thereby asserting an independent and higher claim to moral authority than any national government could claim."[35] The authors write that, as a result, "the Oslo Process legitimized unelected and self-nominated NGOs at the expense of elected governments."[36] This critique erroneously assumes that all states involved in diplomacy are democracies with governments that fairly represent their people. It also mischaracterizes civil society's aims. Civil society brought to the table voices often forgotten in traditional diplomacy, but it did not claim to represent the whole world.

On two points, the Heritage Foundation authors and the NGOs involved in the Oslo Process would likely agree: the convention was adopted with great speed, and it has a humanitarian aim. They reach different conclusions about the significance of these facts, however. Groves and Bromund see the timeline and purpose as evidence of a flawed convention, and would have preferred slower, more careful deliberations that balanced security and humanitarian concerns.[37]

Civil society, and many states, by contrast, view these characteristics as signs of a successful effort to minimize the suffering of civilians in armed conflict as expediently as possible.

A competing treaty process to regulate cluster munitions through the Convention on Conventional Weapons represented the more traditional kind of approach advocated by Groves and Bromund.[38] Negotiations of a proposed protocol began in November 2007, eight months after the start of the Oslo Process, and culminated at the CCW's Fourth Review Conference in November 2011, more than a year after the Convention on Cluster Munitions entered into force. Led by the United States, major users and producers of cluster munitions sought an instrument that would have regulated, rather than prohibited, cluster munitions. The protocol would have banned only certain kinds of cluster munitions, legitimized use of some models for 12 years, and allowed others to be used indefinitely. A large number of Oslo Process states as well as the Cluster Munition Coalition and the International Committee of the Red Cross vehemently opposed this option. They argued that it could threaten the absolute ban on cluster munitions and that having a weak treaty following a strong one would set bad precedent for international law. The Cluster Munition Coalition campaigned strongly against the proposed protocol, and the protocol ultimately failed when a group of 50 states objected, meaning it lacked the consensus required for adoption.[39] The CCW negotiations and the rejection of the protocol show that NGOs and many states are united in their support of the Oslo Process approach and the type of law that it produces.

Proponents argue that a CCW protocol would have attracted more major military powers, but the Convention on Cluster Munitions remains a powerful and effective tool without them. The collaborative Oslo Process led to endorsement of the ban by a wide range of states. As of March 1, 2014, 113 states have joined the treaty and are bound by its object and purpose. Of those, 84 have ratified or acceded, meaning they are bound by the whole instrument.[40] These states include users, producers, stockpilers, and affected states, plus states with no direct relationship to cluster munitions at all. While some major users and producers, such as China, Israel, Russia, and the United States, did not join the treaty, it can still influence how they conduct war. The Mine Ban Treaty proves the power of stigma. The United States, for example, has not used antipersonnel mines since that treaty's adoption.[41] Similarly, since the Convention on Cluster Munitions entered into force in 2010, there has been limited use of cluster munitions, primarily by militaries that routinely violate international humanitarian law, such as Qaddafi's armed forces in Libya and Assad's forces in Syria.[42] These uses received widespread condemnation by the international community.[43]

CONCLUSION

Civil society has continued to play a role in the life of the Convention on Cluster Munitions since its adoption in Dublin. Representatives of the Cluster Munition Coalition participate actively in the annual meetings of states parties. They work to promote strong interpretation and implementation of the convention, sometimes advising states on language for national legislation and sometimes critiquing language that has been proposed. They also advocate for more states to join the convention and serve as a watchdog through the annual publication of the *Cluster Munition Monitor.*

Despite the criticisms discussed above, Oslo Process states have widely praised the role of civil society and survivors. During statements at the convention's adoption on May 30, 2008, they repeatedly thanked the Cluster Munition Coalition and emphasized the importance of the collaborative nature of the Oslo Process. Irish foreign affairs minister Micheál Martin stated, for example, "I would also like to pay tribute here to the Cluster Munition Coalition for their tireless lobbying and their informed advocacy. And I thank in particular the victims of cluster munitions for constantly reminding us of the broader humanitarian context of our negotiations."[44]

Support for civil society's involvement has not waned. At the Fourth Meeting of States Parties in Lusaka, Zambia, in September 2013, Ambassador Steffen Kongstad of Norway said, "We have demonstrated that states, international organisations and civil society can make real progress when working together—even in the field of disarmament, when considerable resources are required, and sensitive issues relating to national security are involved."[45] The Convention on Cluster Munitions illuminates the power NGOs can exercise to influence the creation of international law with a humanitarian focus and shows that a collaborative approach allows them to do so while preserving states' role in diplomacy.

NOTES

1. This article uses the terms "civil society" and "nongovernmental organizations" interchangeably.
2. "The Nobel Peace Prize 1997," Norwegian Nobel Committee press release, October 10, 1997, http://www.nobelprize.org/nobel_prizes/peace/laureates/1997/press.html.
3. Ibid.

4. Stephen D. Goose, "Cluster Munitions in the Crosshairs: In Pursuit of a Prohibition," in *Banning Landmines: Disarmament, Citizen Diplomacy, and Human Security*, ed. Jody Williams, Stephen D. Goose, and Mary Wareham (Lanham, MD: Rowman & Littlefield, 2008), 217.

5. For more information on cluster munitions, including the history of their use, the nature of the weapons, the harm they produce, and the efforts to ban them, see generally Human Rights Watch, *Meeting the Challenge: Protecting Civilians Through the Convention on Cluster Munitions* (2010), http://www.hrw.org/reports/2010/11/22/meeting-challenge-0.

6. International Campaign to Ban Landmines–Cluster Munition Coalition, *Cluster Munition Monitor 2013* (2013), http://www.the-monitor.org/cmm/2013/pdf/2013%20Cluster%20Munition %20Monitor.pdf, pp. 1–2. The number of stockpilers has decreased to 72 states since the convention was adopted. Ibid., 2.

7. Ibid., 1.

8. Bonnie Docherty, "Ending Civilian Suffering: The Purpose, Provisions, and Promise of Humanitarian Disarmament Law," *Austrian Review of International and European Law* 15 (2010): 7–8.

9. International organizations as well as states and NGOs played important roles in the Oslo Process. The International Committee of the Red Cross provided legal advice and analysis throughout the process. The UN Mine Action Service provided technical expertise, while the UN Development Programme helped fund states that needed sponsorship to attend. Human Rights Watch, *Meeting the Challenge*, 124.

10. See Human Rights Watch, *Fatally Flawed: Cluster Bombs and Their Use by the United States in Afghanistan*, vol. 14, no. 7(G) (2002), http://www.hrw.org/reports/2002/12/18/fatally-flawed-0; Human Rights Watch, *Off Target: The Conduct of War and Civilian Casualties in Iraq* (2003), http://www.hrw.org/reports/2003/12/11/target-0; Human Rights Watch, *Flooding South Lebanon: Israel's Use of Cluster Munitions in Lebanon in July and August 2006* (2008), http://www.hrw.org/ reports/2008/02/16/flooding-south-lebanon-0. Human Rights Watch also documented the harm caused by cluster munitions in Georgia in 2008. See Human Rights Watch, *A Dying Practice: Use of Cluster Munitions by Russia and Georgia in August 2008* (2009), http://www.hrw.org/ reports/2009/04/14/dying-practice-0.

11. Human Rights Watch, *Off Target*, 85–87.

12. Human Rights Watch, *Flooding South Lebanon*, 55.

13. Human Rights Watch, *Meeting the Challenge*, 45.

14. Other NGOs also documented the civilian harm of cluster munitions. See, e.g., Handicap International, *Circle of Impact: The Fatal Footprint of Cluster Munitions on People and Communities* (2007), http://www.handicapinternational.be/en/publications/%E2%80%9Ccircle-of-impact%E2%80%9D-report-on-the-human-impact-of-cluster-bombs.

15. The survivors participated as members of the Ban Advocates, a group coordinated by Handicap International, a member of the Cluster Munition Coalition.

16. For Branislav Kapetanovic's account of his accident, see http://www.handicapinternational.be/ en/branislav-kapetanovic.

17. For Soraj Ghulam Habib's account of his accident, see http://www.handicapinternational.be/ en/soraj-ghulam-habib.

18. Oslo Conference on Cluster Munitions, "Declaration," February 22–23, 2007.

19. Convention on Cluster Munitions, Diplomatic Conference for the Adoption of a Convention on Cluster Munitions, CCM/77, Dublin, May 30, 2008, preamble.

20. Ibid., art. 2.

21. Ibid., art. 5.

22. Ibid., art. 6.

23. C King Associates, Norwegian Defence Research Establishment, and Norwegian People's Aid, M85: An Analysis of Reliability (2007), http://www.landmineaction.org/resources/M85%20report.pdf.

24. Ibid., 5–6.

25. John Borrie, Unacceptable Harm: A History of How the Treaty to Ban Cluster Munitions Was Won (New York: United Nations Institute for Disarmament Research, 2009), 189.

26. Human Rights Watch and Harvard Law School International Human Rights Clinic, "User State Responsibility for Cluster Munition Clearance," February 2008, http://www.hrw.org/news/2008/02/19/user-state-responsibility-cluster-munition-clearance.

27. The provision establishes a political rather than a legal obligation because it "strongly encourage[s]" user states who are party to the treaty to assist with clearance. Nevertheless, the provision set was the first of its kind in disarmament law. Docherty, "Ending Civilian Suffering," 41.

28. For information on the Cluster Munition Coalition's advocacy, see Human Rights Watch, Meeting the Challenge, 122–23.

29. Steven Groves and Ted R. Bromund, "The United States Should Not Join the Convention on Cluster Munitions," Heritage Foundation backgrounder, no. 2550, April 28, 2011, http://www.heritage.org/research/reports/2011/04/the-united-states-should-not-join-the-convention-on-cluster-munitions, p. 20.

30. Ibid., 19.

31. Ibid., 20.

32. Human Rights Watch, Meeting the Challenge, 130, 134.

33. Groves and Bromund, "United States Should Not Join," 22.

34. Human Rights Watch, Meeting the Challenge, 121–22.

35. Groves and Bromund, "United States Should Not Join," 20.

36. Ibid., 21.

37. Ibid., 19.

38. Groves and Bromund described the CCW proceedings as "the only forum for all concerned parties to negotiate serious agreements that advance the elaboration of the laws of war and have a chance of being widely ratified." Ibid., 24.

39. For an overview of the CCW's Fourth Review Conference and the proposed protocol, see Docherty, "Ending Civilian Suffering," 42–43.

40. UN Office at Geneva, Disarmament, "Convention on Cluster Munitions: Signatories and Ratifying States," http://www.unog.ch/80256EE600585943/%28httpPages%29/67DC5063EB530E02C12574F8002E9E49?OpenDocument.

41. Landmine and Cluster Munition Monitor, "Country Profiles: United States, Mine Ban Policy," updated December 17, 2012, http://www.the-monitor.org/index.php/cp/display/region_profiles/theme/3141.

42. Cluster Munition Monitor 2013, p. 1. According to the Cluster Munition Monitor, there are unconfirmed reports that government forces from Sudan and Myanmar used cluster munitions in 2012–13. Thailand used cluster munitions along the Cambodian border in 2011. Ibid.

43. As of September 4, 2013, 113 states had condemned Syria's use of cluster munitions through a UN General Assembly resolution and/or independently. "Cluster Munitions: Syria Use Persists," Human Rights Watch press release, September 4, 2013, http://www.hrw.org/news/2013/09/04/cluster-munitions-syria-use-persists. During the convention's Fourth Meeting of States Parties in Zambia in September 2013, 31 states parties and signatories plus the United Nations and the European Union condemned Syria's use of the weapons. "Cluster Munitions: Nations Condemn Syrian Use," Human Rights Watch press release, September 13, 2013, http://www.hrw.org/news/2013/09/13/cluster-munitions-nations-condemn-syrian-use.

44. Statement by Minister Micheál Martin at closing ceremony, Dublin Diplomatic Conference on Cluster Munitions, May 30, 2008, http://www.clusterconvention.org/files/2013/01/Ireland.pdf.

45. Statement by Ambassador Steffen Kongstad at Fourth Meeting of States Parties to the Convention on Cluster Munitions, Lusaka, Zambia, September 9, 2013, http://www.clusterconvention.org/files/2013/09/Steffen-Kongstad.pdf.

*Bonnie Docherty is a senior researcher in the Arms Division at Human Rights Watch and a lecturer on law and senior clinical instructor at the International Human Rights Clinic at Harvard Law School. She has conducted several field missions to document the use and effects of cluster munitions. She was also actively involved in the Oslo Process that produced the Convention on Cluster Munitions.

Original contribution.

A Brief History of "Save Darfur"

*by Andrew Stobo Sniderman**

THE DARFUR LOBBY WAS HISTORIC. BUT WAS IT EFFECTIVE?

If machetes (rise and) fall in Africa and no American voters are listening, do American politicians care? No, says history. "If every member of the House and Senate had received one hundred letters from people back home saying we have to do something about Rwanda," a senator explained in 1994 after the United States stood by while 800,000 people were butchered in three months, "then I think the response would have been different." No one wrote, and popular silence abetted official indifference.

The Darfur lobby changed everything. In the summer of 2003, the government of Sudan and its proxies targeted non-Arab civilians in a region called Darfur. Hundreds of thousands would die, millions would be displaced. But this time, Americans would write, call, march, divest, and lobby in a coordinated multi-year campaign to change their government's foreign policy. This was a dream come true for human rights advocates accustomed to political irrelevance: a genocide in faraway Darfur became a major issue in domestic politics. The Darfur lobby was born, as Rebecca Hamilton recounts in *Fighting for Darfur*, a history of American policy on Darfur between 2003–2010 and the mass movement that sought to direct it. Hamilton, a Harvard-trained lawyer and current Sudan correspondent for *The Washington Post,* knows the movement well because she was once among its leaders.

At the peak of its influence in 2006, the Darfur lobby, led by a sprawling coalition called Save Darfur, shaped American policy and priorities. It had loosened congressional purse strings (to the tune of hundreds of millions of dollars in peacekeeping costs and a billion dollars more in humanitarian aid), constricted Sudan with economic sanctions, and hounded President Bush to send peacekeepers. A White House staffer gushed: "We would meet with Save Darfur and tell them what amount of money was needed, then they would go [to Congress]... and come back with more!" Another administration official complained: getting 100,000 e-mails from activists on the first week of the job "pisses you off."

The Darfur lobby even won the ear of a president. George W. Bush emerges as a surprisingly sympathetic, if constrained, character in Hamilton's many vignettes. Early in his presidency, in the margins of a damning report on the

Clinton administration's response to the genocide in Rwanda, he writes "Not on my watch." In a meeting with Darfur activists, he speaks of a universal "freedom from genocide." Behind closed doors, he reads critical *New York Times* coverage and slams a table to demand more effective policies from his advisors. Publicly, he pushes for armed international protection for Darfuris: "There have to be consequences for murder and rape, which means you have to have a presence on the ground that can use force." He even consents to an International Criminal Court investigation in Darfur, despite his deep-seated opposition to that institution, which leads to a landmark indictment of Sudan's sitting president, Omar al-Bashir. Alas, Bush's enthusiasm for saving Darfur withers in the shadow of his misadventures in Iraq and Afghanistan. Bush "very reluctantly" opts against another U.S. military intervention in a Muslim country, recounts a senior advisor. He then pins his hopes on NATO, and, later on, the UN—largely, it turns out, in vain.

Fighting for Darfur begins with a whirlwind tour of Sudanese history, and reminds us that Darfur is more than a vacuum where people go to die. Ethnic conflict dates back to the 1980s, when members of one African ethnic group warned, presciently, of a "Holocaust." Sudan is the largest country in Africa and site of a brutal civil war between North and South that lasted between 1983–2005 and claimed two million lives. Darfur burned as a historic North/South peace deal was finalized and signed; the international community was forced to divide its attention between a burgeoning crisis and a separate peace within the same country.

How to explain the anomalous outpouring of American sympathy for Darfuris—black (!), African (!!), Muslim (!!!) Darfuris? Some claim that unprecedented social media makes faraway atrocities ever harder to ignore (dude, people are dying on my iPhone), and that the human rights community has cracked the code for political impact (ape the National Rifle Association, but for genocide). There is something to this, but certainly less than its proponents claim, as the muted response to the far-greater human toll in Congo demonstrates.

Rather, the Darfur lobby benefited from a perfect storm for advocacy. First, Colin Powell—responding, it should be noted, to savvy bureaucrats and his conscience, not activists—sparked media and popular interest in September 2004 by declaring that genocide was occurring in Darfur. The "G-word" stirred the first major wave of the Darfur movement's true believers, including members of the Jewish community murmuring "Never again." Second, the widely observed tenth anniversary memorials of the Rwandan genocide happened to coincide with the first year of the Darfur conflict. The mythology of international failure on Rwanda energized activists and elicited promises from politicians.

Third, congressional advocates for Darfur—Democrats like Donald Payne and Republicans like Sam Brownback—were easy converts to the cause, largely because a bipartisan group of legislators had already been engaged on Sudan issues since the 1990s. They had been drawn to the country because of its bloody civil war in the 1980s and 1990s, notably the plight of Christians in Southern Sudan. These same legislators pivoted to Darfur, where the same bad guys, Islamists in Khartoum, were killing new victims.

Finally, and perhaps most critically of all, the drawn-out nature of the crisis—some called it "Rwanda in slow motion"—gave political organizers years to gain momentum. Translating postcards into policy takes time, and activists had plenty as the killing and dying in Darfur dragged on and on. (By contrast, during the 1994 massacres in Rwanda, Clinton's officials refused to utter the G-word, legislators could not locate the country on a map, the image of Black Hawk helicopters plunging in Somalia haunted officials thinking about intervention in Africa, and most Rwandans died in a mere three months.)

What role did the media play? Many editors eventually made Darfur front page news. Mass coverage enabled a mass movement (and vice versa), and journalists seemed as fixated by the G-word as activists. That said, Hamilton cites a study showing that in 2005 the major US television news networks devoted fifty times more news coverage to Michael Jackson than Darfur. The media was also silent during a "deadly 13-month lag" between 2003 and 2004, the first phase of the conflict with the worst fighting and aerial bombing.

The book has its weaknesses, most palpably on China. Incredibly, when it comes to the Chinese, Sudan's largest oil customer and supposed linchpin of the geopolitics of Darfur, Hamilton does not boast a single source in Beijing. Overall, Hamilton relies primarily on interviews, not documents. Sometimes the reader must settle for anonymous opinions, and American officials tend to say they were doing their best. These are the perils of reporting contemporary diplomacy; it is opaque by design, and in the absence of credible fact-checking or Wikileaks we might unknowingly fall in the crevasses between public accounts and actual policy. Exhibit A: the CIA maintained extensive intelligence links with the Sudanese government even during the genocide. These shadows have eluded journalists and await more patient historians.

Not that Hamilton confined herself to talking with Americans—she does a remarkable job reaching key players on Darfur in the UN, International Criminal Court, African Union, Arab League, and Sudan. The result is the most comprehensive account of the international response to the Darfur genocide available.

Along the way, Hamilton introduces the idealists who dreamed of stopping genocide and their government officials who struggled to show them results. We also meet some improbable anti-heroes. Hassan Al-Turabi, the man who welcomed Osama Bin Laden into Sudan, later became a key leader in the Darfur rebel movement. Michael Gerson, the speechwriter who coined the "axis of evil," stuck around for Bush's second term to push the President to do more to help civilians in Darfur, pestering that earned him the epithet "conscience of the White House."

The Darfur lobby was historic, but was it good? Its critics, including Mahmood Mamdani in his acerbic *Saviours and Survivors,* argue that an ignorant lobby is worse than no lobby at all, good intentions notwithstanding. Many activists did not bother to learn about the people they sought to save, and some leaders fudged details to keep it simple for their base and banners. The focus was ending killing rather than understanding Sudan. Hamilton suggests that American officials curtsied too deeply before activist demands at the expense of an effective whole of Sudan policy, notably a focus on the implementation of the North/South peace agreement.

It seems that Hamilton wants it both ways: she criticizes the U.S. government for ignoring Darfur in 2003–2004 as it focused on finalizing the peace negotiations, but she also sides with critics who say the U.S. later neglected the peace deal by focusing on Darfur. Perhaps the facts support her on both counts, but she might also be demanding that the U.S. government do everything, and do it better.

Overall, however, Hamilton thinks the Darfur lobby is a positive development, especially if it morphs into a permanent lobby against mass atrocity. Hamilton thinks the United States is capable of foreign policy that is effective and more human-rights focused, should its citizens demand it. Time will tell.

Hamilton concludes with a sobering assessment: the Darfur lobby was influential at home, but not effective for Darfur. Hamilton calls it a failure with a "silver lining." Yes, humanitarian aid and the eventual deployment of international peacekeepers alleviated much suffering, yet a genocide was implemented with virtual impunity. Even an engaged superpower could not dictate terms to a ruthless regime flush with petro-dollars.

If the splintering of Darfur's rebel movement and the meddling of neighbouring Chad and Libya made a peace deal difficult, the intransigence of the Sudanese state made it impossible. The U.S. and UN blinked when Sudan's president promised to make Darfur "a graveyard" for UN troops. State sovereignty still means a great deal in strong states, even when a sovereign chooses to massacre his own people, and especially when that sovereign has the tacit support of China. President Bush seemed earnest in his desire to do more for Darfur, but he was tarred by Iraq and stymied by China. Hamilton concludes, "The tragedy of the advocacy effort is that the first sustained movement to pressure the US government to fight genocide and mass atrocity arose in response to a crisis where the US itself became less influential." Or: nice try, but better luck next time.

*Andrew Stobo Sniderman is a Sauvé Scholar at McGill University and studied international relations at Oxford University as a Rhodes Scholar. He was, once upon a time, a leader in the Darfur lobby. His writings are collected at www.Stobo.ca.

Sniderman, Andrew Stobo. "A Brief History of 'Save Darfur.'" Review of Fighting for Darfur: Public Action and the Struggle to Stop Genocide, by Rebecca Hamilton. Columbia Journalism Review, March 16, 2011. http://www.cjr.org/critical_eye/a_brief_history_of_save_darfur.php.

Solving War Crimes with Wristbands: The Arrogance of "Kony 2012"

by Kate Cronin-Furman and Amanda Taub*

Have you heard? Joseph Kony, brutal warlord and International Criminal Court indictee, is going to be famous like George Clooney. The reason is *Kony 2012,* a 30 minute film by the advocacy organization Invisible Children, which has gone viral in the 72 hours since its release, garnering over 38.6 million views on You-tube and Vimeo. It has been retweeted by everyone from Justin Bieber to Oprah, and shared on Facebook by seemingly everyone under the age of 25.

The video opens with a perplexing sequence of home movies. A happy couple film their baby's delivery by Caesarean, and he grows into a healthy, smiling tod-dler. Then the scene cuts to Lord's Resistance Army (LRA) leader Joseph Kony in Central Africa, violently preying upon poor villagers. Now we discover the reason for the five minutes we just spent with this bubbly blond child in Los Angeles. He serves as a contrast for the crying children of northern Uganda, who have been victimized by Kony. (Never mind the fact that the LRA left Uganda years ago.)

The movie swirls us through a quickie history of the LRA, a rebel group that terrorized vulnerable civilian populations in northern Uganda for nearly twenty years before moving into the borderlands of South Sudan, Democratic Republic of the Congo, and Central African Republic. It's (justifiably) heavy on the vilifi-cation of Kony, but light on any account of the complex political dynamics that sparked the conflict or have contributed to the LRA's longevity. Instead, we are given a facile explanation for Kony's decades-long reign of terror: Not enough Americans care.

Invisible Children has turned the myopic worldview of the adolescent—"if I don't know about it, then it doesn't exist, but if I care about it, then it is the most important thing in the world"—into a foreign policy prescription. The "invis-ible children" of the group's name were the children of northern Uganda forcibly recruited by the LRA. In the group's narrative, these children were "invisible" until American students took notice of them.

Awareness of their plight achieved, child soldiers are now visible to the naked American eye. And in fact, several months ago, President Obama sent 100 mili-tary advisors to Uganda to assist in the effort to track down Kony. But according to Invisible Children, these troops may be recalled unless the college students of

America raise yet more awareness. The new video instructs its audience to put up posters, slap on stickers, and court celebrities' favor until Kony is "as famous as George Clooney." At that moment, sufficient awareness will have been achieved, and Kony will be magically shipped off to the International Criminal Court to await trial.

This awareness-based approach to atrocity strikes many people as worthwhile. As Samantha Power laid out in brutal detail in her book *A Problem From Hell: America in the Age of Genocide*, the United States has repeatedly failed to intervene to stop genocide and crimes against humanity because of our leaders' belief that public opinion would not support such a decision. In theory, awareness campaigns should remedy that problem. In reality, they have not—and may have even exacerbated it.

The problem is that these campaigns mobilize generalized concern—a demand to do *something*. That isn't enough to counterbalance the costs of interventions, because Americans' heartlessness or apathy was never the biggest problem. Taking tough action against groups, like the LRA, that are willing to commit mass atrocities will inevitably turn messy. Soldiers will be killed, sometimes horribly. (Think Somalia.) Military advice and training to the local forces attempting to suppress atrocities can have terrible unforeseen consequences. Consider the hundreds of victims of the LRA's 2008 "Christmas Massacre," their murderous response to a failed, U.S.-supported attack by Ugandan and Congolese government forces. International Criminal Court investigations often prompt their targets to step up attacks on civilians and aid workers, in an attempt to gain leverage with the court. (Both Kony and Sudanese President Omar Hassan al-Bashir have tried that method.)

The t-shirts, posters, and wristbands of awareness campaigns like Invisible Children's do not mention that death and failure often lie along the road to permanent solutions, nor that the simplest "solutions" are often the worst. (In fairness, you try fitting that on a bracelet.) Instead, they shift the goal from complicated and messy efforts at political resolution to something more palatable and less controversial: ever more awareness.

By making it an end in and of itself, awareness stands in for, and maybe even displaces, specific solutions to these very complicated problems. Campaigns that focus on bracelets and social media absorb resources that could go toward more effective advocacy, and take up rhetorical space that could be used to develop more effective advocacy. How do we go from raising awareness about LRA violence to actually stopping it? What's the mechanism of transforming YouTube page views into a mediated political settlement? For all the excitement around awareness as an end in itself, one could be forgiven for forming the impression that there might be a "Stop Atrocity" button blanketed in dust in the basement of the White House, awaiting the moment when the tide of awareness reaches the Oval Office.

If only there were. Because Americans are, by and large, pretty aware. In addition to the millions who have now watched *Kony 2012*, organizations like the Enough Project, Amnesty International, and STAND mobilize countless more. A Google News search of 2011 archives produces thousands of articles about child soldiers in Africa, rape in the Eastern DRC, and ongoing violence in Darfur.

Treating awareness as a goal in and of itself risks compassion fatigue—most people only have so much time and energy to devote to far-away causes—and ultimately squanders political momentum that could be used to push for effective solutions. Actually stopping atrocities would require sustained effort, as well as significant dedication of time and resources that the U.S. is, at the moment, ill-prepared and unwilling to allocate. It would also require a decision on whether we are willing to risk American lives in places where we have no obvious political or economic interests, and just how much money it is appropriate to spend on humanitarian crises overseas when 3 out of 10 children in our nation's capital live at or below the poverty line. The genuine difficulty of those questions can't be eased by sharing a YouTube video or putting up posters.

Invisible Children has been the target of intense scrutiny from the international development and NGO community for spending less than one third of the funds they raise on actual programs to help LRA-affected populations. (Mia Farrow was unimpressed.) The $1,859,617 that Invisible Children spent in 2011 on travel and filmmaking last year seems high for an organization whose total expenses were $8,894,630 (which includes the cost to make all those bracelets and posters).

However, we're less concerned with the budgetary issues than with the general philosophical approach of this type of advocacy. Perhaps worst of all are the unexplored assumptions underpinning the awareness argument, which reduce people in conflict situations to two broad categories: mass-murderers like Joseph Kony and passive victims so helpless that they must wait around to be saved by a bunch of American college students with stickers. No Ugandans or other Africans are shown offering policy suggestions in the film, and it is implied that local governments were ineffective in combating the LRA simply because they didn't have enough American assistance.

None of us who actually work with populations affected by mass atrocity believe this to be a truthful or helpful representation. Even under horrific circumstances, people are endlessly resourceful, and local actors understand their needs better than outsiders. It's good that Americans want to help, but ignoring the role and authority of local leaders and activists isn't just insulting and arrogant, it neglects the people who are the most likely to come up with a solution to the conflict.

The LRA is a problem worth solving, but how to do so is a complicated question with no easy answers. Americans are right to care but we need to stop kidding ourselves that spending $30 plus shipping and handling for a *Kony 2012* action kit makes us part of the solution to anything.

*Kate Cronin-Furman is a lawyer and a PhD candidate in political science at Columbia University.
Amanda Taub is a lawyer who teaches international law and human rights at Fordham University.

Cronin-Furman, Kate, and Amanda Taub. "Solving War Crimes with Wrist Bands: The Arrogance of 'Kony 2012.'" *Atlantic*, March 8, 2012.

Part 3:
Public Scrutiny and the Drumbeat to War

The previous section discussed NGO strategies to raise public awareness about conflict or crisis situations. Public awareness and scrutiny of war offer the possibility of creating pressure for warring parties to change their behavior, to reform the laws of war, or to persuade international actors to intervene to stop atrocities. Social media and citizen journalism have broadened the range of news providers, enabling the global public to hear from more diverse voices, potentially getting closer to the truth about what is happening in conflict. But can the discourse about conflict on the nightly news or in courtrooms back home actually change the way wars are conducted in faraway battle zones? And with so many of these new voices providing unchecked or biased information, is the advantage of having more information outweighed by the reality that much of it may simply be bad information?

PUBLIC SCRUTINY OF MODERN CONFLICT

Public discourse about war making has become a much more prominent part of modern conflict. How the public reacts to what is happening in a conflict can now have as much of an influence on the outcome of war, and thus to warring parties' strategies, as tactical, battlefield decisions. State militaries—particularly in democracies—depend on public support to continue war fighting. Non-state groups, like insurgent groups or guerrilla movements, may also need some degree of local popular backing in order to receive shelter, arms, new recruits, or other assistance. Reports of behavior that shocks the public—for example the killing of mass numbers of civilians, or the torture of prisoners of war—can sap support, and thus limit military options. On the flip side, public support *for* military intervention—because the public has seen images of atrocities or read about aggressive acts that merit a response—can lead to war even where other political, economic, or military factors counsel against it.

Public reaction to war is central to war-fighting strategies; yet the recent developments in telecommunications have made it harder for warring parties to shape those reactions than in the past. Globalization and new communication technologies have increased public access to information and expanded the media environment. Internet and mobile communications are cheap, widespread, and globally connected, making it much easier for anyone to be a content-producer. Access to information is so pervasive that the narrative of conflict cannot be confined or manipulated as it was in the past.

In many ways, the greater access to public media along with the increased importance of public discourse on war can be a positive force. It can democratize wartime decision making, enabling citizens to have more of a say in everything from whether to intervene, to how war is conducted, to whether the costs of war are appropriately addressed. Global citizens who seek intervention or help from the international community have the opportunity to have their voices heard as never before. Lawyers, journalists, or NGO activists who want to raise concerns about the conduct of war have greater leverage to do so. Many are motivated not only by a belief that the public has a right to know, but also by a belief that greater transparency and accountability will over time lead to limits on unnecessary or extreme acts of violence in war.

But there may also be downsides and risks. While we tend to think of the increased media coverage and public scrutiny as providing more information—a positive addition—they could simply be adding a greater amount of noise, distracting policymakers from critical decision making. In addition, there are no policemen in the globalized media environment. Those who wish to spread misinformation or to distort or manipulate public opinion to ill effect have equal access to a global audience. Some argue the pressure for 24-7, real-time information and the open access for nonprofessional, unvetted sources has created a "race to the bottom," with the most sensational, but not necessarily the most accurate, information getting broader exposure. These factors could create pressure not for better policies or conduct, but for ill-advised ones.

LAWFARE

One of the most prominent issues within modern discourse is whether the conduct of warring parties in the course of war is lawful or not. While laws of war have long existed, the perception of legality has a bigger impact on the strategy and outcomes of war than in the past because of the increased salience of public opinion on war-fighting. Owing to the greater real-time media coverage, violations of domestic or international law may now be relayed back to publics more easily. In countries where abiding by the law is valued, this may provoke backlash or loss of support. In addition, the greater prevalence of lawyers, NGOs, journalists, and other activists in conflict zones collecting information about possible violations makes the threat of legal action—and resulting legal limitations on state parties—much more potent than in the past.

In the first article, "Lawfare: A Decisive Element of 21st-Century Conflicts?," Charles Dunlap, Jr. argues that compliance with the law has become so important among law-abiding modern militaries like those of the United States (the focus of Dunlap's article) that it can now be used against them by less law-abiding opponents. Dunlap refers to the use of law as a weapon or tactic as "lawfare." He gives the example of Taliban fighters in Afghanistan who hid among civilian populations in a deliberate effort to trigger NATO air strikes that would increase civilian casualties. The civilian deaths provoked allegations that NATO had violated the laws of war, and ultimately led to greater restrictions on the use of air strikes.

While Dunlap focuses on the lawfare and counter-lawfare taking place in active conflict zones like Afghanistan, others have used "lawfare" to describe the activities of lawyers, NGOs, and other actors who attempt to use law to constrain or limit the behavior of warring parties, either through advocacy campaigns like those described in the previous section, or through litigation in domestic courts. In recent years, lawyers have brought court cases to challenge the United States' right to detain individuals at its Guantánamo base in Cuba, to limit certain detention and interrogation tactics, and to demand greater public transparency about electronic surveillance, wiretapping, and other intelligence-gathering activities globally. While many of the court cases have not been justiciable, others have had significant effects, owing in large measure to the public awareness and resulting public hostility they generate. Litigation in courts in the United Kingdom and the European Court of Human Rights has created hard limits on the detention policies of member countries. Public outrage over the breadth of electronic surveillance by the U.S. National Security Agency, and threats of legal action, led to a reversal of policies that many U.S. policymakers would otherwise have continued because these methods gathered massive amounts of intelligence data.

Critics argue that this type of litigation is dangerous because it limits what states can do to counter international and national security risks. As Richard Burst, a lawyer and critic of U.S. domestic detainee litigation, wrote, "Should we allow [military] operations to be chilled and disrupted by a stream of discovery requests? . . . Should we rearm [enemy troops] with legal causes of action that will consume significant time and manpower to defend, and further provide them a public platform from which to denounce the United States?"[1]

In the second article, "Lawfare in the Court: Litigation as a Weapon of War?," Nikolaus Grubeck, a barrister in the United Kingdom who has argued cases involving counterterrorism and the laws of war, admits that sometimes such legal review has unintended consequences. For example, because there are fewer jurisdictional issues and less reluctance from courts to hear detention cases, there are now more legal restrictions and sensitivity regarding the detention of suspected enemy combatants than there are for killing them. But he notes such checks are an important part of democracies, even democracies in war. In some cases, checks may even benefit state militaries, rather than simply tie their hands. "Being seen to uphold and respect law and basic humanitarian values can be important in countering violent insurgent tactics," he notes.[2] In addition, "To the extent that 'lawfare' is about upholding legal and ethical standards in both war and peacetime, it is likely to further the cause for which both lawyers and soldiers are fighting."[3]

WAG THE DOG?

A common assumption is that media coverage can shape conduct in war. Negative media coverage of conflict and public pressure resulting from it may lead warring parties to forgo the use of certain weapons or tactics. Many also assume that media coverage for or against military engagement in a crisis situation can actually drive a state party to intervene, or to withdraw. But is this media effect (what some call the "CNN effect") as powerful as it seems?

In "The CNN Effect: Can the News Media Drive Foreign Policy?," Piers Robinson evaluates whether saturated media coverage of a crisis actually can trigger an intervention to prevent or stop a humanitarian crisis. He notes that while some may embrace the idea that the media can encourage attention toward a particular crisis, others fear that intense media attention will "reduce the scope for calm deliberation,"[4] potentially encouraging intervention in situations where it would do more harm than good.

Although Robinson does not find a conclusive answer to whether media can drive intervention, he notes that news media appear to have a greater impact where the policy actors in question are uncertain and the dominant narrative portrayed in or covered by the media unifies around a single proposed course of action. Borrowing a quote from former UN secretary-general Kofi Annan, Robinson notes, "'when governments have a clear policy . . . the television has little impact'; however, 'when there is a problem and the policy has not been thought [through] . . . they have to do something or face a public relations disaster.'"[5]

Peter Viggo Jakobsen, in "Focus on the CNN Effect Misses the Point: The Real Media Impact on Conflict Management Is Invisible and Indirect," argues that public pressure fueled by greater media attention has little effect at the pre-violence phase—that is, in questions of whether to intervene before a conflict spirals out of control and fighting erupts. The "CNN effect" only has the possibility of influencing in a narrow set of interventions to begin with—those involving Western states with large, influential media corps. And even this limited effect is waning because, Jakobsen argues, international news gets increasingly less attention from the public. Finally, the effect is limited because at the point where Western publics might pay attention, the chance for preventive diplomacy has usually already passed.

Yet, although media coverage may not have the direct causal effect on humanitarian intervention that many assume it does, Jakobsen argues that it can have an important impact on which crises, or types of crises, receive global attention: "By ignoring conflicts during the pre- and post-violence phases and by being highly selective in its coverage of conflicts in the violence phase, the media helps to shift focus and funds from more cost-effective long-term efforts directed at preventing violent conflict and rebuilding war-torn societies to short-term emergency relief."[6]

NEW VOICES IN WAR COVERAGE

While Robinson and Jakobsen focus primarily on the role of traditional journalism in driving public discourse on war, many would argue that these outlets have a diminished role vis-à-vis emerging "citizen journalists" or nontraditional media sources. With the expansion of blog readership and social media platforms like Twitter or Facebook, anyone can reach a global audience easily and cheaply. In part because of this free, citizen-produced information, the traditional business model for media is struggling, and foreign-coverage budgets are shrinking. This leads to a cycle of even greater reliance on freelance journalists and citizen reporting.

New media voices provide information in conflict or crisis zones where traditional media cannot or have not gone. In the post-Arab Spring crisis that emerged in Syria, President Bashar al-Assad's regime barred almost all foreign reporters and limited and controlled domestic reporting (domestic press freedom was limited even before the crisis). As a result, citizen activism and reporting became even more prominent, with major broadcast and print media relying on Syrian citizen tweets, Facebook posts, camera photos, and videos as the primary or only source of information in that conflict. Citizens often risked their lives to get such information out. Violence and reprisals are so high in the Syrian conflict—with estimates of over 100,000 killed between 2011 and late 2013[7]— that even tweeting a casualty number or sharing a photo can elicit targeting from one side or the other.

A critique of such citizen journalism is that although it may be providing more, or otherwise unavailable, information, much of it may simply be wrong, detracting from the public understanding of a crisis situation rather than improving it. Reports may be highly subject to manipulation and based on deliberately disseminated false information. In situations like that in Syria, where there are so many diverse sources, readers outside the country may have difficulty determining what is accurate.[8]

While gauging the reliability of reports is a challenge of citizen journalism, many argue that the downsides are outweighed not only by the greater availability of information but by the fact that it comes from a more diverse range of voices. Because more of the global citizenry are engaged in providing information and critiquing other sources, actions in wartime may be held up to even greater scrutiny, enhancing public transparency and accountability in ways that traditional media alone could not have. As one blogger commenting on the citizen journalist phenomenon in Syria noted, "these social media reporters are not only holding government troops and armed groups accountable for their actions, but making mainstream, traditional media more accountable as well." A citizen-journalist featured in the blog notes, "Things cannot be so easily ignored."[9]

In "Could Twitter Have Prevented the Iraq War?"[10] Eric Boehlert argues that social media can help reduce conflict because it represents citizen viewpoints that may be different than traditional media or the policy establishment. Citizens are empowered to challenge both journalists and policymakers from these citizen viewpoints. He maintains that in the run-up to the 2003 U.S. intervention in Iraq, traditional media acted as the drumbeat to war and failed repeatedly to question or challenge the Bush administration. Boehlert contends that social media, primarily Twitter, could have acted as a "media equalizer." Members of the public or organized antiwar activists could have countered what pro-war columnists and statesmen were using as justifications to go to war. Moreover, because of social media, people now have a direct pathway to confront those pushing for war:

> Imagine how Twitter could have been used in real time on February 5, 2003, when Secretary of State Colin Powell made his infamous attack-Iraq presentation to the United Nations. At the time, Beltway pundits positively swooned over what they claimed was Powell's air-tight case for war. (Powell later conceded the faulty presentation represented a "blot" on his record.) But Twitter could have swarmed journalists with instant analysis about the obvious shortcoming. That kind of accurate, instant analysis of Powell's presentation was posted on blogs but ignored by a mainstream media enthralled by the White House's march to war.[11]

Boehlert argues that Twitter users and citizen bloggers might have provided different stories from those covered in mainstream media, or, through sharing functions on social media, given greater currency to media coverage that did provide a different view of facts on the ground.

While social media has the potential to act as a check against traditional media and policymakers, there is nonetheless a risk that these new media voices could bias decision making or coverage in negative ways. In "When Lines Between NGO and News Organization Blur,"[12] Glenda Cooper points out that the increasingly unclear lines between traditional media and citizens or NGOs who provide information with an agenda can skew which issues or which crises get attention. Just as Jakobsen raises concerns about how traditional media have determined which conflicts get international attention and which don't, Cooper worries that citizen or NGO capture of the media space can bias which international crises are responded to. Rather than a determination based on need, the response may come down to whether NGOs are present in a conflict zone or crisis, and whether they have a successful public advocacy strategy. "The more media-friendly the disaster, the more money it attracts."[13] She cautions that similar checks and balances to traditional media sources must be used in the NGO realm, including quality control and fact checking.

While these are all significant concerns, ultimately many NGOs, media, and citizens alike tend to err on the side of getting more information to the public. NGOs have become an increasingly important information provider. As Kimberly Abbott, an analyst working in the field, noted, partnerships between aid agencies, research and advocacy NGOs, and media can fill important gaps in coverage: "Now, with many foreign bureaus of major news outlets shuttered, and the simultaneous growth of more media savvy NGOs, the agencies are doing even more: researching and pitching stories, sharing contacts, developing content and providing logistics, guidance, analysis, opinion and, in some cases, funding. Put simply, without the help of these groups, many foreign news stories would not be told at all."[14]

As you read these selections consider the following questions:

- What do you think about the concept of lawfare? Can litigation or legal advocacy be considered a "weapon of war"?

- Even if lawfare is not a weapon per se, what is its effect on modern conflict? Is it a helpful check reinforcing norms and restrictions on warfare, a dangerous development limiting warring parties' ability to prevent harm, or simply a waste of time?

- Many civil society activists or lawyers hope that as a result of the greater salience of law there may be fewer intentional or avoidable civilian deaths, fewer incidents of torture or cruelty, or lower levels of violence or conflict altogether—in short greater controls and limitations on war as a result of the legal scrutiny. Do you agree that greater transparency and accountability through media or law might accomplish this?

- What do you think the impact of media coverage is on decisions to go to war or not? Can sufficient coverage of atrocities in a far-off land lead to humanitarian intervention?
- How does the selection of which media events get covered affect the fanning or resolution of crises worldwide?
- How do social media developments like Twitter change the discourse about war and conflict situations?
- Does the greater prevalence of actors writing and reporting with a particular motivation or bias (citizen journalists, partisan groups, NGOs) increase or decrease the public's access to information? Is it likely to lead to improved decision making or responses to what happens in war zones, or simply muddy understanding of what is going on?

NOTES

1. Richard Brust, "As DC Circuit Weighs the Future of Guantanamo Inmates, Some Say Judicial Review Can Harm Military," *ABA Journal*, October 1, 2002, http://www.abajournal.com/magazine/article/detention_dilemma_as_d.c._circuit_considers_guantanamo_inmates_can_judicial/.
2. Nikolaus Grubeck, "Lawfare in the Courts: Litigation as a Weapon of War?," in this volume, p. 130.
3. Ibid.
4. Piers Robinson, "The CNN Effect: Can the News Media Drive Foreign Policy?," *Review of International Studies* 25, no. 2 (April 1999): 301.
5. Ibid., 305.
6. Peter Viggo Jakobsen, "Focus on the CNN Effect Misses the Point: The Real Media Impact on Conflict Management Is Invisible and Indirect," *Journal of Peace Research* 37 (March 2000): 132.
7. Agence France-Presse, "Syria Death Toll: More Than 110,000 Dead in Conflict, NGO Says," September 1, 2013, http://www.huffingtonpost.com/2013/09/01/syria-death-toll_n_3851982.html.
8. A *New Republic* article attempted to categorize some of the major sources of citizen journalism and reporting by the reliability of their reporting and vetting. See Nora Caplan-Bricker, "A Guide to Syria's Best Citizen Journalism," *New Republic*, August 29, 2013, http://www.newrepublic.com/article/114532/guide-citizen-journalists-feeding-us-news-syria.
9. Ombline Lucas, "Citizen Journalists: A New Kind of War Reporting," *Magazine of the International Committee for the Red Cross*, February 2012, http://www.redcross.int/EN/mag/magazine2012_2/4-9_extra_1.html.
10. Eric Boehlert, "Could Twitter Have Prevented the Iraq War?" *Salon*, March 18, 2013, http://www.salon.com/2013/03/18/could_twitter_have_prevented_the_iraq_war_partner/.
11. Ibid., 3.
12. Glenda Cooper, "When Lines Between NGO and News Organization Blur," *Nieman Journalism Lab*, December 21, 2009, http://www.niemanlab.org/2009/12/glenda-cooper-when-lines-between-ngo-and-news-organization-blur/.
13. Ibid., 3.
14. Ibid.

Lawfare: A Decisive Element of 21st-Century Conflicts?

by Charles J. Dunlap, Jr.

If anyone doubts the role of law in 21st-century conflicts, one need only pose the following question: what was the U.S. military's most serious setback since 9/11? Few knowledgable experts would say anything other than the detainee abuse scandal known as "Abu Ghraib." That this strategic military disaster did not involve force of arms, but rather centered on illegalities, indicates how law has evolved to become a decisive element—and sometimes *the* decisive element—of contemporary conflicts.

It is not hard to understand why. Senior commanders readily characterized Abu Ghraib in customary military terms as "clearly a defeat" because its *effect* is indistinguishable from that imposed by traditional military clashes. No one debates that the revelations energized the insurgency and profoundly undermined the ability of U.S. forces to accomplish their mission. The exploitation of the incident by adversaries allowed it to become the perfect effects-based, asymmetrical operation that continues to present difficulties for American forces. In early 2009, for instance, a senior Iraqi official conceded that the name "Abu Ghraib" still left a "bitter feeling inside Iraqis' heart."[1]

For international lawyers and others involved in national security matters, the transformational role of law is often captured under the aegis of the term *lawfare*. In fact, few concepts have risen more quickly to prominence than lawfare. As recently as 2001, there were only a handful of recorded uses of the term, and none were in today's context. By 2009, however, an Internet search produces nearly 60,000 hits. Unfortunately, lawfare has also generated its share of controversy.

LAW IN WARFARE

To the best of my knowledge, lawfare as used in today's context first appeared in my 2001 essay for Harvard University's Carr Center.[2] At that time, the term was defined to mean "the use of law as a weapon of war" and, more specifically, to describe "a method of warfare where law is used as a means of realizing a military objective." Today, the most refined definition is "the strategy of using—or misusing—law as a substitute for traditional military means to achieve an operational objective."[3]

The purpose of the lawfare conceptualization in the national security context is to provide a vehicle that resonates readily with nonlegal audiences, particularly in the Armed Forces. Historically, the role of law in armed conflict was variously presented, but often simply as yet another requirement, one to which adherence was a matter of integrity and moral rectitude. As powerful as such values may be as incentives, especially to the militaries of liberal democracies, conceiving of the role of law in more conventional military terms has its advantages. Understanding that the law can be wielded much like a weapon by either side in a belligerency is something to which a military member can relate. It facilitates accounting for law, and particularly the fact and perception of adherence to it, in the planning and conduct of operations.

While recognizing the ever-present ethical responsibility to comply with the law, how does transforming adherence to law into a strategy serve the purposes of the warfighter? The answer is found in the work of Carl von Clausewitz. A man of his times, Clausewitz had little regard for international law as a factor in war.[4] Nevertheless, he was keenly aware of the political dimension, and this is the linkage to today's understanding of lawfare.

Clausewitz's famous dictum that war is a "continuation of political intercourse, carried on with other means" relates directly to the theoretical basis of lawfare.[5] Moreover, his analysis of the "trinity" of the people, government, and military whose "balance" produces success in war is likewise instructive. Specifically, in modern democracies especially, maintaining the balance that "political intercourse" requires depends largely upon adherence to law in fact and, importantly, *perception*.

Legal experts Michael Reisman and Chris Antoniou put it this way:

In modern popular democracies, even a limited armed conflict requires a substantial base of public support. That support can erode or even reverse itself rapidly, no matter how worthy the political objective, if people believe that the war is being conducted in an unfair, inhumane, or iniquitous way.[6]

Some adversaries see opportunity in this aspect of our political culture. Professor William Eckhardt observes:

Knowing that our society so respects the rule of law that it demands compliance with it, our enemies carefully attack our military plans as illegal and immoral and our execution of those plans as contrary to the law of war. Our vulnerability here is what philosopher of war Carl von Clausewitz would term our "center of gravity."[7]

In short, by anchoring lawfare in Clausewitzean logic, military personnel—and especially commanders of the militaries of democracies—are able to recognize and internalize the importance of adherence to the rule of law as a *practical* and necessary element of mission accomplishment. They need not particularly embrace its philosophical, ethical, or moral foundations; they can be Machiavellian in their attitude toward law because adherence to it serves wholly *pragmatic* needs. Thus, the concept of lawfare aims to insinuate law into military thinking in a new way, one that rationalizes it in terms compatible with the realities of 21st-century operations.

Legal "Weaponry"

The new emphasis on law in war derives from the larger, worldwide legal revolution. George Will recently characterized the United States as the "Litigation Nation" to describe how deeply legal consciousness has penetrated American society.[8] Furthermore, international commerce depends upon law, along with a variety of international forums, to operate efficiently. This, in turn, is accelerating a globalization of law. As international law generally penetrates modern life, it tends to influence, as other trends have, the way war is conducted. Add to that the enormous impact of information mediums, from round-the-clock news sources to cell phone cameras that empower almost anyone to record events, and it is easy to understand why incidents that seemingly implicate the international law of war can rapidly have significant ramifications among the body politic.

Commanders today, keenly aware of the devastating impact on operations that incidents such as Abu Ghraib can have, typically are willing partners in efforts to ensure that compliance with the law is part and parcel of their activities. It is no surprise, for example, that the much-heralded counterinsurgency manual devotes a considerable amount of text to law and law-related considerations.[9] Counterinsurgency and other contemporary "irregular warfare" situations are especially sensitive to illegalities that can undermine the efforts to legitimize the government (and those wishing to assist it) that the insurgency is aiming to topple.

The new counterinsurgency doctrine also emphasizes that lawfare is more than just something adversaries seek to use against law-abiding societies; it is a resource that democratic militaries can—and should—employ *affirmatively*. For example, the reestablishment of the rule of law is a well understood component of counterinsurgency and has proven an important part of the success U.S. forces have enjoyed in Iraq.[10]

There are other examples of how legal instruments can substitute for military means and function as an affirmative good. To illustrate: during the early stages of operations in Afghanistan, a legal "weapon"—a contract—was used to deny potentially valuable military information (derived from commercially available satellite imagery) from hostile forces.[11] In addition, although strategists argue that 21st-century threats emerge most frequently from nonstate actors who often operate outside of the law, these actors are still vulnerable to its application. Legal "weaponry," for instance, may well be the most effective means of attacking the financial networks terrorist organizations require to function. Likewise, sanctions and other legal methodologies can isolate insurgencies from the external support many experts believe is essential to victory.

A Tool for the Enemy?

While the employment of legal methodologies can create offensive opportunities for savvy U.S. commanders, too frequently our opponents use an exploitative form of lawfare along the lines of that arising in Abu Ghraib's aftermath. In fact, lawfare has emerged as the principal effects-based air defense methodology employed by America's adversaries today. Nowhere is this truer than in Afghanistan, where the Taliban and al Qaeda are proving themselves sophisticated and effective lawfare practitioners.

Specifically, the Taliban and al Qaeda are attempting to demonize the air weapon through the manipulation of the unintended civilian casualties airstrikes can produce. Their reason is obvious: precision air attacks are the most potent weapon they face. In June 2008, the *Washington Times* reported a Taliban fighter's lament that "tanks and armor are not a big deal. The fighters are the killers. I can handle everything but the jet fighters."[12] More recently, *Newsweek* told of a Taliban commander who, visiting the site of an attack by a Predator drone, marveled at how a "direct hit" was scored on the exact room an al Qaeda operative was using, leading the publication to conclude that a "barrage of pinpoint strikes may be unsettling al Qaeda."[13]

Yet the enemy is fighting back by mounting a massive—and increasingly effective—lawfare campaign. Using the media, they seek to create the perception, especially among Afghanis, that the war is being waged in an "unfair, inhumane, or iniquitous way."[14] Unfortunately, some well-intended efforts at countering the adversary's lawfare blitz are proving counterproductive. For example, in June 2007, a North Atlantic Treaty Organization (NATO) spokesman in Afghanistan insisted that the Alliance "would not fire on positions if it knew there were civilians nearby."[15] A little more than a year later, another NATO spokesman went even further, stating that if "there is the likelihood of even one civilian casualty, we will not strike, not even if we think Osama bin Laden is down there."[16] The law of war certainly does not require zero civilian casualties; rather, it only requires that they not be excessive in relation to the military advantage sought.

Regardless, NATO's pronouncements unintentionally telegraphed an opportunity for lawfare-based strategy by which the enemy could avoid (or manipulate) airstrikes. That strategy is in effect today as evidenced by a November 2008 report wherein U.S. officers advised that the Taliban is "deliberately increasing the risk to civilians" by locating themselves among them.[17] In terms of manipulation, consider an incident in which the Taliban, according to an American official, held a wedding party hostage as they fired on U.S. forces in an "attack designed to draw airstrikes on civilians and stoke anti-American sentiment."[18]

What is frustrating is the fact that revolutionary advances in aerial surveillance technologies and precision munitions have made airstrikes, in the words of Marc Garlasco of Human Rights Watch, "probably the most discriminating weapon that exists."[19] The problem concerns perceptions. Accordingly, Jaap de Hoop Scheffer, the Secretary-General of NATO, correctly recognizes that perceptions are a "strategic battleground" and wants to "prioritize strategic communications" to remind the world "that the Taliban remain the ruthless killers and abusers of human rights that they have always been."[20]

The Taliban is not the only adversary employing abusive lawfare tactics. In their air and ground operations in Gaza in late 2008 and early 2009, the Israelis faced a foe who, according to Israeli officials, flouted international law in an unprecedented manner. Specifically, the New York Times reported:

> Hamas rocket and weapons caches, including rocket launchers, have been discovered in and under mosques, schools and civilian homes, the [Israeli] army says. The Israeli intelligence chief, Yuval Diskin, in a report to the Israeli cabinet, said that the Gaza-based leadership of Hamas was in underground housing beneath the No. 2 building of Shifa Hospital, the largest in Gaza.[21]

It appears that based on its experiences in the 2006 Lebanon War, the Israelis made careful and innovative counter-lawfare preparations for the Gaza operation. Besides using "meticulous technical and human intelligence" to validate targets— as well as employing low collateral damage munitions in strikes—the Israelis also subjected plans to review by military lawyers "huddling in war rooms."[22] In addition, Israel "distributed hundreds of thousands of leaflets and used its intelligence on cell phone networks in Gaza to issue warnings to civilians, including phone calls to some families in high-risk areas."[23]

Perhaps of most interest is the implementation of a concept called "operational verification."[24] According to *Defense News,* almost every Israeli army unit has specially trained teams equipped with video cameras, tape recorders, and other documentation gear. The aim is to "document the story in real time" while there is still a "chance to influence public opinion" about the conduct of the operation.

Anthony Cordesman argues that although he believes that Israel did not violate the law of war and made a "systematic effort to limit collateral damage," there was nevertheless "almost constant negative coverage of Israel in the Arab and Islamic world, as well as in much of Europe," despite Israel's efforts.[25] Consequently, as *Der Spiegel* reported, Israeli officials are "gearing up for a wave of lawsuits from around the world" claiming violations of the law of war.[26] Other news agencies report that the Israeli government is vowing to defend its soldiers against legal attack. Interestingly, *Der Spiegel* characterized the expected legal action in what are in effect lawfare terms in paraphrased Clausewitzian language as a "continuation of the war with legal means."[27]

OPERATIONALIZING LAW

What does all this mean for commanders in 21st-century conflicts? In the first place, it is imperative that warfighters reject interpretations of lawfare that cast the law as a villain. A better, more realistic assessment is set forth by attorney Nathanial Burney:

> [Lawfare] is often misused by those who claim that there is too much law, and that the application of law to military matters is a bad thing that hamstrings commanders in the field. The fact of the matter is that lawfare is out there; it happens. It is not inherently good or bad. . . . It might be wiser for such critics to take it into account, and use it effectively themselves, rather than wish it didn't exist.[28]

Besides the fact that law may sometimes offer ways of bloodlessly achieving operational objectives, it is simply historically untrue that totalitarians who operate outside of humanitarian norms that the law reflects are more likely to succeed. Scholar Victor Davis Hanson points out that the basis for the enormous success of Western militaries is their adherence to constitutional government and respect for individual freedoms, and constant external audit and oversight of their strategy and tactics.[29] Historian Caleb Carr goes a step further by insisting that the "strategy of terror" of waging war against civilians nearly always has proven to be a "spectacular" failure.[30] In short, adherence to the rule of law does not present the military disadvantage so many assume.

Next, the commander must be concerned with "legal preparation of the battlespace." This means that command must ensure that troops have been properly trained to understand the law applicable to the operation and are ready to apply it under extreme stress. In this regard, the 2007 Department of Defense study of Soldiers and Marines in Iraq is troubling as it revealed that only "47 percent of the soldiers and 38 percent of Marines agreed that non-combatants should be treated with dignity and respect, and that well over a third of all soldiers and Marines reported that torture should be allowed to save the life of a fellow soldier or Marine."[31]

Although intensive training and strong leadership may mitigate such attitudes, experts doubt such efforts can wholly prevent incidents from occurring.[32] Furthermore, Stephen Ambrose observed that it is a "universal aspect of war" that when young troops are put "in a foreign country with weapons in their hands, sometimes terrible things happen that you wish had never happened."[33]

This could suggest that the best way to avoid incidents is to limit the number of troops on the ground. Supporting this conclusion is a September 2008 report by Human Rights Watch that found that civilian casualties "rarely occur during planned airstrikes on suspected Taliban targets" but rather "almost always occurred during the fluid, rapid-response strikes, *often carried out in support of ground troops*."[34] Thus, small-footprint operations can limit the risk to civilians, as well as limit the adversary's opportunity for lawfare-exploitable events with strategic consequences.

Legal preparation of the battlespace also requires robust efforts to educate the media as to what the law does—and does not—require. Adversaries today are clever in their relations with the global media, and U.S. forces must be able to respond as quickly (and ideally before inquiries are made) and transparently as possible to lawfare-related incidents. Relationships with the media must be built in advance; once an incident occurs, it is difficult to explain legal complexities or to demonstrate the efforts to avoid unnecessary civilian losses on a timeline that will be meaningful.

Commanders would be wise to emulate the Israeli initiative by establishing "operational verification" teams to record activity in real time in instances where the adversary is employing an effects-based lawfare strategy centered around allegations of war crimes. In any event, multidisciplinary teams of legal, operational, intelligence, and public affairs specialists ought to be organized, trained, and equipped to rapidly investigate allegations of incidents of high collateral damage. Likewise, command and control systems ought to be evaluated for their ability to record data for the purpose of accurately reconstructing processes if required.

"Operational verification" teams could be more than simply sophisticated elements of an information operations effort. Properly organized, trained, and equipped, they can fulfill legitimate public diplomacy needs, but they can also provide near-real-time feedback to commanders as to how operations are being executed. Thus, commanders could rapidly adapt procedures if the empirical data gathered by such teams indicate opportunities to better protect innocents.

Of course, the availability of expert legal advice is absolutely necessary in the age of lawfare. The military lawyers (judge advocates) responsible for providing advice for combat operations need schooling not only in the law, but also in the characteristics of the weapons to be used, as well as the strategies for their employment. Importantly, commanders must make it unequivocally clear to their forces that they intend to conduct operations in strict adherence to the law. Helping commanders do so is the job of the judge advocate.

Assuring troops of the legal and moral validity of their actions adds to combat power. In discussing the role of judge advocates, Richard Schragger points out:

> Instead of seeing law as a barrier to the exercise of the client's power, [military lawyers] understand the law as a prerequisite to the meaningful exercise of power.... Law makes just wars possible by creating a well-defined legal space within which individual soldiers can act without resorting to their own personal moral codes.[35]

That said, commanders should aim not to have a judge advocate at the elbow of every rifleman, but rather to imbue troops with the right behaviors so they instinctively do the right thing on the battlefield. The most effective way is to carefully explain the enemy's lawfare strategies and highlight the pragmatic, real-world impact of Abu Ghraib-type incidents on the overall success of the mission. One of the most powerful motivators of troop conduct is the desire to enhance the security of fellow soldiers. Making the connection between adherence to law and troop safety is a critical leadership task.

Integral to defensive lawfare operations is the education of the host nation population and, in effect, the enemy themselves. In many 21st-century battlespaces, these audiences are not receptive to what may appear as law imposed by the West. In 1999, for example, a Chinese colonel famously argued that China was "a weak country, so do we need to fight according to your rules? No. War has rules, but those rules are set by the West.... [I]f you use those rules, then weak countries have no chance."[36]

To counter such beliefs, it is an essential lawfare technique to look for touchstones within the culture of the target audience. For example, in the early 1990s, the International Committee of the Red Cross produced an illustrated paperback that matched key provisions of the Geneva Convention "with bits of traditional Arab and Islamic wisdom."[37] Such innovations ought to be reexamined, along with creative ideas that would get the messages to the target audience. One way might be to provide audio cassettes in local languages that espouse what are really Geneva Convention values in a context and manner that fit with community religious and cultural imperatives.

The point is to delegitimize the enemy in the eyes of the host nation populace. This is most effectively accomplished when respected indigenous authorities lead the effort. Consider Thomas Friedman's favorable assessment of the condemnation by Indian Muslim leaders of the November 2008 Mumbai attacks:

> The only effective way to stop [terrorism] is for "the village"—the Muslim community itself—to say "no more." When a culture and a faith community delegitimize this kind of behavior, openly, loudly and consistently, it is more important than metal detectors or extra police.[38]

Moreover, it should not be forgotten that much of the success in suppressing violence in Iraq was achieved when Sunnis in Anbar Province and other areas realized that al Qaeda operatives were acting contrary to Iraqi, and indeed Islamic, sensibilities, values, and law. It also may be possible to use educational techniques to change the attitudes of enemy fighters as well.

Finally, some critics believe that "lawfare" is a code to condemn anyone who attempts to use the courts to resolve national security issues. For example, lawyer-turned-journalist Scott Horton charged in the July 2007 issue of *Harper's Magazine* that "lawfare theorists" reason that lawyers who present war-related claims in court "might as well be terrorists themselves."[39] Though there are those who object to the way the courts have been used by some litigants,[40] it is legally and morally wrong to paint anyone legitimately using legal processes as the "enemy."

Indeed, the courageous use of the courts on behalf of unpopular clients, along with the insistence that even our vilest enemies must be afforded due process of law, is a deeply embedded American value, and the kind of principle the Armed Forces exist to preserve. To be clear, recourse to the courts and other legal processes is to be encouraged; if there are abuses, the courts are well equipped to deal with them. It is always better to wage legal battles, however vicious, than it is to fight battles with the lives of young Americans.

Lawfare has become such an indelible feature of 21st-century conflicts that commanders dismiss it at their peril. Key leaders recognize this evolution. General James Jones, USMC (Ret.), the Nation's new National Security Advisor, observed several years ago that the nature of war has changed. "It's become very legalistic and very complex," he said, adding that now "you have to have a lawyer or a dozen."[41] Lawfare, of course, is about more than lawyers; it is about the rule of law and its relation to war.

While it is true, as Professor Eckhardt maintains, that adherence to the rule of law is a "center of gravity" for democratic societies such as ours—and certainly there are those who will try to turn that virtue into a vulnerability—we still can never forget that it is also a vital source of our great strength as a nation.[42] We can—and must—meet the challenge of lawfare as effectively and aggressively as we have met every other issue critical to our national security.

NOTES

1. Kim Gamel, "Iraq to Open Notorious Abu Ghraib Prison," January 24, 2009, available at <www.boston.com/news/middleeast/world/articles/2009/01/25/iraq_to_reopen_notorious_prison/>.

2. Charles J. Dunlap, Jr., *Law and Military Interventions: Preserving Humanitarian Values in 21st Century Conflicts*, Working Paper (Boston: Harvard Kennedy School, 2001), available at <www.ksg.harvard.edu/cchrp/Web%20Working%20Papers/Use%20of%20Force/Dunlap2001.pdf>.

3. Charles J. Dunlap, Jr., "Lawfare Today," *Yale Journal of International Affairs* (Winter 2008), 146, available at <www.nimj.org/documents/Lawfare%20Today.pdf>.

4. Carl von Clausewitz, *On War*, ed. and trans. Michael Howard and Peter Paret (Princeton: Princeton University Press, 1989).

5. Ibid.

6. W. Michael Reisman and Chris T. Antoniou, *The Laws of War: A Comprehensive Collection of Primary Documents on International Laws Governing Armed Conflict* (New York: Vintage Books, 1994), xxiv. Emphasis added.

7. William George Eckhardt, "Lawyering for Uncle Sam When He Draws His Sword," *Chicago Journal of International Law* 431 (2003), 4.

8. George F. Will, "Litigation Nation," *The Washington Post*, January 11, 2009, B7.

9. Field Manual 3–24, *Counterinsurgency* (Washington, DC: Headquarters Department of the Army, December 15, 2006).

10. Michael Gordon, "In Baghdad, Justice Behind the Barricades," *The New York Times*, July 20, 2007, available at <www.nytimes.com/2007/07/30/world/middleeast/30military.html?ref=world>.

11. See John J. Lumpkin, "Military Buys Exclusive Rights to Space Imaging's Pictures of Afghanistan War Zone," October 15, 2001, available at <www.space.com/news/dod_spaceimaging_011015.html>.

12. Rowan Scarborough, "Pentagon Notebook," *The Washington Times*, June 26, 2008, available at <www.washtimes.com/news/2008/jun/26/pentagon-notebook-mcpeak-calls-mccain-too-fat/?page=2>.

13. Sami Yousafzai and Mark Hosenball, "Predators on the Hunt in Pakistan," *Newsweek*, February 9, 2009, 85.

14. Reisman and Antoniou.

15. "U.S. Coalition Airstrikes Kill, Wound Civilians in Southern Afghanistan, Official Says," *International Herald Tribune*, June 30, 2007, available at <www.iht.com/articles/ap/2007/06/30/asia/ASGEN-Afghan-Violence.php>.

16. Pamela Constable, "NATO Hopes to Undercut Taliban with Surge of Projects," *The Washington Post*, September 27, 2008, A12.

17. "Inside U.S. Hub for Air Strikes," November 29, 2008, available at <http://news.bbc.co.uk/2/hi/south_asia/7755969.stm>.

18. Jason Stratziuso, "Official: Taliban Tricking the U.S. into Killing Civilians," November 8, 2008, available at <www.azcentral.com/arizonarepublic/news/articles/2008/11/08/20081108afghanistan1108.html>.

19. As quoted by Josh White, "The Man on Both Sides of Air War Debate," *The Washington Post,* February 13, 2008, A5.

20. Jaap de Hoop Scheffer, "Afghanistan: We Can Do Better," *The Washington Post,* January 18, 2009, B7.

21. Steven Erlanger, "A Gaza War Full of Traps and Trickery," *The New York Times,* January 11, 2009, available at <www.nytimes.com/2009/01/11/world/middleeast/11hamas.html>.

22. Barbara Opall-Rome, "Israelis Document Everything to Justify Strikes," *Defense News,* January 12, 2009, 8.

23. Anthony H. Cordesman, *The "Gaza War": A Strategic Analysis* (Washington, DC: Center for Strategic and International Studies, February 2009), 17, available at <www.csis.org/media/csis/pubs/090202_gaza_war.pdf>.

24. Opall-Rome.

25. Cordesman, ii.

26. Thomas Darnstadt and Christopher Schult, "Did Israel Commit War Crimes in Gaza?" *Der Spiegel,* January 26, 2009, available at <www.spiegel.de/international/world/0,1518,603508,00.html>.

27. Ibid.

28. Nathanial Burney, *International Law* (2007), available at <www.burneylawfirm.com/international_law_primer.htm#lawfare>.

29. Victor Davis Hanson, *Carnage and Culture: Landmark Battles in the Rise of Western Power* (New York: Doubleday, 2001), 450–451.

30. Caleb Carr, *The Lessons of Terror* (New York: Random House, 2002), 11.

31. Department of Defense, "DOD News Briefing with Assistant Secretary Casscells from the Pentagon," May 4, 2007, available at <www.defenselink.mil/transcripts/transcript.aspx?transcriptid=3958>.

32. See William Thomas Allison, *Military Justice in Vietnam: The Rule of Law in American War* (Lawrence: University of Kansas Press, 2007), 92.

33. Stephen E. Ambrose, *Americans at War* (Jackson: University Press of Mississippi, 1997), 152.

34. Human Rights Watch, "'Troops in Contact' Airstrikes and Civilian Deaths in Afghanistan," September 2008, 4, available at <http://hrw.org/reports/2008/afghanistan0908/afghanistan-0908web.pdf>. Emphasis added.

35. Richard C. Schragger, "Cooler Heads: The Difference between the President's Lawyers and the Military's," September 20, 2006, available at <www.slate.com/id/2150050/?nav/navoa>. Emphasis added.

36. John Pomfret, "China Ponders New Rules of 'Unrestricted War,'" *The Washington Post,* August 8, 1999, A1.

37. Michael Ignatieff, *The Warrior's Honor: Ethnic War and the Modern Conscience* (New York: Metropolitan Books, 1998), 149.

38. Thomas L. Friedman, "No Way, No How, Not Here," *The New York Times,* February 17, 2009, available at <www.nytimes.com/2009/02/18/opinion/18friedman.html>.

39. Scott Horton, "State of Exception: Bush's War on the Rule of Law," *Harper's Magazine,* July 2007, available at <www.harpers.org/archive/2007/07/0081595>.

40. David B. Rivkin, Jr., and Lee A. Casey, "Lawfare," February 23, 2007, available at <http://online.wsj.com/article/SB117220137149816987.html>; compare with "The NGO Front in the Gaza War: Lawfare against Israel," February 2, 2009, available at <www.ngo-monitor.org/article/the_ngo_front_in_the_gaza_war_lawfare_against_israel>.

41. Lyric Wallwork Winik, "A Marine's Toughest Mission," *Parade Magazine*, January 19, 2003, available at <www.parade.com/articles/editions/2003/edition_01-19-2003/General_Jones>.

42. Eckhardt.

*Major General **Charles J. Dunlap, Jr.,** USAF, is deputy judge advocate general, Headquarters U.S. Air Force.

Dunlap, Charles J., Jr. "Lawfare: A Decisive Element of 21st-Century Conflicts?" *Joint Force Quarterly*, no. 54 (3rd quarter, 2009): 34–39. http://www.dtic.mil/dtic/tr/fulltext/u2/a515192.pdf.

Used by permission.

Lawfare in the Courts: Litigation as a Weapon of War?

by Nikolaus Grubeck*

In 2001 Major General Charles Dunlap Jr. coined the term "lawfare," defining it as "the use of law as a weapon of war."[1] In his article "Lawfare: A Decisive Element of 21st-Century Conflicts?,"[2] Dunlap identifies "adherence to law in fact and, importantly, perception" as a key factor of success in war. In democratic societies where the rule of law is an integral part of national values, the perception of national armed forces' conduct as lawful is essential to maintaining public support for their operations. He gives numerous examples of how opponents of law-abiding countries—for example, insurgent groups or terrorists—can use a country's concern for legality as a weapon against it.

Increasingly, the battle for perceptions of legality is taking place in the courtroom. In places like the United States and the United Kingdom, an increasing range of cases has invited the courts to deal with matters intricately connected to the way war is waged. But can such litigation amount to "the use of law as a weapon of war?" Have the allegations of misconduct in these cases assisted our enemies by creating negative perceptions of our adherence to law and/or by unduly restricting the ability of our armed forces to operate effectively? Or are war-related cases generally a positive facet of lawfare, demonstrating due process and accountability and thereby supporting military efforts in the field?

This article seeks to provide an overview of how lawfare has played out in the domestic courts of the common law jurisdictions in recent years. While there are dangers to the increased "judicialization" of war, it also brings clear benefits, suggesting that in general litigation relating to war is likely to help rather than hinder our efforts on the battlefield.

The Long Arm of the Law: Courts' Increasing Role in Cases Relating to War

War-related litigation most traditionally comprises court-martial cases concerning alleged wrongdoing by military personnel involved in conflict. Proceedings concerning criminal conduct by individual members of the armed forces are the most established way for courts to become involved in war. His Honor Judge Jeff

Blackett, the judge advocate general of the British Armed Forces, notes that "every military or naval force throughout the ages has needed to create and make use of a dedicated system of military justice."[3] Cases are brought by military or other public prosecution authorities on the basis of existing standards of conduct. They are generally heard by military judges and juries and handled within established structures.

Individual misconduct cases—because of the nature of the misconduct, the way they came to light, or other factors—may garner significant public attention. Examples include the trials regarding the murder and injury of multiple civilians by U.S. Army staff sergeant Robert Bales in Panjwai district in Afghanistan,[4] the extrajudicial execution of an Afghan prisoner by a UK royal marine,[5] and the ongoing court-martial proceedings concerning alleged corruption by Ugandan military officers serving with the African Union Mission in Somalia.[6]

Beyond this, historically civilian courts have often refused to consider claims relating to conduct during armed conflict. The traditional starting point has always been, "where actual war is raging, acts done by the military authorities are not justiciable by the ordinary tribunals."[7] In other words, such cases were not considered appropriate for, or subject to, review by the courts. Different legal systems have established different thresholds regarding what matters the courts are willing to engage with. In many countries, courts remain reluctant to engage. For example, in a case concerning the UK government's refusal to hold an independent inquiry into the circumstances that led to the invasion of Iraq in 2003, Lord Bingham, of the UK House of Lords wrote in a 2008 judgment, "judicial tribunals . . . recognise their limitations as suitable bodies"[8] to resolve such matters. The High Court of Australia has found that certain types of claims, particularly in the area of foreign affairs and national security, by their very subject matter would risk "embarrassing" the court and the executive if they were justiciable.[9] Similarly, the U.S. government has relied on the "political question doctrine"[10] to argue that the killing by drone strike of U.S. nationals in Yemen was in its nature a political issue and thus not fit for adjudication.[11]

Given these jurisdictional limitations, human rights lawyers and organizations seeking to ensure that their own countries are abiding by the laws of war and respecting human rights and policy considerations have focused much energy on simply expanding the jurisdictional space for these cases to be reviewed by courts—with some success. In recent years, judges have become increasingly willing to enter into what courts in the UK have sometimes described as the "forbidden area."[12]

In Europe, the European Court of Human Rights has played a major role in expanding the boundaries of traditional doctrines of justiciability. It has adjudicated upon a wide range of war-related cases. These included, for instance, air and artillery strikes by Russian forces in Chechnya,[13] the boarding of a foreign ship by French naval units off the coast of Africa,[14] the conduct of Turkish and UK forces in Iraq,[15] Macedonia's involvement in the U.S.-led rendition program of terrorism suspects,[16] and the legality of UK military detention in Iraq.[17] The expansive approach taken by the European Court of Human Rights has meant that national courts in Europe are now regularly asked to rule on the legality of war-related conduct by the executive branch.

Similarly, signatories to the European Convention on Human Rights are required to ensure effective independent investigations of deaths resulting from the use of force[18] and allegations of torture[19] if they occur within the convention's jurisdictional space. Jurisdiction extends to individuals under the "effective control" of the relevant state regardless of their geographical location.[20] This means that judicial and quasi-judicial bodies have assumed a much bigger role in reviewing military operations abroad. By way of example, the UK has conducted extensive inquiries into allegations of abuse by its forces during the war in Iraq.[21]

In the United States, the range of war-related cases open to judicial review or automatically triggering a formal inquiry remains much more restricted.[22] Nonetheless U.S. courts have also been drawn into such litigation, primarily in the context of cases relating to captured alleged enemy combatants. Petitions for habeas corpus by detainees held in Guantánamo Bay have established that such detainees are entitled to at least limited due process rights and that U.S. federal courts are able to adjudicate on these.[23] Detainees in other locations outside the United States have been found to have more limited rights[24] but have still been the cause of extensive court proceedings.

In other countries, too, the status and treatment of conflict-related detainees has arguably been the one aspect of war in relation to which the courts have been the most willing to intervene. In the UK, legal cases brought on behalf of individuals in military detention have dealt with issues ranging from claims for habeas corpus[25] to the legality of detention[26] and of onward transfer to national authorities in light of the risk of torture[27] or execution.[28] In Canada the treatment of detainees captured by Canadian forces in Afghanistan has been investigated repeatedly[29] and remains the subject of ongoing litigation.[30] The courts in Australia have also engaged with the issue, refusing to strike out a case relating to the rights of military detainees.[31]

Another aspect of armed conflict that has been the subject of increasing litigation concerns the provision of information relating to war or at least quasi-military operations. In efforts to increase transparency and public accountability over these matters, legal cases have been brought to request information relating to issues such as drone strikes in Yemen,[32] intelligence cooperation on rendition operations,[33] and interrogation techniques employed in Afghanistan.[34]

THE DANGER OF LITIGATION BECOMING A TOOL OF LAWFARE

The reach of the law in conflict-related cases has certainly increased in recent years. Its impact on the conduct of war, and its potential use or abuse as a tool of lawfare, however, remain contentious. The 2005 U.S. National Defense Strategy went so far as to suggest that the existing patchwork of cases might amount to a concerted strategy to "use international fora, judicial processes, and terrorism" to undermine the strength of the nation.[35] Other commentators have dismissed the claims brought in the course of "lawfare litigation" as "usually factually or legally meritless"[36] and have accused the lawyers acting in such cases of being little more than mouthpieces for enemy propaganda.

Of course, most insurgent groups engaged in armed conflict do not tend to bring cases to court.[37] Nonetheless, court cases can have the same effect as some tactics in warfare, and so might be considered "lawfare" as defined by Dunlap. War-related litigation—even if it is brought by public prosecutors, bereaved relatives of service personnel, or human rights activists rather than enemy fighters— may have the effect of undermining the perception of lawful conduct by armed forces and thereby potentially assist the enemy.

One of the most potent examples of lawfare arose from the mistreatment of Iraqi prisoners in Abu Ghraib Prison by U.S. forces. Information about the Abu Ghraib abuses was brought to public light by American investigative journalists, but reinforced by subsequent litigation in several court cases. The trials were closely monitored by an international public and carried serious consequences for U.S. forces. Insurgent groups used the contradiction between America's legal and moral obligation and the actual behavior of some of the U.S. forces to discredit the entire mission and attract support to the insurgency. The damaged perception of American forces' conduct had real military impact on the ground—Dunlap describes it as the U.S. military's "most serious setback since 9/11."[38]

Litigation may also result in narrowing the military's freedom to act as it deems necessary. The UK Supreme Court, in the case of *Smith v. Ministry of Defence*, recently had to rule on negligence claims arising out of the death of several British soldiers in Iraq caused by a friendly fire incident and the detonation of roadside bombs.[39] Traditionally, civil liability has been limited in such cases by the defense of "combat immunity," which exempts acts on the battlefield from review by the courts.[40] The High Court of Australia held in 1940 that "no one can imagine the court undertaking a trial" of "whether the soldier on the field of battle or the sailor fighting on his ship might reasonably have been more careful to avoid causing civil loss or damage."[41]

The claimants in *Smith* did not allege negligence in relation to conduct in the field of battle in Iraq, but argued that the Ministry of Defence had failed to provide the soldiers with adequate training and equipment. The Supreme Court refused to accept that the doctrine of combat immunity could automatically defeat the claims, ruling that the doctrine had to be construed narrowly. The Ministry of Defence therefore could potentially be found liable for negligence. A minority of the Supreme Court judges disagreed with this conclusion, considering that it would make extensive litigation an almost inevitable consequence of any active service operations undertaken by the British armed forces. There was a risk that the threat of such litigation "would affect decision-making and lead to a defensive approach, both at the general procurement and strategic stages and at the tactical and combat stages when equipment was being deployed."

The decision in the case of *Smith* has been described as "the apogee of judicial encroachment," leading to "the legal erosion of British fighting power."[42] It has also been subject to heavy criticism from the executive branch of government, with the UK secretary of state for defense stating that "I am very concerned at the wider implications of this judgement, which could ultimately make it more difficult for our troops to carry out operations, and potentially throws open a wide range of military decisions to the uncertainty of litigation."[43]

THE IMPACT OF CONFLICT-RELATED CASES ON THE CONDUCT OF WAR: NECESSARY CONSTRAINT OR DANGEROUS ENCROACHMENT?

So does all this litigation (and by extension the increasing "judicialization" of war) amount to warfare through courts? Has it led to such an erosion of fighting power as to empower our enemies by critically undermining the extent to which the wider public sees our armed forces as "adhering to law" in their military operations abroad? The answer is arguably no.

As is clear from the brief overview of cases set out above, they have few unifying features other than that all of them relate to war. The motives of the respective claimants differ widely. Some cases are brought by grieving families of soldiers killed in faraway conflicts. Others are pursued by detainees seeking to be released from Guantánamo Bay, or by civil liberties organizations pushing for more judicial oversight of the executive. The development of the law is piecemeal. It depends on the facts of the individual cases and may be influenced by the political realities of the day.

Of course there are dangers to the excessive legalization of the combat environment. Soldiers must be able to fight without fear of being sued for technicalities. Or, as Lord Hope, the deputy president of the UK Supreme Court, put it: "It is of paramount importance that the work that the armed forces do in the national interest should not be impeded by having to prepare for or conduct active operations against the enemy under the threat of litigation if things should go wrong."[44]

In some instances, the case-by-case evolution of the common law has unintended consequences. For example, most judges are instinctively more comfortable with imposing review and regulation in the context of detention rather than combat operations. As a consequence, capturing and detaining enemy combatants is now generally subject to much more guidance and judicial oversight than killing them.

But the increased involvement of the courts in regulating war also has significant positive aspects. As Dunlap points out, situating war within a context of proper legal oversight also contributes to combat power in that is assures troops of the "legal and moral validity of their actions."[45] Court decisions create clear guidance, thereby establishing "a well-defined legal space within which individual soldiers can act without resorting to their own personal moral codes."[46] Demonstrable adherence to ethical and legal standards of warfare as well as genuine accountability achieved through an open and fair court process when things go wrong can also be an effective way of winning battles of public perception, both at home and in theaters of operation abroad. Being seen to uphold and respect law and basic humanitarian values can be important in countering violent insurgent tactics.

For many of those involved in this type of litigation, it is simply part of maintaining democratic controls on armed forces. It constitutes an important check on the exercise of the most severe manifestation of executive power, promotes accountability, and protects fundamental norms. Individual incidents and court decisions might be taken advantage of by a determined enemy. Yet, at a wider level, as Dunlap says, "the basis for the enormous success of Western militaries is their adherence to constitutional government and respect for individual freedoms, and constant external audit and oversight of their strategy and tactics."[47] Insofar as fair and independent oversight by the courts of conduct in war can help visibly uphold the rule of law, overall it is likely to strengthen, not weaken democratically mandated armed forces. To the extent that "lawfare" is about upholding legal and ethical standards in both war and peacetime, it is likely to further the cause for which both lawyers and soldiers are fighting.

NOTES

1. Charles J. Dunlap Jr., "Law and Military Interventions: Preserving Humanitarian Values in 21st Century Conflicts," working paper (Boston: Harvard Kennedy School, 2001), 5, www.ksg. harvard.edu/cchrp/Web%20Working%20Papers/Use%20of%20Force/Dunlap2001.pdf.

2. Charles J. Dunlap Jr., "Lawfare: A Decisive Element of 21st-Century Conflicts?" *JFQ* (*Joint Force Quarterly*), no. 54 (3rd quarter 2009): 35, http://www.dtic.mil/dtic/tr/fulltext/u2/a515192.pdf.

3. Jeff Blackett, *Rant on the Court Martial and Service Law* (Oxford: Oxford University Press, 2009).

4. BBC News, "Staff Sgt Robert Bales Admits Afghan Massacre," June 5, 2013, http://www.bbc. co.uk/news/world-us-canada-22788987.

5. BBC News, "Marine Guilty of Afghanistan Murder," November 8, 2013, http://www.bbc.co.uk/ news/uk-24870699.

6. BBC News, "Uganda Suspends Officers Sent to Somalia on AU Mission," September 16, 2013, http://www.bbc.co.uk/news/world-africa-24116606.

7. Privy Council (Cape of Good Hope), *Ex p Marais* [1902] AC 109.

8. Lord Bingham, UK House of Lords, in R (Gentle) v. Prime Minister (2008) UKHL 20.

9. High Court of Australia, Attorney-General (UK) v. Heinemann Publishing Australia Pty Ltd ("Spycatcher") (1988) HCA 25, which concerned the publication of a book by a former intelligence officer.

10. U.S. Supreme Court, *Marbury v. Madison*, 5 U.S. 1 Cranch 137 (1803).

11. U.S. District Court DC, *Al-Aulaqi v. Panetta*, No. 1:12-cv-01192 (DDC). See further, Scott Shane, "Judge Challenges White House Claims on Authority in Drone Killing," *New York Times*, July 19, 2013, http://www.nytimes.com/2013/07/20/us/politics/judge-challenges-white-house-claims-on-authority-in-drone-killings.html?ref=anwaralawlaki&_r=0.

12. See, e.g., R (Abbasi) v. Secretary of State for Foreign and Commonwealth Affairs (2002) EWCA Civ 1598, which concerned the UK government's responsibilities vis-à-vis a British citizen captured by U.S. forces in Afghanistan and held in Guantánamo Bay.

13. European Court of Human Rights, Case of Abdulkhanov and Others v. Russia, application no. 22782/06 (October 3, 2013).

14. European Court of Human Rights, Case of Medvedyev and Others v. France, application no. 3394/03 (March 29, 2010).

15. European Court of Human Rights, Case of Issa and Others v. Turkey, application no. 31821/96 (March 30, 2005), and European Court of Human Rights, Case of Al Skeini and Others v. the United Kingdom, application no. 55721/07 (July 7, 2011).

16. European Court of Human Rights, Case of El-Masri v. the Former Yugoslav Republic of Macedonia, application no. 39630/09 (December 13, 2012).

17. European Court of Human Rights, Case of Al Jedda v. the United Kingdom, application no. 27021/08 (July 7, 2011).

18. European Court of Human Rights, Case of McCann v. the United Kingdom, application no. 18984/91 (May 13, 2008); concerning the killing of suspected IRA terrorists in Gibraltar by UK Special Forces.

19. European Court of Human Rights, Case of Assenov and Others v. Bulgaria, application no. 24760/94 (October 28, 1998), a case regarding mistreatment in police detention.

20. European Court of Human Rights, Case of Al Skeini and Others v. the United Kingdom, application no. 55721/07 (July 7, 2011).

21. See the Baha Mousa Public Inquiry, http://www.bahamousainquiry.org, and Al-Sweady Public Inquiry, http://www.alsweadyinquiry.org.

22. See, for instance, the U.S. case *Al-Aulaqi v. Panetta*, No. 1:12-cv-01192 (RMC), in which the U.S. government has relied on the "political question doctrine" (U.S. Supreme Court, *Marbury v. Madison*, 1 Cranch 137, 170 (1803), arguing that a drone-strike killing of U.S. nationals in

Yemen was in its nature a political issue and thus not fit for adjudication. (See further, Scott Shane, "Judge Challenges White House Claims on Authority in Drone Killing," *New York Times*, July 19, 2013, http://www.nytimes.com/2013/07/20/us/politics/judge-challenges-white-house-claims-on-authority-in-drone-killings.html?ref=anwaralawlaki&_r=0.)

23. U.S. Supreme Court, *Hamdi v. Rumsfeld*, 542 U.S. 507 (2004), *Rasul v. Bush*, 542 U.S. 466 (2004), *Hamdan v. Rumsfeld*, 548 U.S. 557 (2006), and *Boumedine v. Bush*, 553 U.S. 723 (2008), all cases by Guantánamo detainees challenging their detention and the structures set up to deal with them.

24. U.S. Supreme Court, *Munaf v. Geren*, 553 U.S. 674 (2008), and U.S. Court of Appeals DC Circuit, *Al Maqaleh v. Gates*, 605 F.3d 84 (2010).

25. UK Supreme Court, Rahmatullah v. Secretary of State for Foreign and Commonwealth Affairs, [2012] UKSC 48.

26. High Court of England and Wales, Serdar Mohammed v Ministry of Defence [2014] EWHC 1369 (QB).

27. High Court of England and Wales, R (Evans) v. Secretary of State for Defence [2010] EWHC 1445 (Admin) and R (Serdar Mohammed) v. Secretary of State for Defence [2012] EWHC 3282 (Admin).

28. European Court of Human Rights, Case of Al-Saadoon and Mufdhi v. the United Kingdom, application no. 61498/08 (October 04, 2010).

29. See, for instance, Steven Chase and Graeme Smith, "Harper Government Stonewalled Detainee Probe, Watchdog Concludes," *Globe and Mail*, July 27, 2012, http://www.theglobeand mail.com/news/politics/harper-government-stonewalled-detainee-probe-watchdog-concludes/article4374184/.

30. Canadian Federal Court, Amnesty International Canada and British Columbia Civil Liberties Association v. Chief of the Defence Staff for the Canadian Forces et al., T-324-07.

31. Australian Federal Court, Hicks v. Ruddock [2007] FCA 299.

32. See "Anwar Al-Aulaqi—FOIA Request," American Civil Liberties Union (ACLU), October 19, 2011, https://www.aclu.org/national-security/anwar-al-awlaki-foia-request.

33. Court of Appeal of England and Wales, R (Binyam Mohammed) v. Secretary of State for Foreign and Commonwealth Affairs [2010] EWCA Civ 65.

34. See "Documents Obtained by ACLU Describe Charges of Murder and Torture of Prisoners in U.S. Custody," American Civil Liberties Union (ACLU), April 16, 2008, https://www.aclu.org/national-security/documents-obtained-aclu-describe-charges-murder-and-torture-prisoners-us-custody.

35. See *The National Defense Strategy of the United States of America*, U.S. Department of Defense (March 2005), p. 5, http://www.defense.gov/news/mar2005/d20050318ndsi.pdf.

36. David B. Rivkin Jr. and Lee A. Casey, "Lawfare," *Wall Street Journal*, February 23, 2007, http://online.wsj.com/article/SB117220137149816987.html.

37. Although some relevant cases have been brought by or against individual alleged insurgents.

38. Dunlap, "Lawfare," *JFQ*, no. 54 (3rd quarter 2009): 34, http://www.dtic.mil/dtic/tr/fulltext/u2/a515192.pdf.

39. UK Supreme Court, Smith and Others v. Ministry of Defence (2013) UKSC 41.

40. The standard legal position has been that "there is no civil liability for injury caused by the negligence of persons in the course of an actual engagement with the enemy." Gibbs CJ, High Court of Australia, Groves v. the Commonwealth (1982) 150 CLR 113.

41. Dixon J, High Court of Australia, Shaw Savill & Albion Co Ltd v. Commonwealth (1940) HCA 40; (1940) 66 CLR 344.

42. Thomas Tugendhat and Laura Croft, "The Fog of Law: An Introduction to the Legal Erosion of British Fighting Power," Policy Exchange report, 2013, p. 28, http://www.policyexchange.org.uk/images/publications/the%20fog%20of%20law.pdf.

43. BBC News, "Iraq Damages Cases: Supreme Court Rules Families Can Sue," June 19, 2013, http://www.bbc.co.uk/news/uk-22967853.

44. Lord Hope, UK Supreme Court, Smith and Others v. Ministry of Defence (2013) UKSC 41.

45. Dunlap, "Lawfare," JFQ, no. 54 (3rd quarter 2009): 38, http://www.dtic.mil/dtic/tr/fulltext/u2/a515192.pdf.

46. Richard C. Schragger, "Cooler Heads: The Difference Between the President's Lawyers and the Military's," *Slate*, September 20, 2006, www.slate.com/id/2150050/?nav/navoa.n. Also, quoted in Dunlap, ibid.

47. Dunlap, "Lawfare," JFQ, no. 54 (3rd quarter 2009): 37, http://www.dtic.mil/dtic/tr/fulltext/u2/a515192.pdf.

*Nikolaus Grubeck is a barrister at the bar of England and Wales. He is currently instructed in several legal cases dealing with issues such as military detention in Afghanistan and Iraq, targeted assassinations, and civilian casualties. He previously worked for the United Nations in Afghanistan and Sudan and has conducted missions in many other conflict-affected areas.

Original contribution.

The CNN Effect: Can the News Media Drive Foreign Policy?

*by Piers Robinson**[1]

During the 1980s the proliferation of new technologies transformed the potential of the news media to provide a constant flow of global real-time news. Tiananmen Square and the collapse of communism symbolised by the fall of the Berlin Wall became major media events communicated to Western audiences instantaneously via TV news media. By the end of the decade the question was being asked as to what extent this 'media pervasiveness'[2] had impacted upon government— particularly the process of foreign policy making. The new technologies appeared to reduce the scope for calm deliberation over policy, forcing policy-makers to respond to whatever issue journalists focused on.[3] This perception was in turn reinforced by the end of the bipolar order and what many viewed as the collapse of the old anti-communist consensus which—it was argued—had led to the creation of an ideological bond uniting policy makers and journalists. Released from the 'prism of the Cold War'[4] journalists were, it was presumed, freer not just to cover the stories they wanted but to criticise US foreign policy as well. The phrase 'CNN effect' encapsulated the idea that real-time communications technology could provoke major responses from domestic audiences and political elites to global events.

This review article assesses what is meant by the term 'CNN effect' in relation to western intervention in humanitarian crises. The paper then goes on to look at another, more radical way of thinking about the relationship between news and political elites: the 'manufacturing consent' school of thought which argues that the media does not create policy but rather that news media is mobilised (manipulated even) into supporting government policy. The incompatibility between the CNN effect and manufacturing consent theory is noted. A review is then conducted of recent research into media effects on Western government responses to humanitarian crises. In my view, this research fails to clarify whether or not the news media has (or has not) triggered recent 'humanitarian'[5] interventions. On the other hand, it does offer important insights which I draw upon in order to propose a 'media-policy interaction' model. It is suggested that this model can advance upon CNN effect and manufacturing consent claims by offering an alternative two way understanding of the direction of influence between the media and government. Not only that: it facilitates a rigorous examination of what remain unsubstantiated claims regarding the power of the media to cause humanitarian intervention.

THE CNN EFFECT AND HUMANITARIAN INTERVENTION

If the Gulf War reminded observers of the enormous power that governments had when it came to shaping the media analysis,[6] events after the 1991 conflict appeared to confirm the opposite.[7] In fact, according to Martin Shaw, emotive and often highly critical coverage of Kurdish refugees fleeing from Saddam Hussein's forces,[8] quite literally caused 'the virtually unprecedented proposal for Kurdish safe havens'.[9] Operation Restore Hope in Somalia quickly followed, and once again it was believed that the ill-fated sortie into the Horn Of Africa in 1992 had effectively been forced upon the United States by media pressure.

The two interventions—in Northern Iraq and Somalia—triggered a major debate within academic and government circles. Foreign policy 'experts' in particular were dismayed by what they saw as this unwarranted intrusion by the Fourth estate into the policy process. George Kennan, typically, argued that media coverage of suffering people in Somalia had usurped traditional policy making channels triggering an ill thought out intervention.[10] Other commentators followed Kennan in expressing concern at the dangers of media dictated foreign policy.[11] James Hoge, for example, observed that 'today's pervasive media increases the pressure on politicians to respond promptly to news accounts that by their very immediacy are incomplete, without context and sometimes wrong'.[12] Working from a realist perspective, critics generally decried the CNN effect and stressed the need for elite control of the foreign policy making process.

Within humanitarian circles there was also a good deal of debate about the apparent power of the news media to cause intervention. Indeed, ever since the 1984 Ethiopian famine, there had been much discussion about the purported impact which the media had had upon crises in the Third World.[13] Amongst the most significant works in this genre were the Crosslines Special Report *Somalia, Rwanda and Beyond*[14] and *From Massacres to Genocide*.[15] Both took a decidedly different approach to that of either Kennan or Hoge, and writing from a broadly 'world society' approach applauded the role played by non-state actors in expanding the policy debate beyond the narrow corridors of political power. Furthermore, instead of attacking the irresponsible part played by the media, these writer-advocates actually praised the new activism and sought to harness the perceived potential of the media to encourage humanitarian intervention.

Though standing at opposite ends of the policy debate, crucially both realists and humanitarians took it as read that the news media was capable of driving policy.[16] Rarely if ever did either question the claim that the news media had played a pivotal role in causing recent interventions.[17] In this way, the CNN effect became an untested and unsubstantiated 'fact' for many in foreign policy and humanitarian circles.

MANUFACTURING CONSENT

The underlying assumption of the 'CNN effect' literature is that the news can make policy. Those who talk of the manufacture of consent argue that political elites impel news makers to 'read' global events in a particular way. Thus rather than assuming that the news media influences or determines what governments do, those who adhere to this position maintain that the media is influenced by government and government policy.[18]

Two implicit versions of the manufacturing consent paradigm can be discerned. First, the *executive* version: this insists that news media reports conform to what might loosely be called the official agenda.[19] For example, Robert Entman has shown how the moral outrage framing of US media reports of the 1983 Korean Airline shoot down was consistent with the Reagan administration's 'Evil Empire' rhetoric.[20] The second *elite* version of the manufacturing consent paradigm claims that news media coverage conforms with the interests of political elites, where elites are defined broadly as members of the executive, legislative or any other politically powerful group.[21] This viewpoint has received conceptual clarification through the work of Lance Bennett,[22] who argues that 'mass media news is indexed . . . to the dynamics of governmental debate'.[23] Hence, even when media coverage is critical of executive policy, this simply reflects a 'professional responsibility [for journalists] to highlight . . . struggles within the centres of power'.[24] An important implication of this elite version is that news coverage critical of executive policy is possible when—and perhaps only when—there exists elite conflict over policy.

RECENT RESEARCH

The thesis that the media has the power to move governments is clearly at odds with manufacturing consent theory. However, before attempting to find a way out of this theoretical impasse, it might be useful initially to assess the various attempts made by recent scholars to analyse media effects on humanitarian intervention. I will first of all consider interview based research undertaken by Nik Gowing, Warren Strobel and Larry Minear *et al.*[25] I will then consider two systematic and methodologically rigorous case studies by Martin Shaw, Steven Livingston and Todd Eachus.[26]

Two things are striking about the interview based studies: the difficulty each has in measuring exactly the precise impact which media has on policy, specifically whether or not the media can cause humanitarian intervention; and the significance each attaches to policy certainty (and uncertainty) in determining media influence. Let us deal with each in turn.

Starting with the impact, which the media is supposed to have had upon foreign policy, the various authors struggle for intellectual clarity. Gowing for example admits that media coverage can change 'overall [government] strategy,' though only on very rare occasions.[27] However he never really defines what he means by overall strategy and therefore leaves the reader unsure as to whether the media can cause humanitarian intervention.[28] One detects the same lack of precision in Strobel. He argues at one point that there is 'little evidence of a *push* [i.e. cause intervention] effect... nor is there evidence of a pull [i.e. cause withdrawal] effect'.[29] But elsewhere he speculates that 'televised images of innocents' suffering can be a factor in moving policy.[30] He also asserts that the media 'can exert strong influence' on policy,[31] that it only plays 'a supplementary role',[32] that it can 'have a decided effect',[33] but in the end does not 'cause intervention'.[34] This analytical confusion leaves one unsure as to what role the media does play exactly during humanitarian crises. The same lack of precision can be found in the volume, *The News Media, Civil Wars and Humanitarian Action*. The different contributors to the volume look in detail at US intervention in Northern Iraq 1991. They argue that media pressure built upon a perceived Western obligation toward the Kurds in order to create a rationale for humanitarian intervention.[35] Yet once again it is never clear how important the media was. They could get to grips better here if they differentiated between immediate and underlying cause. For example, the perceived Western obligation towards the Kurds[36] could have been described as the underlying cause of the intervention decision. Media pressure would then be understandable as the immediate factor in causing intervention. Instead, what we are presented with is a good deal of loose speculation about 'complex systems',[37] 'fluid interplay'[38] and a 'rich and diverse relationship' between media coverage and policy outcome[39]—all of which sounds reasonable enough but does little to clarify things or prove a direct causal relationship between news coverage and policy options.

If the interview based research fails to offer clear answers regarding the significance of the CNN effect on humanitarian intervention, it does highlight the key role 'policy certainty' plays in determining media influence. Gowing approvingly quotes Kofi Annan who has observed that 'when governments have a clear policy,... then television has little impact'; however 'when there is a problem, and the policy has not been thought' through 'they have to do something or face a public relations disaster'.[40] Strobel is even more certain. He notes that 'the effect of realtime television is directly related to the ... coherence ... of existing policy'.[41] The contributors to the Minear volume come to much the same conclusion. Indeed, in their view, there is an inverse relationship between policy clarity and media influence. Hence, when policy is unclear or ill defined the media can indeed have some influence on policy; on the other hand, 'the media effect on policy decreases as the clarity of strategic interest increases'.[42]

Moving now to a consideration of the case study based research, Shaw's *Civil Society and Media in Global Crises* contains a useful analysis of the impact that news media coverage is presumed to have had upon the Western decision to intervene in Northern Iraq in 1991. Shaw systematically analyses news bulletins and describes how coverage of the plight of Kurdish refugees became increasingly critical of Western inaction. When media criticism reached a crescendo, Shaw argues that the West was impelled to do something. His central and important claim, therefore, is that coverage of suffering Kurdish refugees actually caused the unprecedented proposal for Kurdish safe havens.[43]

Significantly, Shaw's careful analysis of news bulletins reveals that it was a particular type of coverage that pressured Western leaders to intervene. In his words, 'the graphic portrayal of human tragedy and the victims' belief in Western leaders was skilfully juxtaposed with the responsibility and the diplomatic evasions of those same leaders to create a political challenge which it became impossible for them to ignore'.[44] The important point that Shaw's work reveals here is that the framing[45] of news media reports is crucial in determining their political impact. Media reports do not 'objectively' report humanitarian crises. Rather, they report crises in particular, and often very different, ways. The emotive and graphic coverage of the Kurds clearly pressured politicians to 'do something'. This pressure would not have existed if media reports had been framed in a less emotive and more distancing manner. For example, with regard to the humanitarian crises in Liberia during the 1990s, Minear *et al.* point out that 'the international media ventured into Liberia ... to provide bizarre documentary style coverage from the "Heart of Darkness" rather than news of a serious threat to international peace and security'.[46] The result of this kind of framing was not to heighten but lessen pressure on Western politicians to do something. This insight into framing is a crucial one and will be drawn upon later to propose a media-policy interaction model.

The problem with Shaw's work however is a failure to analyse the policy process itself. He accepts that the 'loss of policy certainty' in the 'aftermath of the

Cold War' may indeed have 'opened up a particular window for the media'.[47] But beyond that he says very little about official policy. As a result he tends to privilege the role of the media while ignoring other possible motivations for the intervention. His claim that the news media precipitated intervention in Northern Iraq during 1991 is certainly plausible; but without a deeper discussion of the policy-makers and how they viewed the situation, his account is rendered less than convincing.

Like Shaw, Livingston and Eachus[48] offer a systematic in depth case study—not by analysing the Iraqi case but by looking at US intervention in Somalia during 1992. They base their discussion on a survey of official statements, the policy process in question and media coverage. As such, it is the most methodologically exacting research considered so far. Interestingly, what drives their discussion is not so much whether the media can influence policy but rather who determines the content of the news and therefore controls its capacity to influence.[49] As such the authors actually assume that media influence on policy can and does occur.[50] Importantly, for Livingston and Eachus, if it turns out to be journalists themselves setting the news agenda, then it might be concluded that the CNN effect was indeed in operation. If on the other hand the news agenda was set by politicians then something else would be going on: but one could hardly talk of a CNN effect. And by carefully unpacking how certain government officials worked hard to get Somalia on the political agenda, Livingston and Eachus convincingly demonstrate how media coverage actually reflected the agendas of certain government officials in Washington. These officials then used this media coverage to influence top executive policy makers to intervene in Somalia. However, because it was government officials (not journalists) setting the news agenda, Livingston and Eachus argue that the CNN effect (as they understand it) was not present in relation to US intervention in Somalia.

Conceptualising the CNN effect in terms of 'who controls the media' is useful because it reflects the debate within foreign policy circles. For foreign policy experts, by focusing upon news media sources this approach can determine if non-elite actors have gained control of the media and therefore the ability to influence policy. This conceptualisation is also effective at highlighting how political actors manipulate the news agenda for their own purposes. I would argue however, that whilst valid for these purposes, defining the CNN effect in this way masks important and unanswered questions regarding the purported power of the media to trigger humanitarian intervention. First, by assuming media influence (as Livingston and Eachus do re Somalia), the conceptualisation forecloses the possibility that other factors might have caused an intervention decision. This is particularly problematic with regard to recent cases of humanitarian intervention where it is plausible that media inspired altruism was not a prime motivation.[51] Second, whilst media coverage has been associated with recent humanitarian interventions it is also the case that media coverage has accompanied instances of non-intervention: for example, non-intervention during the 1990s humanitarian crises in Liberia. The question raised is why intervention occurs in some instances but not others; focusing on the CNN effect as an issue of media control does not explain why news media coverage of humanitarian crises appears only sometimes to cause intervention. Third, defining the CNN effect in terms of who controls the media fails to reflect the humanitarian debate that is concerned not with questions of policy control but the role the news media plays in triggering international responses to humanitarian crises. The questions of if and how the news media causes intervention are of fundamental interest to this debate and require analysis.

THE WAY FORWARD

The five research pieces reviewed, whilst generally failing to determine the impact of media coverage on humanitarian intervention decisions, offer guidance for a constructive move forward in resolving the theoretical impasse between CNN effect and Manufacturing Consent media theory. The idea of policy certainty as a key factor in determining whether the news media impacted on policy was prominent in the work of Gowing, Strobel, Minear *et al.* and in Shaw's case study.[52] The importance of media framing as a key factor in determining the potential of media coverage to elicit pressure for intervention was well illustrated by Shaw[53] when he unveiled the emotive 'do something' framing of the Kurdish crisis. Taken together these insights suggest a theoretical media-policy interaction model that predicts media influence on government policy only when there exists policy that is uncertain and media coverage that is framed to advocate a particular course of action. When there exists uncertain policy *vis-à-vis* an issue the government is unable to feed a plausible and well rehearsed policy line to the media and therefore set the agenda. In this situation journalists are able to frame reports in a way that is critical of government inaction and pressures for a particular course of action. This is when the CNN effect occurs. Interestingly, the idea of media influence when there exists policy uncertainty fits neatly with the elite version of manufacturing consent media theory. As discussed earlier, this version implies that news coverage that is critical of executive policy is possible when there exists elite conflict over policy (i.e. policy uncertainty). Alternatively, when government has a certain policy it will draw upon its substantial resources and credibility as an information source to influence news media output. In these situations, the media serves to 'manufacture consent' for government policy. By identifying the conditions under which Manufacturing Consent and CNN effect occur, the model offers a way beyond the current theoretical impasse between the two theories.

Importantly, the research reviewed in this paper failed to clarify the significance of media impact on humanitarian intervention decisions. The media policy interaction model offers a way forward with respect to this question by providing a theoretical basis upon which to rigorously examine the impact of the news media on intervention decisions. As part of a case study comparison, if uncertain policy and prointervention framing is found to be associated with cases of intervention (and certain policy and media coverage supportive of official policy associated with nonintervention), theoretical support will be found for the claim that the media causes humanitarian intervention. If the opposite is found to be the case then doubt will be cast on claims regarding the power of the media to trigger intervention. Such measuring of independent variables needs to be supplemented via the kind of careful analysis of policy processes demonstrated in the work of Livingston and Eachus. Failure to do this, as we saw with Shaw's work,[54] means that other motivations for intervention can be missed and final conclusions be less than convincing. Research conducted along these systematic and theoretically informed lines would help to clarify the causal impact of the news media on recent intervention decisions. As such it would make up for the shortcomings of the research reviewed here, as well as contribute to both foreign policy and humanitarian debates which take it as read that the media has caused humanitarian intervention.

In summary, the realisation of this research programme would offer a rigorous assessment of what remain unsubstantiated claims regarding the power of the news media in the post Cold War, real-time world. At the same time the media-policy interaction model promises to advance media theory beyond the simple manufacturing consent/CNN effect dichotomy toward a more nuanced understanding of the media-policy relationship.

NOTES

1. The research for this article was funded by the ESRC. For comments on earlier drafts thanks to Eric Herring, Michael Cox, Cécile Dubernet, Clair McHugh, Richard Little, Steve Livingston, Jonathan Mermin, Martin Shaw and two anonymous reviewers.

2. James Hoge, 'Media Pervasiveness', *Foreign Affairs*, 73 (1994), pp. 136–44.

3. Michael R. Beschloss, *Presidents, Television and Foreign Crisis* (Washington DC: The Annenberg Washington Program in Communications Policy Studies of Northwestern University, 1993), Timothy J. McNulty, 'Television's Impact on Executive Decision-Making and Diplomacy', *The Fletcher Forum of World Affairs*, 17 (1993), pp. 67–83.

4. Kevin Williams, 'The Light at the End of the Tunnel' in John Eldridge (ed.), *Getting the Message* (London: Routledge, 1993), p. 315.

5. In this article the term humanitarian intervention is understood to mean the use of military force (non-humanitarian means) being used in order to achieve humanitarian objectives; the interventions in Iraq 1991 and Somalia 1992 are commonly understood (although not necessarily accurately) to fit this definition. It should be noted however that, as Eric Herring argues, the term humanitarian intervention can be problematic. It is often used in relation to any instance of intervention during a humanitarian crisis. As such the term can gloss over instances of humanitarian means being employed to achieve non-humanitarian ends; and intervention during a humanitarian crisis which is motivated and conducted according to non-humanitarian goals.

6. For example see Jean Baudrillard, 'La Guerre de Golfe n'a pas eu Lieu', *Liberation*, 29 March 1991, W. Lance Bennett and David L. Paletz (eds.), *Taken By Storm* (Chicago: University of Chicago Press, 1994), Greg Philo and G. McLaughlin, *The British Media and the Gulf War* (Glasgow: Glasgow University Media Group, 1993).

7. Hoge, 'Media Pervasiveness'.

8. Shaw, *Civil Society and Media in Global Crises* (London: St Martin's Press, 1993), p. 88.

9. Ibid., p. 79.

10. George F. Kennan, 'Somalia, Through a Glass Darkly', *New York Times*, 30 September 1993.

11. For example see Raymond R. Coffey, 'Don't Let TV Cameras Shape Policy', *Chicago Sun-Times*, 10 December 1992, Hoge, 'Media Pervasiveness', Michael Mandelbaum, 'The Reluctance to Intervene', *Foreign Policy*, 95 (1994), pp. 3–18, Jessica Mathews, 'Policy vs TV', *Washington Post*, 8 March 1994.

12. Hoge, 'Media Pervasiveness', p. 137.

13. Most notably Paul Harrison and Robin Palmer, *News Out Of Africa* (London: Hilary Shipman, 1986) and Jonathan Benthall, *Disasters, Relief and the Media* (London: I. B. Taurus, 1993).

14. Edward Girardet, (ed.), *Somalia Rwanda and Beyond* (Geneva: Crosslines Global Report, 1995).

15. Robert Rotberg and Thomas Weiss (eds.), *From Massacres to Genocide* (Cambridge Massachusetts: The World Peace Foundation, 1996).

16. A notable exception to this tendency is Rotberg and Weiss, *From Massacres to Genocide*, who do not assume media influence on government policy.

17. A notable exception being Joanna Neuman, *Lights, Camera, War* (New York: St. Martin's Press, 1996).

18. For example see W. Lance Bennett, 'Toward a Theory of Press-State Relations in the United States', *Journal of Communication*, 40 (1990), pp. 103–125, Noam Chomsky and Edward Herman, *Manufacturing Consent* (New York: Pantheon, 1988), John Eldridge (ed.), *Getting the Message News*, Robert Entman, 'Framing US Coverage of International News', *Journal of Communication*, 41 (1991), pp. 6–27, Daniel Hallin, *The Uncensored War* (New York: Oxford University Press, 1986), Glasgow University Media Group, *War and Peace News* (Milton Keynes: Open University Press, 1985), Philo and McLaughlin, *The British Media and the Gulf War*.

19. For good examples see Chomsky and Herman, *Manufacturing Consent*, Glasgow University Media Group, *War and Peace News*.

20. Entman, 'Framing US Coverage of International News', p. 10.

21. For good examples see Bennett, 'Toward a Theory of Press-State Relations in the United States' and Hallin, *The Uncensored War*.

22. Bennett, 'Toward a Theory of Press-State Relations in the United States'.

23. Ibid., p. 108.

24. Ibid., p. 110.

25. Nik Gowing, 'Real-Time TV Coverage from War', in James Gow, Richard Paterson and Alison Preston (eds.), *Bosnia by Television* (London: British Film Institute, 1996), Larry Minear, Colin Scott and Thomas Weiss, *The News Media, Civil Wars, and Humanitarian Action* (Boulder & London: Lynne Rienner, 1997), Warren P. Strobel, *Late-Breaking Foreign Policy* (Washington DC: United States Institute of Peace Press, 1997).

26. Shaw, *Civil Society and Media in Global Crises*, Livingston and Eachus, 'Humanitarian Crises and US Foreign Policy', *Political Communication*, 12 (1995), pp. 413–429.

27. Gowing, 'Real-Time TV Coverage', p. 88.

28. Ibid., pp. 86–90.

29. Strobel, *Late-Breaking Foreign Policy*, p. 212.

30. Ibid., p. 162.

31. Ibid., p. 216.

32. Ibid.

33. Ibid., p. 219.

34. Ibid., p. 216.

35. Minear *et al.*, *The News Media, Civil Wars and Humanitarian Action*, p. 51.

36. Ibid.

37. Ibid., p. 57.

38. Ibid., p. 46.

39. Ibid.

40. Gowing, 'Real-Time TV Coverage', pp. 85–86.

41. Strobel, *Late-Breaking Foreign Policy*, p. 219.

42. Minear *et al.*, *The News Media, Civil Wars, and Humanitarian Action*, p. 73.

43. Shaw, *Civil Society and Media in Global Crises*, p. 79.

44. Ibid., p. 88.

45. The concept of framing refers to the 'specific properties of … [a] narrative [e.g. media report] that encourage those perceiving … events to develop particular understandings of them,' Entman, 'Framing US Coverage of International News', p. 7.

46. Minear *et al.*, *The News Media, Civil Wars and Humanitarian Action*, p. 48.

47. Shaw, *Civil Society and Media in Global Crises*, p. 181.

48. Livingston and Eachus, 'Humanitarian Crises and US Foreign Policy', pp. 413–429.

49. Ibid., p. 415.

50. Ibid.

51. For example Howard Adelman, 'The Ethics of Humanitarian Intervention', *Public Affairs Quarterly*, 6 (1992), p. 74 argues that strategic concerns over cross border refugee flows are the primary motivation for 'humanitarian' intervention.

52. Gowing, 'Real-Time TV Coverage from War', pp. 85–6, Strobel, *Late-Breaking Foreign Policy*, p. 219, Minear *et al.*, *The News Media, Civil Wars, and Humanitarian Action*, p. 73, Shaw, *Civil Society and Media in Global Crises*, p. 181.

53. Shaw, *Civil Society and Media in Global Crises*, p. 88.

54. Shaw, *Civil Society and Media in Global Crises*.

*Piers Robinson, a senior lecturer at the University of Manchester, has done extensive work on media, war and humanitarian crises. He led a major Economic and Social Research Council project exploring media coverage of the 2003 Iraq invasion. His other work has been cited in publications such as *The Responsibility to* Protect (International Commission on Intervention and State Sovereignty, 2001).

Robinson, Piers. "The CNN Effect: Can the News Media Drive Foreign Policy?" *Review of International Studies* 25, no. 2 (April 1999): 301–309. Copyright © British International Studies Association.

Reprinted with the permission of Cambridge University Press.

Focus on the CNN Effect Misses the Point: The Real Media Impact on Conflict Management Is Invisible and Indirect

*by Peter Viggo Jakobsen**

> *'[Television] has changed the way the world reacts to crises,'*
>
> —Boutros Boutros-Ghali, then United Nations (UN)
> Secretary-General (Gowing, 1994a).

The media ignores most conflicts most of the time. The coverage of the pre- and post-violence phases is negligible at best and only a few armed conflicts are covered in the violence phase. As focus and funds follow the cameras, the 1990s have witnessed a transfer of resources from more cost-effective, long-term efforts directed at preventing violent conflict and rebuilding war-torn societies to short-term emergency relief. Selective media coverage also contributes to an irrational allocation of short-term emergency relief because coverage is determined by factors other than humanitarian need. This invisible and indirect media impact on Western conflict management is far greater than the direct impact on intervention and withdrawal decisions that the debate over the CNN effect focuses on.

INTRODUCTION

There is a general feeling that media coverage, especially television, has had an increased influence on Western conflict management since the collapse of the Soviet Union. Two factors are usually invoked to account for this change. One is the absence of military threats to Western security that has made military intervention a matter of choice rather than compulsion. The scope for legitimate debate concerning the need and utility of using military force has widened, making it possible for the media and the public to wield greater influence than was usually the case during the Cold War, where such decisions could be justified with reference to national security and/or the need to stop the spread of Communism. The second factor perceived to have enhanced the impact of the media is the increased importance of 'real time television' defined as the transmission of pictures less than two hours old. Using mobile satellite dishes, journalists are now able to bring 'real time' coverage of conflicts and disasters all over the globe. Journalists thus have the power to bring atrocities to the attention of Western audiences either instantaneously or hours after they have occurred (Gowing, 1994b).

While most accept that the impact of the media and the public has increased, there is little agreement on what this impact amounts to. This is nowhere clearer than in the discussion of so-called CNN effect which has dominated the debate. Supporters of the CNN effect argue that the media drives Western conflict management by forcing Western governments to intervene militarily in humanitarian crises against their will. The causal mechanism of the CNN effect is usually conceived in the following way: Media coverage (printed and televised) of suffering and atrocities → journalists and opinion leaders demand that Western governments 'do something' → the (public) pressure becomes unbearable → Western governments do something. Many decisionmakers have lent credence to this view. For example, John Shattuck, the US Assistant Secretary of State for human rights and democracy, has claimed that: 'The media got us [the USA] into Somalia and then got us out' (Shattuck, 1996: 174).

Sceptics argue that the influence of the CNN effect is negligible, that a decision to launch a humanitarian intervention is ultimately decided by other factors, and that the CNN effect may actually prevent military intervention because governments fear that televised images of dead soldiers may cause public support behind an intervention to collapse.[1] What are we to believe? Are the media forcing governments to intervene, discouraging them from intervening, or is the importance of the CNN effect exaggerated? The answer provided in this article is that the CNN effect may directly influence decisions to intervene in exceptional situations, but that the CNN debate with its focus on intervention and withdrawal decisions misses the point, obscuring the indirect, invisible, and far greater impact that media coverage has on conflict management. By ignoring conflicts during the pre and post-violence phases and by being highly selective in its coverage of conflicts in the violence phase, the media helps to shift focus and funds from more cost-effective, long-term efforts directed at preventing violent conflict and rebuilding war-torn societies to short-term emergency relief. It also creates a situation where the provision of emergency relief to a large extent is determined by factors which have nothing to do with humanitarian need. These indirect and invisible effects have a far greater impact on Western conflict management than the CNN effect.

The analysis falls in four parts. The first three are structured around the three main phases that efforts to manage a crisis can be divided into: the pre-violence phase, where the objective is to prevent organized, armed violence from breaking out; the violence phase, characterized by efforts to limit or end armed violence;

and finally the postviolence phase, where conflict managers seek to promote peacebuilding and reconciliation in order to create the foundation for a lasting peace. I analyse the influence of the media during each phase before ending with a general discussion of the impact of the media on Western conflict management.

MEDIA COVERAGE AND CONFLICT MANAGEMENT
IN THE PRE-VIOLENCE PHASE

[F]or most commercial networks, the precondition for coverage is crisis. There has to be large-scale violence, destruction, or death before the media takes notice (The Commission on Global Governance, 1995: 95).

During the pre-violence phase, the impact of media coverage on conflict management is negligible for two reasons. First, the media usually fails to take an interest in conflicts before violence or mass starvation kills a large number of people. Second, governments tend to ignore calls for preventive action when media coverage does occur. Kosovo is but the latest case in point.

With so many ongoing and potential violent conflicts around, it will usually take more than warnings from humanitarian nongovernmental organizations (NGOs), UN agencies, diplomats, or international experts to get the international media interested in a simmering crisis. Western publics are most interested in local and national events—newspaper coverage of international news has actually declined during the last 100 years (*The Economist*, 1998: 13–14), and they suffer increasingly from 'conflict fatigue'. Since coverage of conflicts that *might* explode in violence is unlikely to boost ratings, these conflicts are usually ignored.

International news channels and newspapers also pay little attention to the successes of preventive diplomacy. This is partly due to the fact that preventive successes are invisible. When preventive diplomacy succeeds nothing happens and this makes successes hard to find. But the preventive successes that are easy to spot, such as the preventive deployment of UN troops in Macedonia, receive much less coverage than failures. Dramatic pictures of massive human suffering sell better than pictures of UN troops going quietly about their business day in and day out.

When, in spite of these problems, media coverage of simmering conflicts does occur, calls for action are generally ignored. The relevant Western government agencies are more often than not aware of potential violent conflicts; inaction usually is not caused by a lack of early warning but by a lack of political will. The Western powers had plenty of warning that violence was about to break out in former Yugoslavia and in Rwanda, although the scale of the killing in the latter case was unexpected. Governments may fail to take preventive action for a variety of reasons. They may be preoccupied with other more pressing issues, warnings are sometimes wrong and it can be difficult to distinguish false alarms from real ones, preventive success does not win elections because it is invisible and, most importantly, internal conflicts are complex and hard to manage successfully. Policymakers are consequently likely to avoid the difficulties and dangers associated with attempts to manage them until domestic pressures to do so become compelling (see also George & Holl, 1997: 10–12). The direct impact of the media on preventive crisis management is, in short, negligible.

MEDIA COVERAGE AND CONFLICT MANAGEMENT IN THE VIOLENCE PHASE

The CNN effect: Surely it exists, and surely we went to Somalia and Rwanda partly because of its magnetic pull. Surely the world's actions—or inaction—and political leaders' pronouncements are greatly influenced by this effect. (Then chairman of the Joint Chiefs of Staff, US General John M. Shalikashvili, 1995)

Shalikashvili exaggerates. Although the direct impact of the media on Western crisis management is greatest during the violence phase, it remains limited nevertheless. Direct media impact is first and foremost limited by the fact that most violent conflicts are not covered at all; 'silent emergencies' outnumber the 'loud' ones by far. The usual suspects when forgotten, ongoing conflicts are rounded up include: Abkhazia, Afghanistan, Angola, Azerbaijan, Burundi, East Timor (until 1999), Kashmir, Liberia, Moldova, Nagorno Karabakh, Sierra Leone, Sudan, Tajikistan, etc. Media coverage is decided by a host of different factors, most of which have nothing to do with humanitarian need such as: geographic proximity to Western countries, costs, logistics, legal impediments (e.g. visa requirements), risk to journalists, relevance to national interest, and news attention cycles. A trigger event such as an exodus of refugees or a massacre is usually required and the crisis must be photogenic and dramatic: a short bloody war is better than a drawn out stalemate. These factors explain why Somalia made the news in 1991 whereas neighbouring Sudan was ignored although the humanitarian situation was just as bad, if not worse (Livingston, 1996).

The implication is that Western governments can decide for themselves how they want to deal with most violent conflicts.

Further limiting the power of the CNN effect is the fact that it only applies to a subset of Western interventions. The CNN effect is irrelevant when Western governments want to intervene, be it for strategic, humanitarian, or other reasons. The media can obviously not 'drive' governments to do something they want to, and when governments want to intervene, they are usually able to 'drive' the media to mobilize support for the use of force. One example is the Gulf War where the Bush administration perceived compelling, strategic interests to be at stake. Another is the American intervention in Haiti, in 1994, where the Clinton administration intervened to stop an exodus of Haitian refugees for domestic reasons. This intervention, which Clinton administration sought to legitimate by invoking human rights and democracy, was opposed by a majority of the American people and most members of Congress because a clearcut strategic rationale was lacking (Jakobsen, 1998: 60, 123–124). In both cases, the American government used the media to mobilize support for its preferred policies, it was not driven by the media to intervene.

The CNN effect only comes into play when Western governments oppose military intervention in conflicts where massive human rights violations occur. In this context, so the argument goes, televized coverage and newspaper reports may drive the Western great powers to intervene against their will and subsequently to withdraw if casualties are taken. The direct power of the media to drive Western great-power policy in this manner has been exaggerated, however. The CNN effect did not cause the three interventions commonly regarded as the prime examples of media-driven humanitarian interventions: the intervention in northern Iraq to save the Kurds in April 1991, the intervention in Somalia in December 1992 to create a secure environment for the distribution of humanitarian relief, and the intervention in Rwanda in June 1994 which set up a security zone for refugees.

The CNN effect did matter. Calls for intervention were initially rejected (Freedman & Boren, 1992: 52–53; Jakobsen, 1996: 210; Natsios, 1996: 160; Oberdorfer, 1992), and media pressure appears to have been necessary for the subsequent change of policy in all three cases. The televized images and the criticism in the printed media reportedly led British Prime Minister John Major to overrule objections from his advisors and propose the safe haven plan which paved the way for the intervention in Iraq (Gowing, 1994b: 38). Major, one of his advisors put it, 'was being panicked by newspaper headlines' (Brown & Shukman, 1991: 183). Media impact on the American policy in the Iraqi case is less clear. Some American officials indicate that it played a crucial role whereas others believe that the intervention would have occurred in any event due to the importance of maintaining a good relationship with Turkey (Strobel, 1997: 127–131).

In the case of Somalia, Marlin Fitzwater, White House Press Secretary, has claimed that the Bush administration came under pressure 'from every corner' and that television tipped it 'over the top' (Gowing, 1994b: 68). Other officials view the impact of the media as less profound, but it is indisputable that the media coverage in newspapers and television played an important role in helping the officials in favour of an intervention to win the argument within the administration. Without the media coverage, several key members of the Bush administration, including National Security Advisor Brent Scowcroft, acting Secretary of State Lawrence Eagleburger, and Assistant Secretary of State for African Affairs Herman Cohen, believe that the intervention would not have taken place (Strobel, 1997: 141–142).

Finally, sources in Quai d'Orsay (French Foreign Ministry) indicated that public opinion played a key role in convincing the sceptics within a deeply divided French government to reverse the policy of non-intervention in Rwanda (Duteil, 1994; Subtil, 1994; see also Prunier, 1995: 280–282).

Although the CNN effect thus appears to have been necessary for these interventions, it is equally clear that it was insufficient to cause them, and that they were ultimately decided by other factors. Special circumstances helped make the governments particularly susceptible to pressure in each case. Critics held President George Bush and Prime Minister John Major partly responsible for the Iraqi tragedy because they had urged the Iraqi people to overthrow Saddam Hussein, and Western inaction also undermined Bush's New World Order rhetoric (Jakobsen, 1996: 208). Moreover, as mentioned previously, a strategic interest in preserving a good relationship with Turkey also played a role for the Americans.

The Somali intervention came to be perceived as a low-risk operation promising a high humanitarian and political payoff by the Bush administration. It permitted Bush to leave office on a high note and deflected unwelcome pressure for an intervention in Bosnia, while the Pentagon hoped for a public relations boost that would help prevent budget cuts threatened by the incoming President Bill Clinton (Jakobsen, 1996: 209; Strobel, 1997: 137–140).

The French government came under a particularly strong pressure to intervene in Rwanda because media coverage of the genocide began earlier in France than in most other Western states (Moskos, 1996: 22; Winther, 1997: 101), and because the Hutu forces committing the genocide had been trained and armed by France (Jakobsen, 1996: 210).

The principal factor inducing the intervening governments to change their minds and intervene is likely to have been their belief that the interventions could be conducted quickly with a low risk of casualties. Recently defeated in the Gulf War, Iraq was not expected to be willing or capable to put up a fight, and the terrain made it possible to draw a line in the sand and rely on air power to protect the troops (Jakobsen, 1996: 208); Pentagon planners expected opposition to melt away when the marines landed in Somalia (Gellman, 1992); and the French did their utmost to minimize the risk of a clash with the advancing Tutsi army in Rwanda by limiting the scope of the intervention in time and space, removing Hutu sympathizers from the intervention force, establishing contacts with the Tutsi leadership and by arming the force heavily in order to maximize deterrence (Millwood, 1996: 42–43, 48; Prunier, 1995: 287, 293). Clear exit strategies were also in place in all three cases since the UN was [expected] to take over from the intervention forces.

Western 'non-interventions' in the 1990s also suggest that casualty estimates and exit points are decisive when Western governments are reluctant to intervene in humanitarian crises. Western great powers have repeatedly withstood strong media generated pressures to intervene militarily in humanitarian emergencies when the risk of casualties was perceived as high and/or exit points could not be identified. Concern about casualties and quagmires played a major role in Western decisions to withstand media generated pressures for military interventions in Bosnia between 1992 and May 1995, in Chechnya in November to December 1994 where it would have triggered a confrontation with Russia, in Burundi in July 1996, in the Great Lakes region in November 1996, and in Kosovo in June 1998 (Drozdiak, 1998; Evans, 1997: 62–69; Gowing, 1997: 7–11; Jakobsen, 1998: 79–109; Smith, 1998).

The importance of casualties and exit points can also be inferred from the Western intervention practice. The strong reliance on air power in Bosnia in 1995 (Deliberate Force) and Kosovo in 1999 (Allied Force) was designed to reduce the risk of casualties, and the interventions in Somalia, Rwanda, and Albania were all minimalist in nature, guided by a 'zero-casualty approach' and limited in time. Troops were ordered to advance very cautiously, a policy of non-confrontation with the parties was adopted, and demands that the intervening states should engage in systematic disarmament and prolong their intervention were flatly rejected (Greco, 1998: 28; Luttwark, 1993: 22–23; Nundy, 1994). The North Atlantic Treaty Organization's (NATO) Implementation Force (IFOR) conducted its mission in Bosnia in 1996–97 in a similar fashion, refusing to take on any tasks related to the civilian implementation mission that would expose its personnel to risks (Holbrooke, 1998: 327–329, 335–338).

Summing up, the CNN effect has only a limited impact on Western intervention decisions. It is only relevant in a small minority of cases. While media generated pressures made a difference to policy by putting military intervention on the agenda against the will of the Western great powers in the cases of northern Iraq, Somalia, and Rwanda, the decisions to intervene were ultimately decided by other factors, notably low risks of casualties and clear exit points. The importance of these factors was further underlined by the fact that Western great powers have resisted intervention pressures on numerous occasions when the risk of casualties was perceived as high and/or clear exit points could not be identified. The CNN effect consequently is only likely to pave the way for interventions in exceptional circumstances when Western decisionmakers believe that they can be undertaken quickly with few losses.

The argument that the CNN effect may force governments to withdraw against their will is also flawed. It rests primarily on the American decision to withdraw from Somalia, but case-studies of the American decisionmaking process suggest that the televised pictures of the dead soldier being dragged through the streets of Mogadishu merely affected the timing of the withdrawal. The Clinton administration had already begun contemplating a withdrawal when the 18 soldiers were killed on 3 October 1993, and the pressure for the withdrawal, to some extent, was pushing through an open door (Drew, 1994: 322–323; Gowing, 1994b: 27; Strobel, 1997: 177–183). In short, the basis for the argument that the CNN effect has the power to force Western governments to withdraw looks very shaky indeed.

Thus far, I have argued that the direct media impact on Western crisis management in the violence phase is limited. This begs the question of how this limited impact makes itself felt? In conflicts where Western governments are reluctant to intervene and perceive the risk of casualties associated with military intervention on the ground as unacceptable, media generated pressures are likely to result in minimalist policies, which are primarily aimed at demonstrating to their action-demanding publics that 'something is being done' so that ground deployments can be avoided. Western great-power policy towards Bosnia between 1992 and the summer of 1995 is an example of this. UN resolution 770 authorizing the use of all necessary means to facilitate the delivery of humanitarian relief which was adopted in response to media reports about Serbian 'death camps' in August 1992, the American air drops of humanitarian relief beginning in March 1993, the lift and strike policy advocated by the Clinton administration, and the safe haven policy all fall into this category. They were undertaken to defuse pressure for ground troops with the knowledge that they would be ineffective with respect to stopping the humanitarian crisis and the atrocities. Top policymakers in the Bush administration have made no bones about the fact that they regarded the deployment of ground troops as the only effective means of stopping the fighting in Bosnia, and that the principal purpose of resolution 770 and other actions taken during 1992 was to defuse the pressure for such a deployment, which they perceived as too risky (Strobel, 1997: 147–153). Pentagon officials dismissed the air drops as 'gesture politics' regarding them as inefficient (Tisdall, 1993). Top members of the Clinton administration have admitted that the lift and strike policy was unlikely to work, and that it was chosen because it provided a risk-free way to use force so that the deployment of American ground troops into a quagmire could be avoided (Jakobsen, 1998: 89–90). Similarly, the safe area concept was designed to defuse a strong pressure for military intervention on the ground in connection with the Srebrenica crisis in April 1993. Although it was clear from the beginning that significant troop deployments would be required to make the safe area policy work (UN commanders requested 35,000 troops), the Security Council refused to authorize more than 7,500. This made it impossible to disarm the Bosnian units and prevent them from using the safe areas as launching pads for attacks on Serbian forces, and to deter the latter from attacking the safe areas. The crises at Gorazde and Bihac in 1994 and the fall of Srebrenica and Zepa in 1995 were the predictable consequences of this policy (Caplan, 1996: 8–9; Gowing, 1994b: 49–50, 54–55; Owen, 1995: 177–178; Wahlgren, 1998: 170–177, 182).

Hence, the most likely direct impact of media pressure on reluctant governments to intervene during the violence phase is minimalist policies aimed at demonstrating that something is being done, which fall well short of troop deployments but may involve significant funding for humanitarian relief operations.

MEDIA COVERAGE AND CONFLICT MANAGEMENT IN THE POST-VIOLENCE PHASE

> [C]overage of 'unsexy' nation building and development projects,
> or the kind of economic regeneration efforts required to avoid
> conflict, is likely to be negligible at best. (Gowing, 1997: 20)

Media coverage of a conflict is next to impossible to sustain unless Western troops are killed or massacres of civilians occur. If an intervention succeeds in stopping the fighting, the media quickly loses interest in it. After the successful deployment of troops in Somalia in December 1992, media coverage quickly dropped. By February 1993, only a limited number of reporters remained and the reporting on CNN fell sharply, only to pick up again in June when 24 UN peacekeepers were killed and things began to go wrong. Of the 1,300 journalists who had gone to Haiti in September 1994 to cover the US intervention, only a handful remained a month later (Strobel 1997: 169–170, 197–198). The same happened in Bosnia where NATOs mission has received much less coverage than the UN mission that preceded it, precisely because it has been more successful and the fighting has been stopped.

Conflict management in the post-violence phase hence receives the same amount of coverage as the pre-violence phase—very little. The direct impact of the media on crisis management during this phase is, in short, minimal. Mine clearing is only news if Princess Diana is doing it. Coverage, when it does occur, tends to be negative. Most stories concerning long-term development and nation-building projects focus on mismanagement, fraud and corruption, lack of meaningful evaluation criteria, and so on. Stories about so-called 'white elephants'—expensive projects that for some simple reason fail to work—are legion, and they have the unfortunate effect of eroding public and hence governmental support for long-term peacebuilding efforts.

THE GENERAL IMPACT OF MEDIA COVERAGE ON WESTERN CONFLICT MANAGEMENT: POSITIVE OR NEGATIVE?

The 'CNN factor' tends to mobilize pressure at the peak of the problem—
which is to say, at the very moment when effective intervention
is most costly, most dangerous and least likely to succeed.
(Kofi Annan, UN Secretary General, 1998: 170)

It should be clear by now that the impact of media coverage on Western conflict management is less direct than the CNN effect argument suggests. Its direct impact in the pre and post-violence phases is negligible since they receive very little coverage. Direct impact is greater in the violence phase but limited, nevertheless. The CNN effect is only relevant in a small minority of cases, and even though media generated pressure may make a difference to policy by putting military intervention on the agenda in situations when governments are reluctant to use force, interventions are unlikely to follow unless they can be conducted quickly with a low risk of casualties. Since this is rarely the case, media pressures on reluctant governments are most likely to result in minimalist policies aimed at defusing pressure for interventions on the ground.

The neglect of the pre- and post -violence phases has two unfortunate consequences from a conflict management perspective. First, it distorts the public's perception of conflict prone countries and regions. Since success stories are ignored and news is almost always negative, the public gets the impression that contemporary conflicts are irrational and unsolvable, and public support for efforts to do something about them is thereby eroded. This especially has become a problem for the African continent which in the public mind has become a zone of permanent and intractable conflict. Indeed, in the view of one observer, Africa exemplifies 'the coming anarchy' (Kaplan, 1994; see also Gjelten, 1998; Richburg, 1997).

Second, media focus on humanitarian suffering in the violence phase has contributed to a channeling of funds from longterm development projects aimed at preventing conflict from occurring or recurring to short-term emergency relief, although the latter is more cost-effective from a conflict management perspective. Figures from the Organization for Economic Cooperation and Development (OECD) show that the official development assistance (ODA) provided by its members has fallen by more than 20% in constant dollars between 1992 and 1997, and that the 1997 contribution was down to $48.3 billion. Measured in percent of the OECD members' collective GNP, this is the lowest ODA level in 45 years (OECD 1999: 6; Smillie, 1998: 36–38). By contrast, the funds provided for humanitarian relief by OECD members have risen from $845 million in 1989 to close to $5 billion in 1995 (Donini, 1996: 9). While a dramatic increase in the number of people dependent on humanitarian assistance provides a partial explanation of this redistribution of funds (Forman & Parhad, 1997: 2), a clear correlation between media coverage and funding levels in humanitarian emergencies suggests that the media is an important contributing factor. Statistics from the UN Consolidated Inter-agency Humanitarian Assistance Appeals show that appeals for emergencies covered by the media are far more successful than appeals for forgotten emergencies. Crises in the news such as Chechnya (1995–96), the Great Lakes Region (1995–97), Kosovo (1998), Rwanda (1994), and Yugoslavia (1994–95) received 85–100% of their requirements whereas forgotten emergencies received far less (OCHA, 1999).

The relationship between funding and news coverage is also visible within conflicts. From July to September 1994, when media coverage peaked in the Rwanda emergency, funding poured in making it possible to 'do anything'. Once media coverage fell, donations quickly dropped below the requirements, however (Millwood, 1996: 37, 116–117). This also happened in former Yugoslavia where virtually all the funds required were forthcoming until the fighting stopped in late 1995 and media interest fell. In the 1996–98 period, funding levels were down to 55–69% (OCHA, 1999).

While these statistics show that the media has the power to pressure governments to alter their priorities and channel funds to emergencies when they are 'discovered' by the media, they also indicate that the power of the media to affect funding levels is of a fleeting nature. That funding tends to fall as soon as the media moves on suggests that donor governments retain considerable control over funding decisions. However, this does not alter the conclusion that the media contributes to an irrational allocation of resources and to a channeling of resources from long-term development and regeneration projects to short-term emergency relief by demanding that funds be given to emergency 'X' one month and to emergency 'Y' in the next.

The neglect of the pre-violence phase is not all bad, however. Thus, the Organization for Security and Cooperation in Europe's (OSCE) High Commissioner on National Minorities believes that invisibility and quiet behind-the-scenes diplomacy is the key to successful conflict prevention (Gowing, 1997: 33). Lack of media attention is an advantage from this perspective but, as Nik Gowing points out, quiet, behind-the-scenes diplomacy sometimes fails, and he suggests that increased media attention might have preventive diplomacy succeed in Burundi in late 1995 (Gowing, 1997: 19). While more research is needed to clarify the conditions under which media attention respectively hinder and help preventive diplomacy, it seems safe to conclude that the overall impact of the media's neglect of the pre- and post-violence phases on Western conflict management is negative.

If we turn our attention to the violence phase, the impact of media is harder to assess since it has both positive and negative consequences. One of the negative consequences, highlighted in the analysis and the quote by Kofi Annan earlier, is that interventions put on the agenda by the media rarely succeed. Fear of casualties and quagmires will often induce Western governments to adopt minimalist policies aimed at demonstrating that 'something is being done.' As the UN operation in Bosnia demonstrated, humanitarian assistance will often be used as a short-term substitute for effective, and potentially costly, long-term engagement that is aimed at addressing the root causes of the crisis.

The selective nature of the media's conflict coverage creates another problem because funds follow the cameras. As indicated by the previous statistics, well-publicized violent conflicts are well-funded whereas forgotten ones receive much less if any funding, and since the media's choice of conflicts usually has little to do with humanitarian need, this makes for a highly ineffective allocation of funds.

At the operational level, the intense and selective focus on a small number of violent conflicts complicates the task of conflict management in a number of ways. Since well-publicized emergencies receive the lion's share of funds, they also attract most of the humanitarian NGOs. Whereas forgotten emergencies involve relatively few NGOs, the number of NGOs operating in high-profile emergencies will typically exceed 200, and this obviously creates huge coordination problems which reduce operational effectiveness.

Inaccurate or biased reporting may create problems for the military forces and diplomats trying to mediate between the parties. The parties actively try to use the international media to generate support for their policies among Western publics and decisionmakers. Thus, the Bosnian and Croat governments paid

American public relations firms to give them a positive image in the US. The propaganda efforts undertaken by the Bosnians and the Croats were quite successful, and this led to frequent complaints from UN personnel in Bosnia and the peace negotiators that biased, anti-Serb reporting undermined their work (Owen, 1995: 118–119; Rose, 1995: 25). Unfortunately, the UN force in Bosnia compounded the problem by disseminating inaccurate information, and even misinformation, to the press (Gjelten, 1998: 14–17).

The parties also tried to influence the media by firing on their own positions, a fact highlighted by Lewis Mackenzie, UN commander in Sarajevo during the Spring of 1992, who complained at a press conference that it was impossible for him to arrange a ceasefire because he could not 'keep the two sides from firing on their own positions for the benefit of the CNN' (Mackenzie, 1993a: 308).

A final problem related to TV coverage from violent conflicts is that the warring parties may use it as a source of real-time intelligence. The Pentagon was thus concerned that the media would compromise operational safety of its Haiti intervention in 1994 because all the major US television networks had camera crews in place ready to cover it live (Gowing: 1994c). The UN in Bosnia faced similar problems as the parties often used television coverage to target their positions.

The impact of media coverage and public pressure is not without its advantages for conflict managers. First, as already mentioned, media generated public pressure occasionally forces Western governments to take action to mitigate a humanitarian emergency that they would have preferred to ignore. Second, peace negotiators and military commanders can use the media to put pressure on the warring parties. UN commander Lewis Mackenzie, who referred to the media as his 'only major weapon system', used threats to go public on CNN to obtain compliance from the parties on several occasions (Mackenzie, 1993b: 23). The British Colonel, Bob Stewart, who commanded the British contingent in Bosnia between August 1992 and May 1993, used threats to film incidents to get through road blocks and he also found it useful to let the media record agreements on camera because this made the parties more reluctant to break them. Finally, he employed the local media to inform the local population about the purpose of the UN operation and also as a means of countering propaganda and misinformation directed against the UN force (Stewart, 1993: 180, 323–324).

Summing up, the direct impact of the media on Western conflict management is negligible because coverage is limited to a small number of conflicts in the violence phase. The large majority of conflicts are ignored. This serves to shift focus and funds from cost-effective, long-term measures to short-term relief efforts leading to a highly ineffective allocation of resources. This invisible and indirect media impact on Western conflict management exceeds the direct impact generated by the CNN effect by far since the latter only affects a very small number of conflicts. Therefore, the media is probably more of a hindrance than a help for Western conflict management at the general level.

The presence of the media in the mission area has negative as well as positive consequences, but since it cannot be wished away, practitioners must learn to use the media constructively as a conflict management tool. This involves the formulation of clear information and public relation strategies from the outset of an operation to target international as well as local audiences, an ability to provide the media with timely and reliable information, and an ability to inform the local media and the local population about the purpose of the operation in order to counter misinformation and propaganda. The good news is that both the UN and the Western armies have realized this and have made much progress with respect to enhancing their public information capabilities in recent years. NATO's Bosnia operation and recent UN operations illustrate this (DPKO, 1997: part II, para. 94; Shanahan & Beavers, 1997).

NOTE

The author would like to thank Knud Erik Jørgensen, Henrik Larsen, Nils Petter Gleditsch, and the anonymous reviewers for their helpful suggestions on an earlier draft.

1. For analyses arguing that the importance of the CNN effect is exaggerated see Gowing (1994b); Jakobsen (1996); Natsios (1996) and Strobel (1997).

REFERENCES

Annan, Kofi A., 1998. 'Challenges of the New Peacekeeping', in Michael Doyle & Olara A. Otunnu, eds, *Peacemaking and Peacekeeping for the New Century*. Lanham, MD: Rowman & Littlefield Publishers (169–187).

Brown, Ben & Shukman, David, 1991. *All Necessary Means*. London: BBC Books.

Caplan, Richard, 1996. 'Post-Mortem on UNPROFOR', *London Defence Studies* (33). Brassey's for the Centre for Defence Studies, University of London.

The Commission on Global Governance, 1995. *Our Global Neighborhood*. Oxford: Oxford University Press.

Donini, Antonio, 1996. 'The Policies of Mercy: UN Coordination in Afghanistan, Mozambique, and Rwanda', *Occasional Paper* (22). Providence, RI: Thomas J. Watson Institute for International Studies.

DPKO, 1997. *The Comprehensive Report on Lessons Learned from United Nations Assistance Mission for Rwanda (UNAMIR), October 1993–April 1996*. New York: UN Department of Peacekeeping Operations.

Drew, Elizabeth, 1994. *On the Edge: The Clinton Presidency*. New York: Simon & Schuster.

Drozdiak, William, 1998. 'NATO Appeals for Peace in Kosovo', *The Washington Post*, 29 May (A37).

Duteil, Mireille, 1994. 'Rwanda: Pourquoi la France Intervient' [Rwanda: Why France Intervenes], *Point* 1136 (25 June): 14–15.

Evans, Glynne, 1997. 'Responding to Crises in the African Great Lakes', *Adelphi Paper (311)*. London: The International Institute for Strategic Studies.

Forman, Shepard & Parhad, Rita, 1997. 'Paying for Essentials: Resources for Humanitarian Assistance', *Journal of Humanitarian Assistance* (http://www-jha.sps.cam.ac.uk/a/a404.htm) 14 December.

Freedman, Lawrence & Boren, David, 1992. 'Safe Havens for Kurds in Post-war Iraq', in Nigel Rodley, ed., *To Loose the Bands of Wickedness. International Intervention in Defense of Human Rights*. London: Brassey's Defense Publishers (43–92).

Gellman, Barton, 1992. 'Intervene in Somalia: Can Do', *International Herald Tribune*, 30 November.

George, Alexander L. & Holl, Jane E., 1997. *The Warning-Response Problem and Missed Opportunities in Preventive Diplomacy*. Washington, DC: Carnegie Commission on Preventing Deadly Conflict.

Gjelten, Tom, 1998. *Professionalism in War Reporting: A Correspondent's View*. Washington, DC: Carnegie Commission on Preventing Deadly Conflict.

Gowing, Nik, 1994a. 'Instant Pictures, Instant Policy: Is Television Driving Foreign Policy?', *The Independent on Sunday* 3 July (14).

Gowing, Nik, 1994b. 'Real-time Television Coverage of Armed Conflicts and Diplomatic Crises: Does It Pressure or Distort Foreign Policy Decisions', *Working paper 94–1* (June). Cambridge, MA: The Joan Shorenstein Barone Center on Press, Politics and Public Policy, John F. Kennedy School of Government, Harvard University.

Gowing, Nik, 1994c. 'Real-time Television Wins a War', *The Independent*, 27 September (18).

Gowing, Nik, 1997. *Media Coverage: Help or Hindrance in Conflict Prevention?* Washington, DC: Carnegie Commission on Preventing Deadly Conflict.

Greco, Ettore, 1998. 'Delegating Peace Operations: Improvisation and Innovation in Georgia and Albania', *Occasional Paper Series* (7). New York: UNA-USA.

Holbrooke, Richard, 1998. *To End a War: From Sarajevo to Dayton and Beyond*. New York: Random House.

Jakobsen, Peter Viggo, 1996. 'National Interest, Humanitarianism or CNN: What Triggers UN Peace Enforcement After the Cold War?', *Journal of Peace Research* 33(2): 205–215.

Jakobsen, Peter Viggo, 1998. *Western Use of Coercive Diplomacy After the Cold War: A Challenge for Theory and Practice*. New York: Macmillan.

Kaplan, Robert D., 1994. 'The Coming Anarchy', *Atlantic Monthly* 273(2): 44–76.

Livingston, Steven, 1996. 'Suffering in Silence: Media Coverage of War and Famine in the Sudan', in Rotberg & Weiss (68–89).

Luttwark, Edward N., 1993. 'Unconventional Force', *The New Republic* 208(4): 22–23.

Mackenzie, Lewis, 1993a. *Peacekeeper—The Road to Sarajevo*. Vancouver: Douglas & Macintyre.

Mackenzie, Lewis, 1993b. 'Military Realities of UN Peacekeeping Operations', *Rusi Journal* 138(1): 21–24.

Millwood, David, ed., 1996. *The International Response to Conflict and Genocide: Lessons from the Rwanda Experience. Study 3: Humanitarian Aid and Effects*. Copenhagen, Danida.

Moskos, Charles C., 1996. *Reporting War When There Is No War: The Media and the Military in Peace and Humanitarian Operations*. Cantigny Conference Series Special Report. Chicago: Robert McCormick Tribune Foundation (http://www.rrmtf.org/conferences/nowar.htm).

Natsios, Andrew, 1996. 'Illusions of Influence: The CNN Effect in Complex Emergencies', in Rotberg & Weiss (149–168).

Nelson, Mark M., 1991. 'EC Leaders Demand Kurds Be Given "Safe Haven" in Iraq. Plan to Send Aid', *Wall Street Journal*, 9 April.

Nundy, Julian, 1994. 'Balladur Takes a Moral Stance on Intervention', *The Independent*, 23 June.

Oberdorfer, Don, 1992. 'The Path to Intervention: A Massive Tragedy We Could Do Something About', *The Washington Post*, 6 December (A1).

OCHA 1999. *Financial Tracking Database for Complex Emergencies*. United Nations Office for the Coordination of Humanitarian Affairs (http://www.reliefweb.int/ocha_ol/).

OECD, 1999. *1998 Development Co-operation Report: Highlights*. Organization for Economic Co-operation and Development (www.oecd.fr/dac/pdf/HIGH1-EN.pdf).

Owen, David, 1995. *Balkan Odyssey*. London: Victor Gollancz.

Prunier, Gerard, 1995. *The Rwanda Crisis, 1959–1994: History of a Genocide*. London: Hurst & Company.

Richburg, Keith B., 1997. *Out of America: A Black Man Confronts Africa*. New York: Basic Books.

Robinson, Piers, 1999. 'The CNN Effect: Can the News Media Drive Foreign Policy?', *Review of International Studies* 25(2): 301–310.

Rose, Michael, 1995. 'A Year in Bosnia: What Has Been Achieved', *Rusi Journal* 140(3): 22–25.

Rotberg, Robert I. & Weiss, Thomas G., eds., 1996. *From Massacres to Genocide: The Media, Public Policy, and Humanitarian Crises*. Cambridge, MA: The World Peace Foundation.

Shalikashvili, John, 1995. 'Humanitarian Missions Challenge Military and Media', *Defense Issues* 10(54).

Shanahan, Stephen W. & Beavers, Garry J., 1997. 'Information Operations in Bosnia', *Military Review* 77(6): 53–62.

Shattuck, John, 1996. 'Human Rights and Humanitarian Crises: Policy-making and the Media', in Rotberg & Weiss (169–175).

Smillie, Ian, 1998. 'Relief and Development: The Struggle for Synergy', *Occasional Paper* (33). Providence, RI: Thomas J. Watson Institute for International Studies.

Smith, R. Jeffrey, 1998. 'NATO Albania Deployment Less Likely', *The Washington Post*, 28 May (A30).

Stewart, Bob, 1993. *Broken Lives: A Personal View of the Bosnian Conflict*. London: HarperCollins Publishers.

Strobel, Warren P., 1997. *Late-Breaking Foreign Policy*. Washington, DC: United States Institute of Peace.

Subtil, Marie-Pierre, 1994. 'Le Projet d'intervention Fraçaise au Rwanda Suscite de plus en plus de Critiques' [The French plan for intervention in Rwanda triggers more and more criticism], *Le Monde*, 23 June (1, 4).

Tisdal, Simon, 1993. 'Clinton Team Split Over Bosnian Force', *The Guardian*, 20 March (11).

Wahlgren, Lars-Eric, 1998. 'Start and End of Srebrenica', in Wolfgang Biermann & Martin Vadset, eds, *UN Peacekeeping in Trouble—Lessons Learned from the Former Yugoslavia*. Aldershot: Ashgate Publishing Group (168–185).

Winther, Cecilie, 1997. 'The International Response to the Conflict and Genocide and in Rwanda', in Knud Erik Jørgensen, ed., *European Approaches to Crisis Management*. Kluwer Law International (83–105).

*Peter Viggo Jakobsen is a faculty member at the Royal Danish Defence College, Institute for Strategy.

Jakobsen, Peter Viggo. "Focus on the CNN Effect Misses the Point: The Real Media Impact on Conflict Management Is Invisible and Indirect." *Journal of Peace Research* 37, no. 2 (March 2000): 131–143, copyright © 2000 by *Journal of Peace Research*.

Reprinted by permission of SAGE.

Could Twitter Have Prevented the Iraq War?

by Eric Boehlert*

Responding to a barrage of criticism he received for a factually inaccurate and flawed column he wrote this month about the sequestration battle, *New York Times* columnist Bill Keller wrote a follow-up blog post to detail how critics had hounded him online, especially via Twitter.

Denouncing the social media tool's tendency to produce what he called mean and shallow commentary, Keller lamented Twitter's suddenly pervasive power. "It is always on, and it gets inside your head," he wrote, adding, "there is no escape." Indeed, within days of writing his column, Keller felt compelled to pen a lengthy piece about his Twitter encounter.

The columnist painted an unpleasant picture of being hounded and "bull[ied]" on Twitter for merely expressing "an unpopular view." But as the tenth anniversary of the United States-led invasion of Iraq approaches, I couldn't help thinking back to when columnists like Keller, and newspapers like the *New York Times*, where Keller became executive editor in July 2003, helped cheer the nation to war. To date, that conflict has claimed the lives of nearly 8,000 U.S. service members and contractors and more than 130,000 Iraqi citizens, and is projected to cost the U.S. Treasury more than two trillion dollars. (The *Times*' public editor later called the paper's prewar coverage "flawed journalism.")

Thinking about the historic failure of the *Times* and others in the media a decade ago, I couldn't help wish that Twitter had been around during the winter of 2002–2003 to provide a forum for critics to badger writers like Keller and the legion of Beltway media insiders who abdicated their role as journalists and fell in line behind the Bush White House's march to war. I wouldn't have cared that recipients might have been insulted by the Twitter critiques or seen them as mean and shallow, the way Keller does today. Sorry, but the stakes in 2003 were too high to worry about bruised feelings.

Looking back, I wish Keller and other pro-war columnists had been "bullied" (rhetorically) as they got almost everything wrong about the pending war. I think the revolutionary peer connection tool would have been invaluable in shaming journalists into doing their jobs when so many failed to. (Keller later admitted the invasion was a "monumental blunder.")

Twitter could have helped puncture the Beltway media bubble by providing news consumers with direct access to confront journalists during the run-up to the war. And the pass-around nature of Twitter could have rescued forgotten or buried news stories and commentaries that ran against the let's-go-to-war narrative that engulfed so much of the mainstream press.

Considering the central role the lapdog media played in helping to sell President Bush's pre-emptive invasion, I wonder if Twitter could have stopped the Iraq War.

Make no mistake, the nascent liberal blogosphere was raising its collective voice against the war in 2003 and calling out the press for its lapdog ways. In fact, one of the catalysts for the rapid expansion of the liberal blogosphere one decade ago was the ingrained sense of frustration. Progressive often searched in vain for passionate and articulate anti-war voices within the mainstream media. (And when they found a champion, Phil Donahue, he was summarily fired just weeks before the invasion.) Denied a voice, they created their own platform, liberal blogs.

The problem was the liberal blogosphere got the war story right, but they did it in something of a bubble. It was a bubble the mainstream media bolstered to isolate their progressive critics; to isolate and marginalize the new band of rowdy citizen journalists. Still new enough in 2002 and 2003 that they didn't necessarily command journalists' respect, and lacking the technological ability to reach into newsrooms, liberal blogs were often ignored by media elite, despite the fact the blogs were raising all the questions about the pending war.

Why am I convinced Twitter would have made an impact? The same reason Keller mentioned in his blog post this month: It's always on. Every Beltway newsroom is now wired to Twitter. It's today's media nervous system, the way The Drudge Report supposedly was during the Clinton years. It's the current that powers each news cycle. It's the first warning signal for breaking news and it's supplementing cocktail chatter that forms conventional wisdoms.

In 2009, *America Journalism Review* noted some of the benefits that Twitter offered reporters:

> It can provide instantaneous access to hard-to-reach newsmakers, given that there's no PR person standing between a reporter and a tweet to a government official or corporate executive.

It's that same lack of a filter, and that power to communicate directly with journalists, that can make it so influential. They may not always choose to respond, but like all Twitter users, journalists regularly tap the 'Connect' icon to follow what people are saying to them and about them.

So yeah, it's the best place to tweak the press and get an instant response. I'm not talking about trolling and name calling. I'm talking about flagging dubious work, the way critics used Twitter to spread the word about the obvious holes in Bill Keller's recent sequestration column.

And Keller isn't alone. Take David Brooks' *Times* piece a few weeks back, in which he erroneously suggested Obama hadn't issued a proposal to avoid the looming sequestration other than raising taxes on the rich. Thanks to the wild-fire messaging of Twitter, Brooks' column became something of a laughing stock by noon on the day it was published. And like Keller, Brooks felt the need to quickly respond to the criticism; to *apologize*. That kind of a real-time debunking, and a debunking that was read inside every newsroom, was precisely what liberals lacked ten years ago. They lacked an intimate amplifier that found its media mark every time.

With the interactivity of Twitter, journalists, I think, feel a much stronger urge to defend their work and to not let legitimate criticism go unanswered. Ignoring Twitter, and specifically ignoring what people are saying about your work on Twitter, isn't really an option the way turning a blind eye to anti-war bloggers may have been ten years ago.

As the *New York Times* recently noted:

The harshest judges of those in news media are often others in the news media, and, with the benefit of Twitter, that intrajournalistic watch-dog role can be performed simultaneously with the journalism being criticized.

That description appeared in a *Times* piece about the angry reaction that erupted on Twitter when journalists were called together for President Obama's first news conference after the Sandy Hook, CT., school massacre. After Obama made public how the administration would respond to the tragedy, the assembled scribes then promptly ignored the issue pressed Obama on budget tactics. Media critics flipped out on Twitter and the *Times* wrote that up as news.

Think back to the night of Bush's final, pre-war press conference on March 6, 2003. Laying out the reasons for war, Bush mentioned Al Qaeda and the terrorist attacks of September 11 thirteen times in less than an hour. Yet not a single journalist challenged the presumed connection Bush was making between Al Qaeda and Iraq, despite the fact that U.S. allies had publicly questioned any such association.

With Twitter, media condemnations would have been instant that night and somnambulant journalists certainly would have felt the public sting.

Or imagine how Twitter could have been used in real time on February 5, 2003, when Secretary of State Colin Powell made his infamous attack-Iraq presentation to the United Nations. At the time, Beltway pundits positively swooned over what they claimed was Powell's air-tight case for war. (Powell later conceded the faulty presentation represented a "blot" on his record.) But Twitter could have swarmed journalists with instant analysis about the obvious shortcoming. That kind of accurate, instant analysis of Powell's presentation was posted on blogs but ignored by a mainstream media enthralled by the White House's march to war.

Now, I realize the social media tool has been credited with helping *start* a revolution, but stopping an invasion that the full force of the Bush administration was determined to wage? Doesn't that seem like a stretch?

My point is Twitter could have altered, in important ways, the media coverage, especially during the run-up to the war when the Beltway press experienced something close to collective malpractice. It could have helped shame journalists into rediscovering the notion of skepticism.

A year after the war began, then-*Washington Post* editor Leonard Downie downplayed any role the media may have played in helping launch the invasion. He insisted people who opposed the war "have the mistaken impression that somehow if the media's coverage had been different, there wouldn't have been a war."

I disagree. It would have been far more difficult for Bush to have ordered the war of choice with Iraq—and sold the idea at home—if it weren't for the bountiful help he received from the mainstream media, and particularly the stamp of approval he received from so-called liberal media institutions such as the *Washington Post*, which in February of 2003 alone, editorialized in favor of war nine times. (Between September 2002 and February 2003, the paper editorialized *twenty-six times* in favor of the war.)

Ten years ago, Twitter could have also performed the Herculean task of making sure brave news stories that did raise doubts about the war didn't fall through the cracks, as invariably happened back then. With swarms of users touting the reports, it would have been much more difficult for reporters and pundits to dismiss important events and findings.

For instance, Twitter could have trumpeted the news that on October 10, 2002, retired Marine General Anthony Zinni, the former head of Central Command for U.S. forces in the Middle East, delivered a keynote address at a Washington think tank where he outlined his grave concerns about the Bush administration's war with Iraq. (The *Washington Post* devoted just 300 words, on page 16, to Zinni's deeply prophetic warning.)

Twitter could have spread the word about the Associated Press' January 18, 2003 dispatch, "Inspectors Have Covered CIA's Sites of 'Concern' and Reporter No Violations," which documented how more than a dozen inspected Iraqi weapons facilities had failed to produce any evidence of Saddam's alleged arsenal.

Twitter could have championed the work of the *Washington Post's* Walter Pincus, who was writing insightful, skeptical war stories, but ones his editors refused to put on page-one. Pieces like "Bush Clings To Dubious Allegations About Iraq," "U.S. Lacks Specifics on Banned Arms," "Alleged al-Qaida Ties Questioned; Experts Scrutinize Details of Accusations Against Iraqi Government," and "Making the Case Against Baghdad; Officials: Evidence Strong, Not Conclusive."

And Twitter could have touted John Barry's March 3, 2003 piece in *Newsweek:*

Hussein Kamel, the highest-ranking Iraqi official ever to defect from Saddam Hussein's inner circle, told CIA and British intelligence officers and U.N. inspectors in the summer of 1995 that after the gulf war, Iraq destroyed all its chemical and biological weapons stocks and the missiles to deliver them.

In other words, Twitter could have been the megaphone—the media equalizer—that war critics lacked ten years ago. And yes, for pro-war columnists like Bill Keller who later admitted they got the Iraq story very wrong, Twitter back then might've meant enduring some "bullying" critiques.

Given the dire consequences of the war, it would've been worth it.

*Eric Boehlert, a former senior writer for Salon, is the author of *Lapdogs: How the Press Rolled Over for Bush.*

Boehlert, Eric. "Could Twitter Have Prevented the Iraq War?" Salon.com. Monday, March 18, 2013. http://www.salon.com/2013/03/18/could_twitter_have_prevented_the_iraq_war_partner/.

This article first appeared in Salon.com, at http://www.Salon.com. An online version remains in the Salon archives. Reprinted with permission.

When Lines Between NGO and News Organization Blur

*by Glenda Cooper**

[. . .]

"Dear Sir. My name is Mohammed Sokor . . . from Dagahaley refugee camp in Dadaab. There is an alarming issue here. People are given too few kilograms of food. You must help."[1] Was this a note—as The Economist asked—delivered to a handily passing rock star-turned-philanthropist? An emotional plea caught on a BBC camera?

No, Mr. Sokor from Kenya is a much more modern communicator than that. In 2007, he texted this appeal to the mobile phones of two United Nations officials in London and Nairobi. He had found the numbers by surfing the Internet in a café at the north Kenyan camp.

The humanitarian world is changing. New information and communication technology is altering how we report, where we report from, and most of all, who is doing the reporting. These developments coincide with mainstream media coming under increasing financial pressure and withdrawing from foreign bureaux. This is a trend that extends beyond the United States. In early 2009, the think tank POLIS together with Oxfam published a report warning that international coverage is likely to decrease under the new public service broadcasting regime being worked out in the U.K. And in 2008, the U.K. tabloid the Daily Mirror said as part of the latest round of job cuts they were abolishing the post of foreign editor altogether. Meanwhile, citizen journalists and NGOs have been rushing to fill the gap. The mainstream media, getting free filmed reports and words, often sees this as a win-win situation. This raises three key issues:

- Do these new entrants to humanitarian reporting mean that we are seeing more diverse stories being told and more diverse voices being heard? Does the fundamental logic of reporting change?

- Are viewers/readers aware of the potential blurring of the lines between aid agencies and the media when NGOs act as reporters?

- How are aid agencies being affected by citizen journalists acting increasingly as watchdogs?

MEDIA AND AID AGENCIES: A SYMBIOTIC RELATIONSHIP

The relationship between the media and aid agencies used to be well-defined and almost symbiotic in nature. This section will capture the essence of this relationship by taking a critical stance. The subsequent sections will then look at how this relationship is changing as well as the role citizen journalists play in this context.

The former UN emergency relief coordinator, Jan Egeland, has talked about the way the world's disaster victims are caught up in a "kind of humanitarian sweepstakes... and every night 99 percent of them lose, and one percent win." The one-percent winners usually owe their good fortune to media coverage.

To illustrate the argument, the table below shows the death toll in the December 2004 tsunami as judged by the UN Special Envoy, and the number of stories written in British newspapers (Dec. 19, 2004 to Jan. 16, 2005) as recorded by Lexis Nexis.[2]

> Indonesia: 167,000 dead or missing; 343 stories
>
> Sri Lanka: 35,000 dead or missing; 729 stories
>
> Thailand: 8,200 dead or missing; 771 stories

The death toll in Indonesia dwarfs that of Sri Lanka and Thailand—it is roughly 20 times that of Thailand—yet Indonesia received barely half the media coverage as Thailand. Not only was it quicker, easier and cheaper for the media to get to Sri Lanka and Thailand than to Indonesia, but there were many more tourists blogging, sending in photographs, and filming from the first two areas, contributing those vital shots of the wave as it happened.

This media coverage translated into increased aid. So many aid workers poured into Sri Lanka that they were dubbed a "second tsunami." In the year after the tsunami, a Disasters Emergency Committee evaluation noted that Indonesia had suffered 60 percent of the damage but received only 31 percent of the funding.[3]

But the tsunami was such an extraordinary event—perhaps it was a one-off? Not at all. Another example is provided by the difference in media coverage after the acute natural disasters in Burma and China in spring 2008. In Burma, the military junta tried to keep the international media out during Cyclone Nargis, while the Chinese authorities allowed the media in to follow the Sichuan earthquake. Figures reported in the Times on May 22, 2008—20 days after Nargis and 10 days after the quake—showed that despite Burma having almost twice as many people dead or missing, China was attracting far more aid.

These examples show that the more media-friendly the disaster, the more money it attracts. In the past, at its most extreme, disaster coverage has been a kind of moral bellwether for the nation.[4] Aid agencies follow these waves of coverage and in turn provide access and footage to the media. Yet when covering famines, earthquakes, or tsunamis, the media have not always prioritized establishing objectivity, and aid agencies have not always sought to correct the lack of balance.

New Ways of Reporting Disasters

In the past the relationship between aid agencies and journalism, as described above, prospered because only a few people had access to places where important events happened—or information about significant events occurring. Now, new technologies—including SMS, mobile video and the Internet—increasingly offer ordinary people the ability to reach audiences they could never have reached before. Dan Gillmor has described the December 2004 tsunami as a "turning point" that set in place this new dynamic. While not the first event to use user-generated content (UCG), it was perhaps the first disaster where the dominant images we remember come not from journalists but from ordinary people. As Tom Glocer, head of Reuters, noted, none of Reuters' 2,300 journalists or 1,000 stringers were on the beaches when the waves struck.

Since then the speed, volume, and intensity of citizen journalism have all increased rapidly. In early 2005, the BBC received, on average, 300 emails a day. By mid-2008, this had risen to between 12,000 and 15,000, and the corporation employed 13 people around the clock solely to deal with UCG. With photographs and video the increase has been even more extreme. Two years ago, the BBC received approximately 100 photos or videos per week. Now they receive 1,000 on average and 11,000 in unusual circumstances. "It used to be exceptional events such as the tsunami or 7/7," says Vicky Taylor, former head of interactivity, BBC, referring to the July 2005 London Tube bombings. "Now people are seeking out news stories and sharing information."[5]

People are adapting different forms of media to make their words and pictures available to a wider audience. The microblogging site Twitter broke the news of the Chinese earthquakes, and Burmese bloggers used the social networking site Facebook to raise awareness of the 2007 protests. Also in Burma, many of those who sought to get out information about Cyclone Nargis opted to use email through Gmail and, in particular, its messaging service Google Talk, because the junta found Gmail more difficult to monitor.[6]

As new actors enter the formerly privileged information-sharing sphere dominated by the mainstream media and aid agencies, there are increased possibilities of more diverse stories being told, and more diverse voices being heard. In the past, those affected by humanitarian crises have traditionally been spoken for by aid agencies or mainstream reporters. For example, Michael Buerk's seminal BBC report in 1984 which alerted the world to the famine in Ethiopia featured only two voices—his own and that of a (white) MSF doctor.[7]

Yet this is changing. As Sanjana Hattotuwa, of the Sri Lankan NGO Centre for Policy Alternatives, wrote: "citizen journalists [in Sri Lanka] are increasingly playing a major role in reporting deaths, the humanitarian fallout and hidden social costs of violent conflict."[8]

In January 2008, Ushahidi (which means testimony in Swahili) was set up by four bloggers and technological experts. As Lokman Tsui explains in his essay in this series, the mashup used Google Earth technology to map incidents of crime and violence with ordinary people reporting incidents via SMS, phone or email. Ushahidi has been so successful that it was awarded a $200,000 grant from Humanity United to develop a platform that can be used around the world, and the website received an honourable mention in the 2008 Knight-Batten awards.

As Ory Okolloh, one of Ushahidi's founders, says, "There were not many 'scoops' per se but in some cases we had personal stories, e.g. about the victims, pictures that were not being shown in the media, and reports that were available to us before they hit the press. We were able to raise awareness (and for that matter learn of) a lot of the local peace initiatives that the mainstream media really wasn't reporting."[9]

Another Knight-Batten award winner is Global Voices, a nonprofit citizen media project set up at Harvard in 2004 which now has around 400,000 visits a month and utilizes 100 regular authors. It mainly links to blogs but is increasingly using Facebook, Twitter, Livejournal, and Flickr as well.

However, it is important to critically assess the significance and the impact of this trend. Verification of citizen journalism is difficult, hoaxing is an ever-present possibility, and the outpouring of material does not always elucidate. As Sarah Boseley of the Guardian reflected on her paper's three-year commitment to report on the Ugandan village of Katine, when the paper gave out disposable cameras to the villagers in the hope of getting a new perspective, "most of them," she said, "just took pictures of their cows."

And such voices are most commonly framed in accordance with traditional news standards rather than challenging them. Citizen journalism may also unwittingly skew the definition of what is important towards the unexpected or the spectacular and the dramatic, focusing, for example, on a natural catastrophe such as an earthquake rather the long-term famine. As Thomas Sutcliffe of the Independent commented: "The problem with citizen journalists—just like all of us—is that they are incorrigible sensationalists."[10]

DIFFERENT NARRATORS—MORE DIVERSE VOICES?

But if every citizen with a cellphone or Internet access can become a reporter, where does this leave the traditional gatekeepers (journalists) and the gatekeepers to disaster zones (aid workers)?

As pointed out above, in the past, journalists turned to aid agencies to get access to disasters and "real" people. The agencies received a name-check in return for facilitating access. The result was a symbiotic relationship in which it was to the advantage of both sides that the humanitarian "story" was as strong as possible. With the growth of UGC, this control of the story has disappeared. As John Naughton, professor of public understanding of technology at the Open University, agrees: "UGC is now blowing that [relationship] apart."[11]

As a result, three trends have developed. First, aid agencies have turned themselves into reporters for the mainstream media, providing cash-strapped foreign desks with free footage and words. Second, they have also tried to take on citizen journalists by utilizing the blogosphere. Third, the agencies are simultaneously facing challenges from citizen journalists who are acting as watchdogs and critics and who can transmit their criticisms to a global audience.

The origins of the first trend stretch back as far as the 1990s and the emergence of the 24-hour news cycle combined with, as Nik Gowing points out, aid agencies having to salvage their reputation after accusations of misinformation during the Rwandan genocide.[12] The two agencies who led this charge in the U.K. were Oxfam and Christian Aid. They both hired former journalists to run their press operations as pseudo-newsrooms. Both agencies pushed the idea of press officers as "fireman" reporters—on the ground as soon as possible after a disaster occurred to gather and film information themselves. Oxfam protocol written for their UK press office in 2007, for example, demanded that a press officer sent to a disaster should use an international cellphone, a local cellphone, a satellite phone, a laptop (capable of transmitting stills and short video clips), and a digital camera.[13]

Perhaps the clearest example of this development occurred during Cyclone Nargis, when a package filmed by Jonathan Pearce, a press office at the aid agency

Merlin, led the BBC Ten O'Clock News on May 18, 2008. (Pearce also wrote a three-part series on the subject for the Guardian.) In the two and a half minute report—which was revoiced by BBC correspondent Andrew Harding—all but 32 seconds had been filmed by Merlin. In many cases, such collaborations have worked out well; news organizations receive content at little or no cost, while aid agencies are able to further their mission and reach larger audiences. But there has also been a potentially dangerous blurring of lines.

Fiona Callister, of the Catholic charity CAFOD, said her press office sometimes provided features that went in UK national newspapers unchanged—just re-bylined with the name of a staff feature writer.[14] And in a piece from the Observer entitled "In Starvation's Grip," with three bylines—Tim Judah, Dominic Nutt, and Peter Beaumont[15]—it is not made clear that two of the authors were Observer journalists and one a Christian Aid press officer.

For some, this is a necessary evil; they would say that NGOs are the only entities seriously funding foreign reporting. The distinguished photographer Marcus Bleasdale said recently, "[o]ver the last ten years I would say 80–85 per cent [of my work] has been financed by humanitarian agencies. To give one example, in 2003 I made calls to 20 magazines and newspapers saying I wanted to go to Darfur. Yet I made one call to Human Rights Watch, sorted a day rate, expenses and five days later I was in the field."[16]

Bleasdale has had a long and distinguished career, especially in Darfur. But there are concerns about what might happen in less experienced hands than his. Dan Gillmor has called humanitarians acting as reports "almost-journalism." Some observers argue that as aid agencies become reporters and conform to dominant media logic, they lose opportunities for advocacy and also any credibility they formerly possessed. Yet the real problem appears to be as Gillmor warns: "They're falling short today in several areas, notably the one that comes hardest to advocates: fairness."

Certainly broadcasters now appear to be less laissez faire about using NGOs as their unpaid reporters than in the past. The Merlin package used by the BBC was so keen to mention its debt that Merlin was given numerous name-checks. This—in the U.K. at least—may be linked to a heightened sense of responsibility after a succession of scandals in 2007 that revealed "faked" footage in documentaries, and which resulted in both the BBC and the major commercial channel ITV being censured. These scandals themselves did not have anything to do with NGOs but added to a climate of caution in news as well as documentaries. Certainly by acknowledging the provenance, it absolved the news organizations of responsibility if the footage should later prove controversial—especially given that recent crises have included Burma and Gaza.

Second, aid agencies are also adapting by seeking to become citizen journalists themselves. The Disasters Emergency Committee, in its 2007 Sudan appeal, persuaded the three UK party leaders to each record a message that could be put up on YouTube. Save the Children has launched its own "fly on the wall" documentary from Kroo Bay in Sierra Leone. Rachel Palmer of Save the Children said that while numbers remained relatively small, those who clicked onto the site spent on average 4.5 minutes there. But the main success was not explaining development but to "bear witness . . . to show people the similarity between their own children and an eight-year-old in Sierra Leone."[17]

And in 2008, the British Red Cross even ventured into the world of alternate reality games to build the game Traces of Hope written by the scriptwriter of Bebo's KateModern. Aimed at 15- to 18-year-olds in the U.K., it attempted to engage players and introduce them to the consequences of the trauma of war, and how the Red Cross helps victims of conflict.

While NGOs are educating themselves in new media, however, they are facing a challenge: citizen journalists are increasingly becoming watchdogs for NGOs, thus consolidating a third trend.

In her 2006 report for the UN Special Envoy, Imogen Wall points out that in Aceh there were two to three mobile phones per refugee camp. When I visited Banda Aceh in 2007, aid agencies had found to their cost that instead of being grateful beneficiaries there was an articulate and determined population using new media (such as texting, and digital photographs) effectively when they felt the reconstruction process was not going quickly enough. They would use such methods often in collaboration with traditional media such as the local newspaper Serambi Indonesia or the local TV news programme Aceh Dalamberita.

"The community is smart in playing the media game," says Christelle Chapoy of Oxfam in Banda Aceh. "We have had the geuchiks (village chiefs) saying quite openly to us—if you don't respond to our demands we will call in the media."[18]

This may mean unwelcome criticism, or, at its most severe, it can put people in danger. Those aid agencies who find themselves attacked online in one area may find more serious consequences in other parts of the world. As Vincent Lusser of ICRC said: "In a globalised media environment, people even in remote conflict areas are connected to the Internet. Therefore our colleagues in Kabul have to think that what happens in Afghanistan can affect our colleagues elsewhere in the world."

CONCLUSION

Citizen journalism can mean that more diverse voices—for example, earthquake survivors in Pakistan, tsunami survivors in Banda Aceh or bloggers in Burma—are being heard. This new wealth of angles can act as a corrective to the previous patriarchal approach where reporters and aid agencies acted as mouthpieces. Neither aid agencies nor the traditional media can return to the control they had in the past. The old certainties about the gatekeeping role that aid agencies had—and journalists utilized—have gone, and both sides are grappling with this new world.

It is important not to be too idealistic about citizen journalism. Without checks and balances, UGC can spread misinformation and even be used as a dangerous weapon—witness the ethnic hatred spread by SMS messages in the aftermath of the December 2007 Kenyan elections.

New media has also seen a potential blurring of boundaries between journalists eager for material but strapped for cash, and aid agencies fighting in a competitive marketplace and using more creative means to get stories placed. If journalists use aid workers' words and footage they must clearly label it as such. If they are accepting a trip from an aid agency—so-called "beneficent embedding"[19]—then they should be honest about it.

If aid agencies act as reporters they must consider whether they are acting as journalists or as advocates. While journalists—if sometimes imperfectly—work on the principle of impartiality, the aid agency is usually there to get a message across: to raise money, to raise awareness, to change a situation. When they act as journalists this often becomes blurred. The danger, as Gillmor points out, is a growth in "almost journalism," a confusion both for aid agencies as to what they are trying to do, and for the viewer/reader about what they are being presented with.

For those agencies who are turning from traditional media to using their own websites, the key point is that to be successful, such footage and websites need to be of as good quality as those produced by traditional media for sophisticated consumers. The associated cost privileges the efforts of larger and well-funded NGOs.

Meanwhile agencies must realize that they are not the only ones grappling with new media. Citizen journalists have the potential to act as NGOs' watchdogs, as the mainstream media retreat from foreign reporting. As the experience in Aceh and elsewhere shows, local people are not just grateful beneficiaries; instead, they can be articulate and angry critics.

And finally new information and communication technologies that enable these developments cannot be ignored. The Economist reports that following

Mr. Sokor's appeal, the WFP did boost rations in the Dagahaley refugee camp. Is that blunt text message a harbinger of things to come?

NOTES

1. The Economist 2007
2. Cooper 2007
3. Vaux 2005
4. Moeller 1999
5. Interview with Vicky Taylor, May 7 2008
6. Interview with Samanthi Dissanayake, BBC producer, 7 May 2008
7. Buerk 1984
8. Hattotuwa 2007
9. Email from Ory Okolloh, September 5, 2008
10. Sutcliffe 2007
11. Interview with John Naughton, November 27, 2006
12. Gowing 1998
13. Oxfam 2007
14. Telephone interview with Fiona Callister, August 29, 2007
15. Judah, Nutt, and Beaumont, 2002
16. Bleasdale 2008
17. Phone interview Jan 20, 2009
18. Interview, Banda Aceh, 30 Apr 2007
19. Cottle and Nolan 2007

REFERENCES

Bleasdale, M. Speaking at "The News Carers: Are Aid Groups Doing too much Real Newsgathering? A Debate at the Frontline Club." New York, February 28, 2008.

Cooper, G. "Anyone Here Survived a Wave, Speak English and Got a Mobile? Aid Agencies, the Media and Reporting Disasters since the Tsunami." The 14th Guardian Lecture. Nuffield College, Oxford, November 5, 2007.

Cottle, S. and Nolan, D. "Global Humanitarianism and The Changing Aid-Media Field." *Journalism Studies* 8, No. 6 (2007), pp. 862–878.

Gowing, N. "New Challenges and Problems for Information Management in Complex Emergencies: Ominous Lessons from the Great Lakes and Eastern Zaire in Late 1996 and early 1997." Conference paper given at Dispatches from Disaster Zones conference, May 1998.

Hattotuwa, S. "Who's Afraid of Citizen Journalists?" In TVEP/UNDP, *Communicating Disasters. An Asia-Pacific Resource Book*, 2007.

Judah, T., Nutt, D. and Beaumont, P. "In Starvation's Grip." The Observer, June 9, 2002.

Moeller, S. *Compassion Fatigue: How the Media Sell Famine, Disease, War and Death.* New York: Routledge, 1999.

Oxfam. "Guide to Media Work in Emergencies." Internal document, Oxfam GB, Oxford, 2007.

Sutcliffe, T. "Ethics Aside, Citizen Journalists Get Scoops." The Independent, January 2, 2007.

*Glenda Cooper is a journalist and academic. She is an associate member of Nuffield College, Oxford. She was a visiting fellow at the Reuters Institute for the Study of Journalism 2007–8 and the 2006–7 Guardian Research Fellow at Nuffield. She is a consulting editor at the *Daily Telegraph*.

Cooper, Glenda. "When Lines Between NGO and News Organization Blur." Nieman Journalism Lab website, December 21, 2009, 12:30 p.m. http://www.niemanlab.org/2009/12/glenda-cooper-when-lines-between-ngo-and-news-organization-blur/.

Used by permission.

Part 4:
The Cost of Making a Difference:
Balancing Risk in Modern Conflict

The NGOs, lawyers, activists, and journalists who have figured prominently so far in this compendium are driven to help civilians caught in conflict, to prevent abuses or atrocities from taking place, or to capture the truth of what is happening in conflict so that a global audience can be more engaged in these issues. But given increasing risk to civilians in conflict zones, what are the costs of such activities, and are they worth it?

REPORTING AND RISK IN CONFLICT ZONES

In the last two decades, the risks to those covering war have increased. The Committee to Protect Journalists reported that "a journalist is killed in the line of duty somewhere around the world once every eight days."[1] The year 2012 was the deadliest on record, according to some studies, in particular because of increased targeting in Syria, Somalia, and Brazil, and continuing high death tolls in places like Pakistan and Yemen.[2]

The changing face of the media corps may be one factor for increased targeting. As media industry woes have forced downsizing, media outlets rely more on freelance journalists or information from citizen reporting instead of fielding and supporting large numbers of permanent overseas staff. This means that a larger proportion of the writers in these dangerous zones lack some of the safety nets that traditional journalists have—including comprehensive insurance, emergency medical services or coverage, or kidnapping and ransom support. During the 2011 armed revolution in Libya, acclaimed freelancer Tim Hetherington was killed by shelling on the front lines. Colleagues later found that basic first aid training, which often is not available for freelancers, would have saved his life.

The freelance relationship results in less institutional liability for the risks these freelance journalists take in the field, which may lead editors to push for riskier reporting without fully weighing the consequences. In a searing reflection on freelance reporting from Syria in 2013, Italian journalist Francesca Borri noted that editors' bottom lines and intense competition between journalists for limited publishing opportunities create a race to the bottom that forces freelancers to the front line more frequently. She writes, "[T]he editors back in Italy only ask us for the blood, the bang-bang."[3] In addition, with stories averaging $70 apiece, she argues, journalists must cut safety measures to cut costs:

> In places like Syria, ... sleeping in this rebel base, under mortar fire, on a mattress on the ground, with yellow water that gave me typhoid, costs $50 per night; a car costs $250 per day. So you end up maximizing, rather than minimizing, the risks. Not only can you not afford insurance—it's almost $1,000 a month—but you cannot afford a fixer or a translator. ... If you happen to be seriously wounded, there is a temptation to hope not to survive, because you cannot afford to be wounded.[4]

The blurring of lines between citizen or partisan journalism and objective reporting may also increase the risks to traditional journalists. In a story discussing the killing of two Al-Aqsa TV cameramen by Israeli missiles (Al-Aqsa is run by Hamas and often has coverage leaning in that direction), *New York Times* journalist and editor David Carr argues that the presence of some individuals with partisan ties among the information-gatherers can increase the chances that all journalists may be targeted:

> At a time when news outlets in the United States are cutting foreign operations for monetary reasons, cheap and ubiquitous technology has lowered the entry barrier for others who want to engage in journalism, some of whom are already in the theater of conflict and may have partisan motives. Many of those newer players are young and inexperienced in ways that make them particularly vulnerable in the middle of dangerous conflicts. Other journalists have close affiliations with partisan forces in these conflicts. As news media organizations become increasingly politicized, all journalists risk ending up as collateral casualties because they are working adjacent to outlets viewed as purveyors of propaganda.[5]

Finally, the around-the-clock global media environment, and the public's (or at least the newsroom editor's) insatiable demand for real-time information direct from the front lines, may also increase pressures for journalists to push the envelope and put themselves in danger. In the first article, "The Price of a Scoop: Two Dead,"[6] Tunku Varadarajan weighs whether these risks are worth it. In 2009, *New York Times* reporter and British citizen Stephen Farrell was kidnapped along with an Afghan colleague while reporting on civilian casualties in a dangerous area of Afghanistan. He was subsequently rescued by British forces, but his Afghan colleague and one of the rescuing British troops were killed in the rescue. Noting that Farrell rejected advice from British forces not to go to the area where he was ultimately kidnapped, Varadarajan argues "Fine military people spend huge amounts of thought and energy on trying to avoid casualties. Farrell's reckless rejection of their obviously correct advice was a choice as massive as its consequence for his dead Afghan associate."[7]

While Varadarajan suggests that sometimes journalists are too cavalier, he also appreciates that getting information to the public takes risks. "Reporters often, and rightly, inject themselves into dangerous settings to provide information that is important to the public. The coverage of wars has always involved a balance between the risks taken by the reporter and the value of the information that can only be gained by physical proximity to a fight."[8]

Where journalists are not willing to take risks, or the risks are simply too high, coverage of a conflict may be incomplete. The way that security risks and precautions affect journalistic coverage is the focus of Patrick Cockburn's "Embedded Journalism: A Distorted View of War." Cockburn discusses the resurgence of "embed journalism," in which the way the journalist gathers information is by traveling with military troops, relying on their transportation, food, shelter, and other resources. Embedding is not new; in World War I and World War II it was the most common way that stories from the front line were fed back home. But since the U.S. engagement in Vietnam (1959–75), journalists have often eschewed embedded reporting because it has been viewed as a way for governments or militaries to control or "spin" how war was presented to the public.[9]

The security situation in Afghanistan and Iraq led to a resurgence of embedded reporting, and has revived the debate over whether and how this practice might bias coverage of war. "Given that al-Qa'ida and the Taliban target foreign journalists as potential hostages, it is impossible to roam around Iraq or Afghanistan without extreme danger," Cockburn notes.[10] While he argues that embedded journalists can still take an independent viewpoint, Cockburn admits that some skewing is inevitable, as "journalists cannot help reflecting to some degree the viewpoint of the soldiers they are accompanying."[11] Embedding can affect which stories or locations are reported on, as journalists go only where a military escort is available and willing to transport them. It can also lead to a focus on following the conflict in military terms, leaving out the political or social dimensions that might ultimately be more important for conflict resolution. Cockburn argues that "above all, the very fact of a correspondent being with an occupying army gives the impression that the conflicts in Iraq and Afghanistan, countries which have endured 30 years of crisis and warfare, can be resolved by force."[12]

Thus while embedding may be better than no coverage at all, as it certainly informs the public of some aspects of the conflict, it is an illustration of how increasing security risks in these environments can prevent full understanding of a war. If only a limited view of the war is being presented to the public, and that view is susceptible to control by warring parties, then such reporting runs the risk of undermining journalists' goals of improving public awareness and public accountability.

NGO SECURITY DILEMMAS

Journalists are not the only ones in the cross-fire. Humanitarian aid workers and advocates from NGOs are killed, injured, kidnapped, and threatened at increasing rates in conflict zones worldwide, sometimes as a direct target of warring parties and sometimes as a hazard of their work. For example, in 2005 Marla Ruzicka, founder of the Center for Civilians in Conflict, the organization that was a focus in Sarah Holewinski's article in Part 2, was killed by an improvised explosive device in Baghdad, Iraq. While engaged in documenting civilian casualties and advocating for compensation for civilian victims of U.S. forces, she herself became a victim of war.[13]

As Scott Baldauf notes in the third article, "Helpers in a Hostile World: The Risk of Aid Work Grows," by 2010 the number of aid workers killed globally had nearly tripled from a decade before.[14] While attacks on foreign aid workers tend to capture bigger foreign news headlines, studies suggest that 79 percent of staff targeted between 1997 to 2005 were local aid staff.[15] Many possible factors have led to the increased risk for NGOs in conflict zones. The ambiguity of modern conflict—the blurring of lines between civilians and combatants, between wartime and peacetime, and between what is a battlefield and what is a safe space—can increase the chances that aid workers will get caught in the midst of the fighting. Changes in tactics are also increasing aid workers' risk. With more non-state armed groups seeking out "soft targets" that have a political or representational value, civilian aid workers are a more attractive target than in the past. The promise of a global media spotlight focused on such killings or kidnappings may have incentivized wider use of these tactics. Finally, the sheer number of aid workers now engaging in these danger zones may also be a factor—some studies have suggested that the overall number of aid workers in conflict zones has increased dramatically in the last 10 years, such that while the number of attacks has increased, the level or rate of attacks is the same.[16]

Revisiting some of the debates about the impact of the politicization of aid, Baldauf also notes that in places like Pakistan, recent policy developments have helped ratchet up hostility against aid workers to extreme levels. Because part of the U.S. strategy since the September 11 attacks has been to win Pakistani hearts and minds through aid, foreign aid has become inextricably linked with extremely unpopular U.S. foreign policy in the public perception. Statistics suggest that the vast majority of attacks on aid workers and NGO advocates are still taking place in a handful of countries: Afghanistan, Pakistan, Somalia, and Sudan.[17] In almost all these countries, U.S. counterterrorism or counterinsurgency operations have been prominent, but whether U.S. engagement and aid policies have led to more attacks on aid workers in these four countries, or whether the attacks simply reflect the internal conflict dynamics of each country, is an open debate.

Regardless of the cause, Baldauf notes that NGOs are finding new ways to deal with these situations, adjusting their tactics and strategies so they can continue to work in difficult and often life-threatening environments. The humanitarians whom Baldauf interviews are constantly balancing how to protect staff without limiting the lifesaving aid they provide. As an adviser for Oxfam Great Britain, Heather Hughes, explains in Baldauf's story, "Globally we do accept a higher level of risk for certain kinds of work, where there is a humanitarian imperative, such as camps where if we pull out then people will die."[18] At the same time, though, sometimes protecting staff or protecting access demands compromises—such as cooperating or even providing humanitarian aid to repressive or corrupt governments or to armed groups taking part in the conflict. This requires balancing staff safety with the need to ensure that that these tactics do not cause more harm than good in the overall environment (the type of concerns discussed Part 1).[19]

CONCLUSION

Despite the heightened risk, aid workers, human rights activists, journalists, and other globally active citizens who have featured prominently in this book will likely continue to risk their lives for these causes. Although there are those in it for adventure, glory, or money, the majority are working for what they believe to be right in situations of extreme wrong. They are seeking to mitigate the costs of war by treating the wounded, and supporting critical food and shelter needs. They are trying to limit the worst excesses of war, by outlawing certain weapons or tactics, or calling to account warring parties who slaughter civilians, or engage in torture. They are trying to shine a spotlight on the horrors of war, so that a global public might see and judge for itself.

To many not in this field, the choices these journalists and NGO workers make may seem crazy. Is coverage of a story worth eight months in captivity, as *New York Times* journalist David Rohde was forced to endure?[20] Was taking a particular victim's testimony worth Marla Ruzicka's life? In each individual case, the answer is almost certainly no. But many of these civilians believe that without some calculated risks, the causes for which they are striving would never be advanced.

Considering the fragile and complex environments in which these individuals work, success is not guaranteed, or even all that likely. In many of the countries where this work is taking place, war is not an aberration but has ebbed and flowed for generations. Great efforts and great strides can be taken, with real success resulting, only to be set back by a renewed surge in violence, a change in the conflict dynamics. Worse still, as many of the articles in this book have illustrated, even the most well-intentioned efforts run a risk of being co-opted or of creating unintended consequences. Human rights and humanitarian campaigns that sought to stop suffering instead created perverse incentives, attracting the dollars and attention that are the oxygen for continued conflict. Advances in global media that seemed to open the possibility for greater truth and accountability for what happens in war have opened equal opportunities for misinformation and propaganda. Given these setbacks and failures, are the often fatal consequences of such work worth it?

Acclaimed war reporter Marie Colvin was killed in the Syrian conflict in 2012, after decades of working in war zones and assuming great personal risk—notably in 2010 a grenade cost her an eye and caused other serious injuries. Several years before her death, in a speech honoring journalists killed in the course of their reporting, she weighed in on such questions: "We always have to ask ourselves whether the level of risk is worth the story. What is bravery, and what is bravado?"[21] But while she admitted there are difficult choices, and that sometimes reporters and their staff make the "ultimate sacrifice," she never doubted that it was worth it. "The public have a right to know what our government, and our armed forces, are doing in our name. Our mission is to speak the truth to power. We can and do make a difference in exposing the horrors of war and especially the atrocities that befall civilians."[22]

As you read these selections, consider the following questions:

- Is the value of getting information to the public worth the lives of journalists lost each year? What about the civilians or military personnel put at danger by the risks journalists assume?

- Is embedded journalism an inherent conflict of interest, likely to bias reporting too much in favor of the troops whom journalists are relying on for protection, food, and transport? Why?

- As discussed in the Cooper article in Part 3, there has also been an emergence of "embeds" with NGOs. Is the potential for bias more likely with military or NGO embeds? Does the potential of military or warring-party bias pose a greater risk of thwarting public accountability than does NGO bias?

- How would you advise a humanitarian NGO trying to judge the risks of continuing to operate in areas such as Somalia (as featured in the Baldauf article)? Is there a right way to balance risks to staff lives versus the potential for continuing to safe lives?

- Are the efforts that humanitarians, human rights activists, and journalists undertake, as described in this book, worth the risk to them or others around them? Why or why not?

Notes

1. Frank Smyth, "Will UN Plan Address Impunity, Security for Journalists?" Journalist Security blog, Committee to Protect Journalists, November 13, 2012, http://www.cpj.org/security/2012/11/will-un-plan-address-impunity-security-for-journal.php.

2. The International Press Institute (November 21, 2012) found 2012 to be the deadliest year so far in its tracking: http://www.freemedia.at/home/singleview/article/2012-deadliest-year-on-record-for-journalists.html. Also, the Committee to Protect Journalists found a 49 percent increase in journalists killed in 2012 from the previous year, citing "the war in Syria, a record number of shootings in Somalia, continued violence in Pakistan, and a worrying increase in Brazilian murders," http://www.cpj.org/2013/02/attacks-on-the-press-killed-in-2012.php.

3. Francesca Borri, "Woman's Work: The Twisted Reality of an Italian Freelancer in Syria," *Columbia Journalism Review*, July 1, 2013 (not paginated), http://www.cjr.org/feature/womans_work.php.

4. Ibid.

5. David Carr, "Using War as Cover to Target Journalists," *New York Times*, November 25, 2012, http://www.nytimes.com/2012/11/26/business/media/using-war-as-cover-to-target-journalists.html?_r=0.

6. Tunku Varadarajan, "The Price of a Scoop: Two Dead," *Forbes*, September 14, 2009, http://www.forbes.com/2009/09/13/stephen-farrell-new-york-times-rescue-afghanistan-opinions-columnists-tunku-varadarajan.html.

7. Ibid.

8. Ibid.

9. Acclaimed human rights activist Aryeh Neier writes, "Up until the Vietnam War, journalists had generally covered armed conflicts as partisans for their own side. . . . In Vietnam, however, many Western journalists—clad as civilians—questioned the conduct of military operations, and, in the United States and elsewhere, helped to create public doubts about the war." Aryeh Neier, *The International Human Rights Movement: A History* (Princeton, NJ: Princeton University Press, 2012), 4.

10. Patrick Cockburn, "Opinion: Embedded Journalism: A Distorted View of War," *Independent*, November 23, 2010, http://www.independent.co.uk/news/media/opinion/embedded-journalism-a-distorted-view-of-war-2141072.html.

11. Ibid.

12. Ibid.

13. See, e.g., Phillip Robertson, "Marla Ruzicka, RIP," Salon.com, April 18, 2005, http://www.salon.com/2005/04/18/marla/.

14. Scott Baldauf, "Helpers in a Hostile World: The Risk of Aid Work Grows," *Christian Science Monitor*, February 10, 2012, http://www.csmonitor.com/World/Global-Issues/2012/0210/Helpers-in-a-hostile-world-the-risk-of-aid-work-grows.

15. Abby Stoddard, Adele Harmer, and Katherine Haver, "Providing Aid in Insecure Environments: Trends in Policy and Operations," Overseas Development Institute Humanitarian Policy Group Report 23 (September 2006), http://www.humanitarianoutcomes.org/sites/default/files/pdf/ProvidingAidinInsecureEnvironments-Full.pdf.

16. See, e.g., Stoddard, Harmer, and Haver, "Providing Aid."

17. Humanitarian Outcomes, Aid Worker Security Report, 2012, pp. 1–3, http://www.humanitarian outcomes.org/sites/default/files/resources/AidWorkerSecurityReport20126.pdf.

18. Baldauf, "Helpers in a Hostile World."

19. Ibid.

20. See, e.g., David Rohde, "Held by the Taliban: A Five Part Series," *New York Times*, October 17–21, 2009, http://www.nytimes.com/2009/10/22/world/asia/22epilogue.html.

21. Marie Colvin, "Our Mission Is to Report These Horrors of War with Accuracy and Without Prejudice," *Guardian*, February 22, 2012, http://www.theguardian.com/commentisfree/2012/feb/22/marie-colvin-our-mission-is-to-speak-truth.

22. Ibid.

The Price of a Scoop: Two Dead

by Tunku Varadarajan*

What should one make of the tale of Stephen Farrell—the seemingly reckless New York Times reporter who was rescued by British soldiers on Sept. 9 after spending four days as a captive of the Taliban? A soldier died in the course of his rescue, leading sections of British public opinion to go ballistic, accusing Farrell not merely of selfishness, but of moral responsibility for the soldier's death. Is this reaction fair and justified?

Stephen Farrell was a British citizen reporting from Afghanistan. He'd received very strong advice from British troops to stay out of a Taliban-controlled sector into which he was planning to venture in search of a story. Ignoring that advice, Farrell entered the sector with his Afghan interpreter. Both men were seized by the Taliban within hours, and held captive in conditions that led the British to fear for the life of one of their citizens—hence the rescue mission, in which a British soldier was killed. (The hapless interpreter died, too.)

Let me begin by inverting the moral question and asking *not* whether Farrell— whose action in defiance of advice had generated an entirely avoidable need for rescue—bears moral responsibility for the soldier's death, but whether the Brits were entitled not to seek to rescue him. The rational answer has to be "yes." After all, the disregard of specific advice has to have some consequence. And did not Farrell assume the risk of some harm befalling him? So why not allow him to suffer the effects of his own recklessness? Fine military people spend huge amounts of thought and energy on trying to avoid casualties. Farrell's reckless rejection of their obviously correct advice was a choice as massive as its consequence for his dead Afghan associate.

Yet as the actual fact of the rescue demonstrates, matters other than mere reason are in play here. There is a long political and moral tradition in democratic societies by which endangered citizens are sought to be safeguarded. Rescues of this kind—of foolish hikers in mountains, of stubborn homesteaders who stay put in a flood, of gung-ho journalists in the enemy's lair—are a hallmark of civilization. Had Farrell been left to die in Talib hands, the British would have been the first to regard a failure to rescue him—or a failure to contemplate a rescue—as a blot on their escutcheon. So however inclined one might be to hold Farrell in contempt as a reckless Pulitzer-grubber, the question of leaving him to die simply does not arise in a great and self-sacrificial society like Britain (or the U.S., for that matter).

Could one argue—as defenders of Farrell inevitably will—that there is another moral claim competing against the one that asserts that Farrell was responsible for the soldier's death? To wit: the need to get information of public value, for which journalists must—and do—take risks. And isn't the military always asking journalists not to go places, for what might indelicately be described as cover-your-ass reasons? Nobody wants to be blamed if something goes wrong, so it's always easier to exhort cautious behavior. Besides, the "dangerous war zone" argument can also be used by governments to hide all manner of beastly things. Just think of the Sri Lankan army recently, in its final offensive against the Tamil Tigers; or the Israelis in Gaza last December. I have no doubt that there would have been fewer civilian deaths if the press had been around in both cases.

To continue in this vein: Surely the enterprise of journalism would be much poorer if all journalists heeded every government edict. To some extent, does not the enterprise of democracy and informed consent depend on people like Farrell? Pushing the limits is an inherent aspect of press behavior: How else to get past the known to the unknown? Reporters often, and rightly, inject themselves into dangerous settings to provide information that is important to the public. The coverage of wars has always involved a balance between the risks taken by the reporter and the value of the information that can only be gained by physical proximity to a fight. The question is whether Farrell's particular incursion, against advice, was foolhardy rather than courageous.

That said, let us put moral questions to one side and ask what—now—the duty of The New York Times is. What price should it pay for the trouble caused by its reporter? Here's my answer: If The New York Times really does subscribe to this philosophy—the public's right to know, the journalist's duty to be skeptical of authority, etc. —it should reimburse the British government for the cost of the mission to save Farrell (even if it means taking another loan from Carlos Slim) and compensate the dead soldier's family. (That it should compensate handsomely the family of the Afghan interpreter who died is not even open to discussion.) After all, the military has quite enough on its plate not to have to worry about extracting reporters from deadly contretemps of their own making.

Farrell took a huge risk on behalf of his for-profit employer to give it an edge in the news business. Afghanistan is an extremely competitive beat; and war and competitive journalism make for a very perilous—and profitable—alloy. So whereas one would be loath to corral and stifle reporters, why can't there be some financial incentive for journalists to behave responsibly when they venture into battlegrounds? Why not bill publications for the cost of a rescue and require journalists to give half the royalties from any books they write to the military, in the event of a costly rescue?

Embedded here is a broader question regarding the costs and benefits of war reporting. As the Farrell tale demonstrates, journalists tend only to consider the benefits, but not the costs, of their actions. This is a problem in a country like the U.S. in which the majority supports the military in its endeavors, but the press is disproportionately from a minority that reflexively dislikes the military and is suspicious of its motives—and so intuitively discounts the costs of journalistic actions to the effectiveness of our forces.

In other words, Farrell is emblematic of a growing schism between the people and the press. But no great society would gag its Farrells, or keep them out of a war zone. That's just the way it is, and always should be.

UPDATE: On Sept. 18, 2009, by Tunku Varadarajan: Today's New York Times adds another bitter flavor to this story. The newspaper hides away—at the very bottom of page A10—a photograph of mourners in Wootton Bassett, England, as they watched the hearses of two British soldiers killed in Afghanistan. As the paper puts it in the accompanying caption: "One soldier died in a firefight in Helmand Province, the other in Kunduz Province in the rescue of a reporter for The New York Times who had been held by the Taliban." My respect for Bill Keller, the paper's editor, would have gone up by a notch or two if he'd had the sensitivity—and the class—to publish this heart-rending photograph on page one, above the fold.

Instead, the photo—like the soldier who died rescuing the Times reporter—was buried.

*Tunku Varadarajan, a professor at New York University's Stern Business School and a fellow at Stanford's Hoover Institution, is executive editor for opinions at *Forbes*. He writes a weekly column for *Forbes*.

Varadarajan, Tunku. "The Price of a Scoop: Two Dead." Forbes.com (blog), September 14, 2009. http://www.forbes.com/2009/09/13/stephen-farrell-new-york-times-rescue-afghanistan-opinions-columnists-tunku-varadarajan.html.

Embedded Journalism:
A Distorted View of War

*by Patrick Cockburn**

Embedded journalism earned itself a bad name in Iraq and Afghanistan. The phrase came to evoke an image of the supposedly independent correspondent truckling to military mentors who spoon-feed him or her absurdly optimistic information about the course of the war. To many, the embedded journalist is a grisly throwback to First World War-style reporting, when appalling butchery in the trenches was presented as a series of judiciously planned advances by British generals.

Many allegations against the system of "embedding" journalists, mainly with the American or British military, are unfair. Accompanying armies in the field is usually the only way of finding out what they are doing or think they are doing. Nor is there an obvious alternative way for correspondents to operate today. Given that al-Qa'ida and the Taliban target foreign journalists as potential hostages, it is impossible to roam around Iraq or Afghanistan without extreme danger.

It was not always so. When I first started writing articles in Northern Ireland in the early 1970s, it was probably safer to be a journalist than anything else. I used to joke that newly formed paramilitary groups appointed a press officer before they bought a gun. A few years later in Lebanon, militias gave journalists letters allowing us to pass safely through their checkpoints. The Lebanese are a newspaper-reading people and I used to hand out local newspapers as a friendly gesture to bored militiamen on guard duty. But it was also in Lebanon, from 1984, that Iranian-backed groups started to kidnap journalists as an effective way to pressurise governments and publicise the kidnappers' cause.

In these circumstances, over-reliance on "embedding" as the primary method of gathering information may have been inevitable, but it produces a skewed picture of events. Journalists cannot help reflecting to some degree the viewpoint of the soldiers they are accompanying. The very fact of being with an occupying army means that the journalist is confined to a small and atypical segment of the political-military battlefield.

"Embedding" also puts limitations on location and movement. Iraq and Afghanistan are essentially guerrilla wars, and the successful guerrilla commander will avoid fighting the enemy main force and instead attack where his opponent is weak or has no troops at all. This means that the correspondent embedded with the American or British military units is liable to miss or misinterpret crucial stages in the conflict.

Much of the British and American media reporting in Afghanistan since 2006 has been about skirmishing in Taliban strongholds such as Helmand and Kandahar provinces in the south of the country. Problems are often reduced to quasi-technical or tactical questions about coping with roadside bombs or lack of equipment. Until recently, there was little reporting or explanation of how the Taliban had been able to extend their rule right up to the outskirts of Kabul.

In late 2001, in the days just after the defeat of the Taliban, I was able to drive from Kabul to Kandahar without hearing a shot fired. By last year, I could not move without risk beyond the last police station in the south of the capital. A few miles down the road to Kandahar, Taliban motorcycle patrols were setting up temporary roadblocks and checking all who came through.

This year, it is worse. The Taliban are trying, with a fair measure of success, to counter the allied offensive in the south by spreading their rule in northern Afghanistan, taking control of much of Kunduz and Baghlan provinces and cutting Nato's supply routes to Tajikistan and Uzbekistan.

Just before the war of 2001, I travelled though the Hindu Kush mountains from just north of Kabul through Badakhshan province in north-east Afghanistan to Tajikistan. The journey took four days but there were no Taliban, though they still held much of the rest of Afghanistan. I could not make the same journey today because even in Badakhshan, overwhelmingly Tajik and supposedly anti-Taliban, the insurgents are beginning to make inroads.

A danger of "embedding" is that it puts journalists in the wrong place at the wrong time. In November 2004, the US Marines stormed the city of Fallujah, west of Baghdad, which had been seized by insurgents. The troops were accompanied by almost all the Baghdad foreign press corps, at great risk to themselves. Their accounts and pictures of the battle were compelling and the outcome was an undoubted victory for the US.

But reports of American success were misleading because the insurgents had used the concentration of US forces around Fallujah to launch their own assault against the much larger city of Mosul in northern Iraq, which they briefly captured. The Iraqi army and police fled, 30 police stations were occupied, and $40m-worth of arms seized by the insurgents. Given that Mosul is Iraq's third-largest city, it was a stunning reversal for the US-led forces, but it was virtually unreported since there were no American troops there and hence no embedded journalists.

There is a more subtle disadvantage to "embedding": it leads reporters to see the Iraqi and Afghan conflicts primarily in military terms, while the most important developments are political or, if they are military, may have little to do with foreign forces. It has become an article of faith among many in the US that the American military finally won the war in Iraq in 2007–08 because it adopted a new set of tactics and sent 30,000 extra troop reinforcements known as "the surge." US troop casualties fell to nothing and Iraqi casualties dropped from their previous horrendous levels. This explanation was deeply satisfying to American national self-confidence and rescued the reputation of the US army. In the months before the 2008 presidential election, it became impossible for any American politicians to suggest that the "surge" had not succeeded without attracting accusations of lack of patriotism.

Yet the developments that ended the worst of the fighting in Iraq mostly had little to do with the US, which was only one player in a complex battle. The attacks on the US military came almost entirely from Sunni Arab insurgents, but by 2007, the Sunni were being heavily defeated by the predominantly Shia security forces and militias and could no longer afford to go on fighting the Americans as well. Al-Qa'ida had overplayed its hand by trying to take control of the whole Sunni community. The Sunni were being driven from Baghdad, which is now an overwhelmingly Shia city. Facing the annihilation of their community, the Sunni insurgents switched sides and allied themselves with the Americans. In this context it was possible for the US to send out penny packets of troops into Sunni areas which were desperate for defenders against Shia death squads and al-Qa'ida commanders demanding that they send their sons to fight.

But the same sort of tactics cannot be replicated in Afghanistan, where conditions were very different. Despite this, until a few months ago, it had become the accepted wisdom of American opinion pages and television talking heads that the US army had found an all-purpose formula for victory in its post-11 September wars. The author of victory, the present US commander in Afghanistan, General David Petraeus, became America's most popular, prestigious and unsackable military officer. The failure hitherto of "surge" tactics to work in southern Afghanistan has begun to undermine this faith in the new strategy, but American and British policy is still modelled on the "surge": foreign forces backed by Afghan troops will gain control on the ground; they will then hold it and prevent the Taliban coming back; and, then, finally, they will hand over power to Afghan soldiers, police and officials sent from Kabul.

It is unlikely ever to happen this way. As in Iraq, military actions on the ground in Afghanistan don't make much sense separate from political developments. The Afghan government is notoriously crooked and is regarded by most Afghans as a collection of racketeers. All the media reports of small unit actions whose ultimate purpose is to install the rule of Kabul in southern Afghanistan make little sense since the government is so feeble that it barely exists. In some 80 per cent of the country the state does not exist.

"The reality of the war in Afghanistan," one diplomat told me, "which embedded journalism never reveals, is that 60 per cent of the Afghan government soldiers sent to Helmand or Kandahar desert as soon as they can. They are mostly Tajiks terrified of being sent to the Pashtun south. They are taken from the training camps and put on buses and the doors are locked before they are told where they are being posted." But it is these same terrified soldiers, often not even speaking the language of local people, who are at the heart of Nato's plan for victory in Afghanistan.

It is worth asking how well the Iraq and Afghanistan wars have been reported. Could the average newspaper reader and television viewer gain an approximate idea of what was happening in both countries over the past eight years?

War reporting is easy to do, but difficult to do well. Wars rouse such passions that editors and senior producers in home offices seldom retain healthy journalistic scepticism. They develop oversimplified ideas about what the story is, be it "hard-won victory" or "bloody stalemate." Viewers and readers expect drama from conflict and think they know what it looks like. The first pictures from the wars in Afghanistan in 2001 and Iraq in 2003 were dominated by shots of great gouts of fire rising from missiles exploding in Baghdad and Kabul.

But this melodrama was deceptive, obscuring what had really happened. The most important fact about these two wars was that, in their first, conventional warfare stage, they barely took place at all. Taliban fighters faded away to their villages or moved across the border into Pakistan. In Iraq Saddam Hussein's most elite and pampered units dissolved and went home as soon as they could.

It was very difficult to tell all this to news desks at the time. News organisations get geared up for war and feel short-changed when told that not much is really happening. I had followed the retreating Taliban from Kabul to Kandahar in 2001 and saw little fighting along the road. In a substantial city such as Ghazni there were half a dozen Taliban dead, mostly killed in gunfights over ownership of government cars. In Iraq 18 months later, there were plenty of burnt-out Iraqi army tanks on the roads but, when I looked inside, most had been abandoned before they were destroyed by air strikes.

The US and British governments drew precisely the wrong lessons from the failure of the Taliban and the Iraqi army to fight. In both cases, President Bush and Tony Blair had been warned that they were entering a quagmire and instead they had apparently won easy victories. They arrogantly believed they were in control of events while in fact they were only powerful players, who ought to have been paying attention to how Afghans, Iraqis, Iranians, Syrians and Pakistanis were reacting to their actions. Their blindness is easy to criticise in retrospect, but at the time, this sense of American omnipotence was shared by most of the US media.

In one respect I found Iraq easier to report than the Afghan war. In Britain the split was so deep over the war that from the beginning, there were plenty of sceptics willing to believe that they were being lied to by the government and that the venture was going badly. American correspondents had a more difficult time because their home offices were still nervous of being seen as unpatriotic well into 2005. Three years later, American correspondents on the ground were often appalled to see self-declared pundits on Iraq firmly claiming on their own television channels or in newspapers that the "surge" was a famous victory. Iraqis were still dying in their hundreds, but as soon as the US military ceased to suffer casualties, US television largely stopped reporting Iraq.

The Iraq war may have been a "last hurrah" for the US media because so much of it has slimmed down or gone out of business in the past few years. The British media have never put enough resources into reporting either war to cover them properly. The BBC was the only television company to maintain a permanently staffed office in Baghdad. Most newspapers covered it episodically. This was partly because reporting wars is always very expensive and is particularly costly in Iraq and Afghanistan because of the need to pay security companies. In some cases these realised that their job was to enable correspondents to get to the story with the least possible danger, but others behaved like prison guards in their determination to keep correspondents safe. I remember Robert Fisk and I receiving a text message from one distinguished and brave British correspondent in another part of Baghdad regretting that he could not meet us at our hotel because his head of security had decided that our proposed lunch was "not an operational necessity."

The dangers inevitable in covering Iraq had another effect. Much of the best reporting has been done by experienced reporters who knew Iraq before 2004. After that, it became very difficult for young correspondents to have any sort of "learning curve" because anybody hoping to "learn from their mistakes" in Iraq was not going to live very long. Halfway through the Iraq war, one bureau chief lamented to me, saying: "The only fairly safe place for me to send young reporters, who haven't been to Iraq before, is on 'embeds,' but then they drink up everything the army tells them and report it as fact." The best reporting in any single publication during the height of the sectarian slaughter in Iraq in 2006–07 was in *The New York Times*, which got round this dilemma by simply hiring experienced and highly regarded correspondents from other newspapers. Even so, despite the risks, it was always possible to report Iraq and Afghanistan from outside the embrace of the military, as was shown by extraordinarily brave people such as Ghaith Abdul-Ahad and Nir Rosen, who risked their lives mixing with insurgents and militiamen.

I used to get a certain amount of undeserved applause at book festivals by being introduced as a writer "who has never been embedded," as if I had been abstaining from unnatural vice. "Embedding" obviously leads to bias, but many journalists are smart enough to rumble military propaganda and wishful thinking, and not to regurgitate these in undiluted form. They know that Afghan villagers, interviewed in front of Afghan police or US soldiers, are unlikely to say what they really think about either. Nevertheless, perhaps the most damaging effect of "embedding" is to soften the brutality of any military occupation and underplay hostile local response to it. Above all, the very fact of a correspondent being with an occupying army gives the impression that the conflicts in Iraq and Afghanistan, countries which have endured 30 years of crisis and warfare, can be resolved by force.

*Patrick Cockburn is Middle East correspondent for the *Independent*.

Cockburn, Patrick. "Embedded Journalism: A Distorted View of War." *Independent*, November 23, 2010. http://www.independent.co.uk/news/media/opinion/embedded-journalism-a-distorted-view-of-war-2141072.html.

Reprinted by permission.

Helpers in a Hostile World:
The Risk of Aid Work Grows

*by Scott Baldauf**

Aid workers may be an idealistic sort, but they're not naive. They know the risks of crossing oceans or pressing through to remote areas to build tent cities, run feeding stations, or treat the sick in what are by definition the most dangerous and least hospitable corners of the planet.

In the decade since Sept. 11, those risks have only increased as members of the US military and other government agencies have joined the ranks of those doing humanitarian aid work.

In 2010, some 242 aid workers were killed, up from 91 a decade before, according to a survey by Humanitarian Outcomes, underscoring how many attacks on aid workers have become intentional, rather than a side effect of war. It's an environment in which the Navy SEALs may be called upon for help, as they were in the recent rescue of two aid workers from the grip of Somali kidnapping gangs.

Yet while individual cases—in a Yemeni town, a region of Sudan, a district of Somalia—may give the impression that aid groups are on the retreat, the reverse is true. Humanitarian aid budgets by donor nations have grown 10-fold between 1998 and 2008. And while the work has become much more dangerous, aid workers are honing their ability to negotiate with unsavory regimes and find new paths to achieve traditional humanitarian goals.

Among the first aid groups to go into conflict zones or disaster areas, and the last to leave, is Doctors Without Borders, known primarily by its French name, Médecins Sans Frontières. But even MSF has had its staffers expelled from Sudan and Sri Lanka and pulled its staff from aid camps in some of the neediest sections of Somalia and the northern Kenyan border because of attacks in recent years.

Michael Neuman, who has headed MSF missions in North Sudan and Niger and has run logistics in battle zones like Chechnya and Kosovo, recently co-wrote a book, "Humanitarian Negotiations Revealed," about the strategies MSF uses in an increasingly hostile world. He says the key in a war zone is to make the best of a bad situation, mediate with local authorities to create working space, and judge success by how many lives one saves.

"People have to realize there was no golden period of humanitarian aid," says Mr. Neuman. "In 1990, after the fall of the Berlin Wall, we hoped the world would be easier to work in. . . . But then we faced Somalia in the early '90s and the Bosnian war and the genocide in Rwanda, and we had enough examples to let you know that times had not changed."

Neuman's book looks at a number of case studies in which local MSF staff made judgment calls, at times deciding to overlook a government's inhumane actions—such as the aerial bombing of civilian areas in Yemen in 2009 or the shelling of Tamil civilians by the Sri Lankan Army in 2009—in order to maintain health facilities for larger dependent communities.

What aid groups need to do, Neuman says, is use their ethical and practical judgment to design projects that help as many people as possible and to "make sure they are not causing more harm than good."

Heather Hughes, the global security adviser for Oxfam Great Britain in London, agrees that aid groups have to make decisions based largely on whether the reward of making a difference—in saving lives at Somali refugee camps, for instance—is worth the risk of losing staff members in what appear to be targeted attacks.

Such attacks, Ms. Hughes says, force aid groups to question not just their security protocols but also their reason to be in a risky zone. "Globally, we do accept a higher level of risk for certain kinds of work, where there is a humanitarian imperative, such as camps where if we pull out then people will die," she says.

Working in the Line of Fire

If aid workers are getting targeted, it's because they work on the front lines of what is effectively a broader war for political control. In Afghanistan, where US troops and contractors have taken on traditional development work—building schools, digging wells, training hospital personnel—aid workers complain that villagers have difficulty distinguishing between aid workers and combatants.

"The diplomacy, defense, and development approach has had a very significant impact on the humanitarian sector because it's essentially poked the nose of political processes and military processes into traditionally humanitarian spaces and has attempted to co-opt that for political and foreign-policy purposes," says Nic Lee, director of the Afghanistan NGO Safety Office in Kabul. "It undermines the ability of legitimate humanitarian agencies to . . . make it clear that they're acting in an impartial, independent way, and they're not part of a broader foreign-policy process."

DEEP HOSTILITY IN PAKISTAN

Nowhere is the hostility toward foreign aid workers more evident than in Pakistan. Following the devastating flooding of the Indus River in 2010, and again in the spring of 2011, aid workers moved in to help the displaced. Some quickly became targets.

Perhaps the most high-profile of several recent cases is that of Warren Weinstein, a veteran aid worker kidnapped from Lahore, from where he had worked helping small and medium businesses to develop for more than a decade. Al Qaeda in the last week of January released a video saying they would release him if the United States stopped its attacks in Afghanistan, Pakistan, Somalia, and Yemen, but did not provide evidence he was in their custody.

"Now the sense is that no area is safe in Pakistan anymore except for Islamabad," says a translator for a multinational nongovernmental organization who has lived in Pakistan for years (he was unable to give his name because he isn't authorized to talk to the media). "Even those areas traditionally considered safe, like Punjab and Sindh, are no longer so."

BLURRY MOTIVES FOR ATTACKERS

In Somalia, where two MSF workers were killed in Mogadishu last December, and two more kidnapped from a Kenyan-based refugee camp this year, workers can no longer assume that their lifesaving work will be their best protection. Somalia is a clan-based society, where the death of a local fighter in a US drone strike may prompt the dead fighter's clan to kidnap or kill a Western aid worker in revenge.

"The US government recently conducted a successful operation to get two aid workers, and judging from the mood of the Somali community and the way this is discussed on Somali language radio, the majority of Somalis are in favor of that outcome," says Rashid Abdi, a consultant for International Crisis Group in Nairobi, Kenya. "But ... it is not going to be an easy terrain for aid workers to work in the future."

*Scott Baldauf is a staff writer for the *Christian Science Monitor*.

Baldauf, Scott. "Helpers in a Hostile World: The Risk of Aid Work Grows." *Christian Science Monitor*, February 10, 2012. http://www.csmonitor.com/World/Global-Issues/2012/0210/Helpers-in-a-hostile-world-the-risk-of-aid-work-grows.